CYCLING

The

Bicycle Touring Nationwide

John Smith

BICYCLE BOOKS

FROM

Motorbooks International

Publishers & Wholesalers

First published in 1997 by Motorbooks International Publishers & Wholesalers, 729 Prospect Avenue, PO Box 1, Osceola, WI 54020-0001 USA

© John M. Smith, 1997

All rights reserved. With the exception of quoting brief passages for the purposes of review no part of this publication may be reproduced without prior written permission from the Publisher

Motorbooks International is a certified trademark, registered with the United States Patent Office

The information in this book is true and complete to the best of our knowledge. All recommendations are made without any guarantee on the part of the author or Publisher, who also disclaim any liability incurred in connection with the use of this data or specific details

We recognize that some words, model names and designations, for example, mentioned herein are the property of the trademark holder. We use them for identification purposes only. This is not an official publication

Motorbooks International books are also available at discounts in bulk quantity for industrial or sales-promotional use. For details write to Special Sales Manager at the Publisher's address

Library of Congress Cataloging-in-Publication Data
Smith, John M.
        Cycling the USA/John M. Smith
               p. cm.
        Includes bibliographical references (p.   ) and index.
        ISBN 0-933201-84-2 (pbk.: alk. paper)
        1. Bicycle touring—United States—Guidebooks. 2. United States—Guidebooks. I. Title.
GV1045.S56   1997
796.6′4′0973—dc21   97-10348

Printed in the United States of America

Table of Contents

Chapter 5
Midwestern States **47**

Chapter 6
Southern States **83**

Chapter 7
Western Interior States **132**

Acknowledgments

A great number of people have helped to make this book a reality, and I would like to thank them all. Our love of cycling has resulted in *Cycling the U.S.A.*, which I hope will serve as a helpful companion on journeys from California to Maine, Florida to Alaska, and everywhere in between.

In particular, I would like to thank the tourist offices and the state bicycle coordinators who assisted me in so many ways. Their insights on specific routes were as valuable as the photos and maps they so kindly provided. The maps and photos used in this book are acknowledged. (If a photo is not acknowledged, it's the author's.)

I would also like to thank all the people who contributed tips and ideas, whether directly, by way of the internet or on the phone, or indirectly, through articles in books, magazines, and newspapers.

I would like to thank Marg and Rose, for their driving and marketing help.

Columbia Sportswear earned my gratitude for providing topnotch rain gear for my last cycling expedition (from the Canadian border to the southern United States). As stated elsewhere in the book, proper preparation and clothing certainly add to the cycling experience, and Columbia's rain gear did just that (at one point even in the vicinity of a hurricane).

The roads and pathways I crisscrossed would have been bleak and bumpy without the many friends I met along the way in the U.S.A.— they have given me such wonderful memories, and I am grateful.

I would like to thank my publisher for believing in this book.

Finally, I would like to thank my wife, Marion, and our family, who have supported me in so many ways in the writing—and living of this book (even dropping me off at the beginning or picking me up at the end of some of the cycling tours described in *Cycling the U.S.A.*).

Chapter 1

Bicycle Touring in the U.S.A.

A merica's landscape is vast and varied, offering the avid cyclist wondrous opportunities for adventure. *Cycling the U.S.A.* outlines specific routes across this magnificent land, as well as individual tours within each region and state. This book is equally suitable for both U.S.A. residents and visitors from abroad who are looking to discover the country by bicycle.

Using This Book

Cycling the U.S.A. contains at least one specific, detailed route for each state. Other tours for the state are also suggested, but are not described in the same depth. In all, you'll find more than 200 tours and routes suggested here—enough to keep you pedaling for years.

It is also recommended that you consult good regional or state readings in conjunction with using this book, which focuses mainly on describing the routes, to plan your rides. Sources for further reading are listed in the appendix.

Because of the extremes of terrain and climate in the U.S.A., the book has been divided into regions. Chapters 4 to 8 begin with general information about that region (including cycling terrain, climate, etc.), followed by the specific suggested routes for each state within that region. Chapters 9 and 10 cover Alaska and Hawaii. Chapter 11 details specific routes for exploring the U.S.A. on extended tours.

Each detailed tour description includes:
- the distance of the trip (in miles and kilometers)
- the suggested number of days for that trip
- the difficulty of the tour:
    1. Easy–quite level
    2. Moderate–some hilly or challenging sections
    3. Strenuous–very challenging
- the type of tour:
    1. Loop route (you end where you started, but by way of a different route)
    2. Return trip (you return along the same route)
    3. One-way tour (you begin at one point and end at another)
- information on getting to your starting point and back from your destination
- accommodations available on that route
- helpful addresses for tourist/cycling information

- a map of the route
- a description of the specific route, with points of interest indicated
- other suggested routes

Getting to the Starting Point

The U.S.A. is easily traveled by train, plane, boat, and motor vehicle. Bus service is available in each of the 50 states. Boats dock at many

These cyclists enjoy the spectacular scenery of South Dakota's Badlands National Park. *Photo courtesy of the South Dakota Board of Tourism*

of the larger ports. There are more than 14,000 airports. Although passenger rail service is minimal when compared with that in Europe, Amtrak does connect most major cities and is especially useful along the East Coast. Each tour description includes information about getting to the start of your route.

Transporting Your Bicycle

If transporting your bicycle by plane or train, be prepared to take it apart and pack it in a box. Boxes are sometimes available at the airport or station, but you can get one in advance from a bike shop (for a price, they'll even pack it properly for you). Some airlines make you sign a waiver form to indicate that they are not responsible for any damage to your bike, but if the worst happens, your household insurance should cover at least part of the loss. Some airlines allow a bicycle as your first piece of luggage; others consider it excess baggage and charge a flat fee for the bike. Check before you fly.

Visiting the U.S.A.

Visitors from most foreign countries will need a valid passport or some other acceptable form of identification. Although Canadian visitors are not required to have a passport, proof of citizenship, such as a birth certificate, must be available.

Restricted items often require special licenses. Information about restricted food items, for example, are explained in the booklet, "Traveler's Tips," available by writing: Department of Agriculture, 6505 Belcrest Road, Hyattsville, MD 20782.

If you need to bring medicines with you, you should carry the prescription form or have a written statement from your doctor. For more information, contact the Food and Drug Administration, Import Operations Unit, Room 12-8 (HFC-131), 5600 Fishers Lane, Rockville, MD 20857.

Additional helpful leaflets, "Trademark Information for Travelers" and "Pet, Wildlife, and U.S. Customs" are available by writing: U.S. Customs, P.O. Box 7407, Washington, D.C. 20044.

The driving age, the legal age for the consumption of alcoholic beverages, littering fines, fishing license fees, and other such laws vary from state to state. It's your responsibility to obey state laws.

Maps and Information

The addresses and phone numbers of tourist bureaus are given in chapters 4 to 10. These tourist bureaus will send you free maps and information about their area: The quality of that information varies from bureau to bureau. Some will even help you plan your stay, while others have very limited resources. Other pertinent addresses and phone numbers for cyclists are also included in these chapters, and you'll find still more in the appendix.

Cycling in the U.S.A.

When sharing the road, always cycle with the traffic and obey the rules of the road. Your bicycle should be equipped with a good horn or bell and, if riding at night, you should have lights front and back; it's the law in many states.

Chapter 2

Visiting the U.S.A. From Abroad

Geography

From tropical wetlands to Arctic wilderness, from alpine heights to the vastness of the Plains, the U.S.A. has it all.

If you want to cycle along the rugged coastline, try a trip through the states of Washington, Oregon, and California, or ride through Acadia National Park in Maine.

If you prefer an adventurous, wilderness experience, try cycling in Alaska or through Death Valley.

If you want to try some of the most spectacular mountain scenery anywhere, ride in the Rocky Mountains of Montana, Colorado, and Wyoming.

If you prefer quiet, rural settings, travel New York's Catskills and Adirondacks, Vermont's Champlain Valley, Pennsylvania's Amish area, or Kentucky's Bluegrass Country.

For a picturesque island setting, try riding in Hawaii, in Washington's Puget Sound, or through the Florida Keys.

Simply put, the settings for adventure are numerous and spectacular!

Time Zones

The United States has 6 time zones.

When it's 3 p.m. in Hawaii and 4 p.m. in Alaska, it's 5 p.m. in Los Angeles, California (Pacific Time), 6 p.m. in Denver, Colorado (Mountain Time), 7 p.m. in Chicago, Illinois (Central Time), and 8 p.m. in Washington, D.C. (Eastern Time).

Health, Water, and Food

Visitors are advised to obtain or extend health insurance coverage before departing for the U.S.A. If you take a prescription drug, bring a copy of the prescription with you, in case an American doctor needs to renew it for you.

Although the U.S.A. has a good supply of fresh water, contaminants are found in many of the lakes and rivers; therefore, when camping it's advisable to boil your water. Even that may not be sufficient at higher altitudes where the temperature for boiling is lower and the chance of encountering giardia is higher. There you'll need chemical treatment to make water safe. The easiest solution is to stick to public drinking supplies—at restaurants, gas stations, park visitor centers and rest stops—whenever possible.

The U.S.A. has stringent food-service restrictions; you can eat with confidence in the great variety of food service establishments that you will encounter on your cycling trip.

Money Matters

Visitors to America are encouraged to exchange funds for American dollars at either a bank or foreign currency exchange outlet in their own country. Banking hours in the United States vary, but banks are generally open from at least 10 a.m. to 4 p.m.; many are open longer.

It's not advisable to carry large amounts of cash, and many American businesses will not accept personal checks—especially those from out of town, state or country. If you have a U.S. or Canadian banking account, Automatic Teller Machines (or ATMs) are widely available for making cash withdrawals. The safest and most practical options are credit cards and travelers' checks, either of which can be replaced if lost or stolen.

Measurement

The U.S.A. does not operate under the metric system. Use the following guidelines:

Distance
1 mile = 1.6 kilometers
1 kilometer = 0.6 miles

Temperature
Fahrenheit to Celsius
C = 5/9 x (F-32)
For example, 77F = 5/9 x (77-32) = 25C

Celsius to Fahrenheit
F = (9/5 x C) + 32
For example, 20C = (9/5 x 20) + 32 = 68F

Weights, sizes, volumes
Metric to U.S.
1 kilogram (kg) = 2.2 pounds (lbs)
1 liter (l) = 1.8 pints (pts)
1 meter (m) = 3.28 feet (ft)
1 meter (m) = 1.09 yards (yds)
1 centimeter (cm) = 0.39 inch (in)

U.S. to metric
1 pound (lb) = 0.45 kilograms (kgs)
1 foot (ft) = 0.3 meter (m)
1 inch (in) = 2.54 centimeter (cm)
1 yard (yd) = 0.91 meter (m)
1 Imperial gallon (gal) = 4.5 liters (l)
1 U.S. gallon (gal) = 3.8 liters (l)

Chapter 3

Pre-Trip Planning

Part of the exhilaration of bicycle touring—whether in the United States or elsewhere—is the independence you derive from traveling with just a bicycle and what you are carrying; it is, therefore, very important to plan wisely to ensure a safe and comfortable journey.

The Individual and the Group

Cycling the U.S.A. is intended to help both the independent traveler and those cycling in groups. If you enjoy cycling alone, as I do, this book can help you organize your itinerary. Groups can also plan tours with the help of this book. For further assistance, a list of bicycle touring companies is given in the appendix.

Planning Your Trip

Careful planning is essential, especially for longer trips. Find out as much as you can about your planned route (the road conditions, width of paved shoulder, accommodations available, etc.). *Cycling the U.S.A.* was written to help you with this planning. But it never hurts to get more information. Contact the tourism bureaus along the route. If you are a member of an automobile club (such as the American Automobile Association or the Canadian Automobile Association), it can provide you with maps and information. You can also purchase specific cycling routes (if you still feel that this is necessary) from such organizations as Adventure Cycling (pertinent addresses and phone numbers are included in the appendix).

Study the maps and read the information to prepare for your tour, but don't be rigid; a certain amount of flexibility on the road will help you have a good trip. (Having an inclination about the day's destination, however, is a good idea so you can arrange for motels, bed and breakfasts, camping facilities, etc.).

By carrying the proper equipment including repair kit, clothes, and supplies), and carefully planning your route, there will be less stress on you during the actual ride.

Another part of good planning for a longer trip is proper conditioning. Don't just decide to set out on a long journey without doing some training and preparation for the ride. Build up some miles on your bicycle by going on regular, short journeys; include some longer routes, too. Get your body accustomed to cycling. Proper exercise and diet will also help to prepare your body. Most important of all, prepare yourself psychologically; if you are determined to complete a particular ride, then you probably will.

What To Pack For Your Bicycle Trip

Your touring plans will dictate what gear is needed. If you plan to camp out and cook, then a stove, tent, and sleeping bag are essential items; if, however, you plan to stop at motels or bed and breakfasts and eat in restaurants, you'll need less gear (and more money).

Clothing can vary, depending on your planned route and the time of year, but a general rule is to carry as little as possible. Take wash-and-wear clothing. Even in summer it's best to wear layers of clothing. Begin with proper underwear or bike shorts that prevent moisture from being trapped against your skin; wear another shirt, sweater, and a nylon wind breaker in succeeding layers; as you warm up, simply peel away the layers.

Here is a list of the items you can want to carry, depending on the conditions of your specific trip:

Bicycle Gear
bicycle helmet
handlebar bag with map pouch
battery-operated lights (front and rear)
horn or bell
tire pump
lock
carriers and panniers
rear view mirror
cycling gloves
reflective safety vest
water bottle(s)
odometer
tool kit and spare parts

Tool Kit
freewheel remover
tire levers
tire patch kit
spoke tightener
chain lubricant
chain tool
rag/cloth
pliers
spare inner tube
nylon cord
bungee cords
duct tape
screwdrivers
wrenches and Allen keys
knife
crank tool

Additional Bike Gear (if room is available)
pressure gauge
extra spokes
spare brake shoes
spare batteries and bulb for your light
spare chain links
spare nuts and bolts
spare brake and gear cables

Clothing
shorts
bike shorts
long-sleeved shirt
shirts
sweater
nylon wind breaker
slacks/long pants/skirts
swimming trunks/suit
thermal tights and shirt
socks
underwear
sweat pants
rain gear
shoes

A group of cyclists stop for some ice cream at "Ben and Jerry's Ice Cream Factory" in Waterbury, Vermont.

Supplies
toothbrush and toothpaste
soap and towel
pocket knife
sunglasses
sunscreen
insect repellent
razor
maps
first aid kit (including lip balm, bandages,
    antiseptic, pain relief)
credit cards
money
liniment
camera and film
notebook and pen
comb/brush
watch

Camping Supplies (if you will be camping out)
ground sheet
sleeping bag
tent
food containers
pots
food
dishes
mugs
dish towel/cloth
cutlery
fuel
stove
matches
can opener
dish-washing liquid
scouring pad

Chapter 4

East Coast States

The East Coast States can be divided into two smaller regions: New England (Connecticut; Maine, Massachusetts; New Hampshire; Rhode Island; Vermont) and the Mid-Atlantic States (New Jersey; New York; Pennsylvania).

The Appalachian Mountains stretch through the East Coast States (the Longfellow Mountains in Maine; the White Mountains in New Hampshire; the Green Mountains in Vermont; the Catskill Mountains in New York; the Allegheny Mountains in Pennsylvania), and the Appalachian National Scenic Trail, a hiking path of almost 2,000 miles (3,300 kilometers) begins in Maine and stretches through several of the East Coast States and into the Deep South. During the summer, daily high temperatures in this region are likely to be in the 80s, although temperatures in the 90s are quite possible. Usually, temperatures are lower in the mountains and on the coast.

Connecticut
• **The Connecticut River Valley and the Southeastern Shore**
Distance: 48 miles/80 kilometers
Duration: 1–3 days
Rating: Easy
Type: One-Way Tour
Access: Middletown is in south-central Connecticut, south of Hartford, and on the Connecticut River. Ocean Beach is just south of New London, near the southeastern corner of the state. New London is a port city and also has an airport.
Accommodations: Many services are available along this route.
Route Description: Middletown is the site of the Wesleyan Potters Exhibit and the Head of the Connecticut Regatta each year. This city is also home to the Olin Memorial Library and the Center for the Arts. Cycle south on No. 17, east on No. 155, and south on No. 154, following the Connecticut River to Higganium, Haddah, and Tylerville. Cross the river from Tylerville to East Haddam, and ride southeast on No. 82 and No. 156 to North Lyme, Hamburg, Black Hall, South Lyme, and Rocky Neck State Park (offering camping facilities and hiking trails), on the south shore. Continue cycling east from Rocky Neck State Park on No. 156 to Niantic and Waterford. You will pass several beautiful estates along the Niantic River.

Cycle south on No. 213 to Harkness Memorial State Park and New London (founded by a group of Puritans in 1646). Benedict Arnold

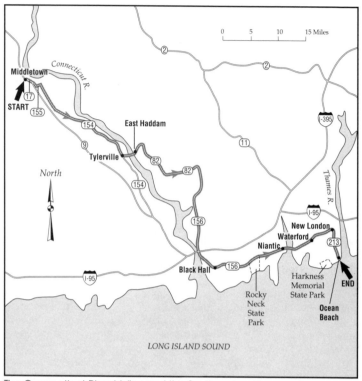

The Connecticut River Valley and the Southeastern Shore

watched the burning of New London in 1781 from what is now called "Ye Ancientest Burial Grounds." Other points of interest in New London include Lyman Allyn Art Museum, John Winthrop, Jr. Monument (commemorating the founder of New London), Monte Cristo Cottage (the boyhood home of dramatist Eugene O'Neill), the Statue of Nathan Hale, the Coast Guard Academy, and the downtown historic district (including Nathan Hale's Schoolhouse, the Captain's Walk, and Whale Oil Row). The annual Yale-Harvard Regatta is held in New London.

You can take a ferry from New London, Connecticut, to Block Island, Rhode Island. (For more information, see the Optional Tours heading).

Complete your tour by cycling from New London along the west bank of the Thames River to the New London Lighthouse (one of the oldest in the U.S.A.) and Ocean Beach.

The cycling has been relatively flat and easy as you have biked along the Connecticut River from Middletown to Black Hall and then along the southeast coast of Connecticut to New London and Ocean Beach.

Boating, swimming, fishing, and hiking are all popular recreational activities in the Connecticut River Valley and along the southeast coast of the state.

Other Tours
• **Ride to New Haven**

Cycle west on No. 1 from New London to New Haven, a town designed by the Puritans in the early 1600s. It's now the home of Yale University. Guided tours of the campus are available.

• **Take a Ferry to Block Island, Rhode Island**

A ferry ride from New London, Connecticut, will take you to Block Island, Rhode Island. Explore this scenic area, which serves as a summer home for many artists. For reservations, contact: Nelseco Navigation Co., P.O. Box 428, New London, CT 06320; phone (203) 442-7891.

• **Eastern Loop Tour**

Uncas, chief of the Mohicans and friend of the colonists, won an important battle just north of Norwich (on No. 12). Continue riding north on No. 12 to Lisbon, west on No. 138 to Jewett City, and north on No. 169 to Canterbury and Brooklyn. Cycle west on No. 6 to Willimantic, where you will find the Windham Textile and History Museum (which is dedicated to showing the textile industry as it was in southern New England during the Industrial Revolution). Then complete the 50-mile (83-kilometer) loop by taking No. 32 back to Norwich.

• **The Litchfield Hills and Farmington Valley**

The wooded Litchfield Hills, in the northwest part of the state, contain Connecticut's highest elevations.

Cycle east on No. 118 from Litchfield (the birthplace of Harriet Beecher Stowe, author of *Uncle Tom's Cabin*) to Harwinton. Then bike on No. 4 to Burlington, Unionville and Farmington, which has a long main street laid out on a river terrace. Ride north on No. 10 to Avon (nearby Talcott Mountain State Park offers panoramic views of the Farmington Valley) Follow the Farmington River as you ride north on No. 202 to Penwood State Park and Simsbury. Near Simsbury is Stratton Brook State Park, which features some bicycle trails. Cycle west, past Stratton Brook State Park, on No. 309 to North Canton, north on No. 179 to Canton Center, and southwest on No. 202 to Nepaug and Torrington. Complete this 66-mile (110-kilometer) loop tour by returning to Litchfield.

For more information on this area, contact: Farmington Valley/West Hartford Visitors Bureau, P.O. Box 1550, Avon, CT 06001; phone (203) 674-1035; 1-800-468-6783.

Connecticut Contacts
Bicycle Coordinator, Connecticut Department of Transportation, 2800 Berlin Turnpike, P.O. Box 317546, Newington, CT 06131-7546; phone (203) 566-6450.

Coalition of Connecticut Bicyclists, Inc., P.O. Box 121, Middletown, CT 06457; phone (203) 287-9903.

Connecticut Valley Tourism Commission, 393 Main Street, Department 3A, Middletown, CT 06457; phone (203) 347-6924.

Southeastern Connecticut Tourism; phone 1-800-222-6783.

State of Connecticut Department of Economic Development, 865 Brook Street, Rocky Hill, CT 06067-3405; phone 1-800-282-6863.

Maine
• **Acadia National Park**

Distance: 70 miles/117 kilometers
Duration: 2–5 days
Rating: Moderate
Type: Loop Tour
Access: Bar Harbor is southeast of Bangor, on Mount Desert Island, and at the entrance to Acadia National Park (on No. 3). Ferry service is available between Bar Harbor, Maine and Yarmouth, Nova Scotia (addresses given above).
Accommodations: Full services available in Bar Harbor. Acadia National Park offers camping facilities.
Route Description: A natural destination for cyclists, Acadia National Park has good paved roads as well as magnificent off-road riding on a network of gravel pathways that meander through lush forests, around mountains and lakes, and along the Atlantic Ocean shoreline.

Activities in Acadia National Park include whale-watching, sailing aboard a windjammer, partaking in a lobster clambake, fishing, sunbathing, and exploring the rugged coastline and the lobster ports.

Cycle south from Bar Harbor on No. 3, where you will pass the Jackson Laboratory, one of the world's largest centers for basic biomedical research dealing with mammalian genetics; findings are applied to the studies of cancer, heart disease, diabetes, obesity, and birth defects.

Cycle on a loop road, past Sand Beach. Pause at Thunder Hole to watch 40-foot spouts of water explode out of a tidal cavern. After you pass Otter Point, rejoin No. 3, and bike northwest to Somesville. Then ride south on No. 102 to the lobster ports of Southwest Harbor and Bass Harbor (from Bass Harbor, you can take a ferry to Swans Island, which provides access to nearly traffic-free cycling through some pretty fishing villages). Cycle northeast from Bass Harbor to West Tremont and Seal Cove, and continue in a loop around to Somesville.

Ride north on No. 198 to Town Hill and then east to Hulls Cove, on Frenchman Bay. Cycle southeast to your destination, Bar Harbor.

Acadia National Park has more than 100 miles (165 kilometers) of hiking trails and more than 50 miles (85 kilometers) of bicycle trails. The terrain is hilly, and there are some challenging climbs in the park. Whether you stay on the paved seashore roads or choose to explore the miles of gravel carriage roads, you will see some of Maine's most spectacular scenery.

Other Tours
• **Nova Scotia, Canada**

Take the ferry from Bar Harbor, Maine to Yarmouth, Nova Scotia, where you can explore part of Nova Scotia (for detailed routes in Nova Scotia, refer to my book, *Cycling Canada*).

• **Grand Manan Channel Loop**

Cycle from Machias, in southeastern Maine, to East Machias (on No. 1). Then take No. 191 along the Manan Channel and into Quoddy Head State Park. Bike north to Lubec, and across the Lubec Narrows to Campobello Island (the summer home of President Franklin

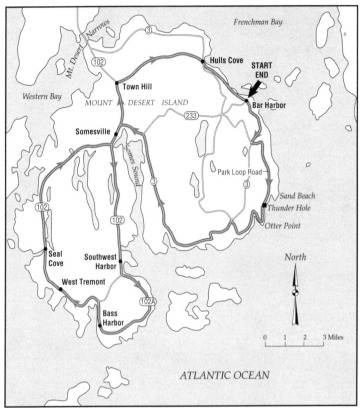

Acadia National Park

Delano Roosevelt, in New Brunswick, Canada). Return on No. 189 to Whiting and then on No. 1 back to Machias, completing this 72-mile (120-kilometer) trip.

• Island Hopping

Cycle along the southern coast of Maine, from Damariscotta—about 50 miles (85 kilometers) east of Portland—to Stonington, where fishing shanties line the shore and weathered docks on pilings extend out into the tranquil harbor. You will ride to Pemaquid Point (where Maine's first settlement was founded in the 1600s), Port Clyde (where you take a ferry to Monhegan Island and see the highest cliffs along the New England shore; several hiking trails lead to scenic outlooks), Rockland (where a ferry will take you to Vinalhaven Island and North Haven Island), Lincolnville (where a ferry will lead you to miles of easy cycling on Islesboro Island), and on to Stonington (where yet another ferry takes you to Isle au Haut, which offers a scenic outlook of the area's islands). This rolling coastline tour will include some challenging climbs and enchanting views.

For ferry information between Port Clyde and Monhegan Island, contact: Monhegan-Thomaston Boat Line, P.O. Box 238, Port Clyde, ME 04855; phone (207) 372-8848.

- **The Aroostook Valley Trail**
    This gravel surfaced rails-to-trails route takes you 18.5 miles (31 kilometers) through a landscape of potato fields and wooded areas in northeastern Maine (near the New Brunswick border). You will ride from Caribou to Washburn, with a side trip possible to historic New Sweden.

- **Across Maine**
    In my previous book, *Cycling Canada*, I described my continental crossing, which included a challenging passage through Maine that took me through the Longfellow Mountains. The route is about 237 miles (395 kilometers) long. Cycle east on No. 2 from Gorham, New Hampshire to Newport, Maine. Then travel on quiet country roads as you ride northeast to Lagrange. Take No. 6 ("The International Lakeland Trail") to the New Brunswick border. There will be a particularly challenging section from Springfield to Topsfield (on No. 6) as you cycle through the vast forests. I even met a black bear on this stretch of road!

Maine Contacts

Bicycle Coordinator, Department of Transportation,
    16 State House Station, Augusta, ME 04333; phone (207) 287-3131;
    FAX (207) 287-2896.
Bureau of Parks and Recreation, State Office Bldg., Augusta, ME 04333.
C.N. Reservations Bureau, P.O. Box 250, North Sydney, Nova Scotia,
    Canada B2A 3M3; phone (207) 288-3395 (for ferry information
    between Bar Harbor, Maine and Yarmouth, Nova Scotia).
Maine Publicity Bureau, 97 Winthrop Street, Hallowell, ME 04347.
Marine Atlantic, Eden Street, Bar Harbor, ME 04609; phone
    (207) 288-3395; 1-800-341-7981 (for ferry information between
    Bar Harbor, ME and Yarmouth, N.S.).

Rumford, Maine

Massachusetts

• **Cape Cod Area**

Distance: 180 miles/300 kilometers
Duration: 4–7 days
Rating: Moderate
Type: One-way Tour
Access: Cape Cod juts out into the Atlantic Ocean, forming the most prominent feature of the coastline. This peninsula is a very popular summer resort area. Plymouth is southeast of Boston on No. 3A. Plymouth and Provincetown are both accessible by boat, as well as by road.
Accommodations: Full services are found at Plymouth, Provincetown, and at many of the towns along this route.
Route Description: Begin your tour in the northern corner of this area, at Plymouth, on Plymouth Bay. The Pilgrims landed at Plymouth Rock in December 1620, to found the first permanent settlement north of Virginia. The *Mayflower II,* moored at State Pier, is a reproduction of the ship that carried the Pilgrims to the New World. Other places of interest include Plymouth Rock, Pilgrim Hall Museum, *Mayflower* Society Museum, and the Pilgrim Monument. While in the Plymouth area, you could take a whale-watching cruise or visit the Cranberry World Visitors Center, which explains the history, cultivation, and uses of the cranberry.

Cycle south on No. 3A to Plimoth Plantation, which gives a living history look at seventeenth century Plymouth. Then continue on No. 3A around Cape Cod Bay, passing several beautiful beaches and lookout points.

Cross the Cape Cod Canal, and cycle south on the bicycle path to the Shore Road and follow it (No. 28A) along Buzzards Bay to Falmouth, a point of departure for ferries to Martha's Vineyard and Nantucket. Take the ferry from Falmouth to Oak Bluffs, on Martha's Vineyard. Its beautiful beaches, New England charm, and proximity to Cape Cod make this island a very popular resort area. It's also a great area for cycling, as you can take a paved bike path from Oak Bluffs to Edgartown (5 miles or 8 kilometers) and from Edgartown to South Beach (2 miles or 4 kilometers).

Return to Edgartown, the island's oldest European settlement, and then cross to Chappaquiddick Island, cycling to Wasque Point and back. Then take the 7-mile (11- kilometer) paved bike path to Vineyard Haven. Ride on Beach Road and Seaview Avenue back to Oak Bluffs, and then take the ferry from Martha's Vineyard to Nantucket Island.

Nantucket Island was first settled by whites in 1659; today it's a popular artists' haven and summer resort area. The island's narrow streets make it more suitable for biking than for driving cars. You'll get great views from the Nantucket Cliffs as you cycle west along Cliff Road and Eel Point Road. Then ride along the Maddaket Harbor to Maddaket. You can return to Nantucket on the paved bike trail. There are also paved bicycle paths leading from Nantucket to Surfside (3 miles or 5 kilometers) and Siasconset (6 miles or 10 kilometers). After exploring the island, board the ferry back to Cape Cod, arriving at Hyannis Port.

Hyannis Harbor Tours, Whale Watcher Cruises, and Cape Cod Scenic Railroad excursions are available from this popular resort area. Craigville Beach (near Hyannis Point) is the largest beach on the cape. A memorial to John F. Kennedy can be found on Ocean Street in Hyannis, and the Kennedy Compound is at Hyannis Port.

Leave Hyannis by cycling east on No. 28, north on Yarmouth Road, and northeast on No. 6A to Dennis. Here you will find a 25-mile (42-kilometer) paved bike path—the Cape Cod Rail Trail, which slices through forests and cranberry bogs as you ride to Wellfleet. At Wellfleet, ride north on No. 6 as you cycle along a section of the Cape Cod National Seashore. You will follow miles of coastline, windswept sand dunes, marshland, dense forests, and glacial cliffs.

You will pass picturesque fishing villages with weathered cottages and lighthouses on your way to Provincetown, the site of the first landing of the Pilgrims, and the destination of this tour. This northern tip of

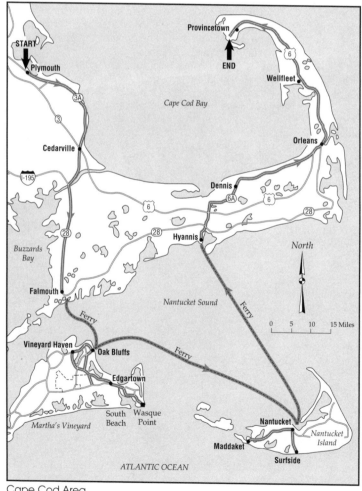

Cape Cod Area

the Cape Cod area is an excellent spot from which to take a whale-watching trip or a dune buggy ride. There are also 8 miles (13 kilometers) of paved bike paths here.

As you make your way from Plymouth, in the northwest, to Provincetown, in the northeast, you will find that some of the roads can be crowded with tourists. Compensating for the crowds, however, are the many paved bicycle paths you ride, and the gently rolling terrain they cross.

Other Tours
• **The Greater Boston Area**

Several paved bicycle paths are available, including the Paul Dudley White-Charles River Bike Path (with 18 miles or 30 kilometers of trails from the Museum of Science, along the Charles River) and the Minuteman Bikeway (a 10.5-mile or 17-kilometer route to the Arlington, Lexington, and Bedford areas). The Minuteman Bikeway will take you near Concord, where you can visit the Minuteman Statue, Sleepy Hollow Cemetery, and the site of Thoreau's cabin on Walden Pond. For a copy of the "Minuteman Bikeway Brochure," contact: Friends of the Minuteman Bikeway, Planning and Community Development, Town Hall, 730 Massachusetts Avenue, Arlington, MA 02174; phone (617) 641-4891.

• **Salem to Cambridge**

Salem, northeast of Boston, is perhaps most famous for its "Witchcraft Trials" of 1692. Salem is now home to the Salem Witch Museum, the House of the Seven Gables Historic Site (inspirational for Nathaniel Hawthorne's book), and the Salem Maritime National Historic Site. Bike northwest on No. 1A, No. 16, and No. 28 to Cambridge, where you can visit Harvard, the oldest university in the country. Old Cambridge is a

"The Mayflower" is on display in Plymouth, Massachusetts. *Photo courtesy of Massachusetts Department of Tourism*

View the cranberry bogs near Plymouth, Massachusetts. *Photo courtesy of Massachusetts Department of Tourism*

series of blocks around the perimeter of Harvard Square, and its buildings reflect nearly 400 years of history. The Longfellow National Historic Site (which was the poet's home from 1837–1882) is also in Cambridge.

• Salem to Cape Ann

Take No. 1A north and No. 127 northeast from Salem, following the rocky coastline. You will ride through Manchester-By-The-Sea and arrive at Gloucester. Do a loop around Cape Ann by riding north on No. 127 to Pigeon Cove and then returning to Gloucester, passing through Rockport (completing the 30 miles/50 kilometers route). This is a great area for a whale-watching expedition. Also, both Rockport and Gloucester are known for their art colonies. Gloucester is home to the Cape Ann Historical Association's Museum, which exhibits paintings by several Cape Ann artists.

• The Mohawk Trail

This 63-mile (105-kilometer) route in northwestern Massachusetts, from Williamstown to Orange, follows what was once an Indian trail. Now a scenic, paved route, you will cycle along the Deerfield River and face some challenging climbs through the Berkshire Hills. Ride east on No. 2 to North Adams, where you can visit Western Gateway Heritage State Park and Natural Bridge (a water-eroded natural bridge of white marble). Continue on No. 2, crossing the Hoosic River, to Savoy Mountain State Forest, Mohawk Trail State Forest (both state forests offer camping, fishing, and hiking), Shelburne Falls (with several interesting potholes by the Deerfield River), Greenfield, Riverside, Farley, and Erving State Forest. Then ride on No. 2A to your destination, Orange.

- **Worcester County**
    Worcester County has several paved bicycle paths, including a 22-mile (37-kilometer) lakes and reservoirs tour, beginning at Westminster, and a 33-mile (55-kilometer) route that begins in Barre and follows the banks of the Quabbin Reservoir. For complete route information, write for the pamphlet, "Bike Routes of Northern Worcester County," available from the Worcester County Convention and Visitors Bureau, 33 Waldo Street, Worcester, MA 01608.

- **Norwottuck Rail Trail**
    This 8.5-mile (14-kilometer) paved trail begins in Northampton (in western Massachusetts) and takes you past Amherst College to Station Road (in South Amherst). The route includes a spectacular crossing of the Connecticut River on a long railroad bridge. For a copy of the "Norwottuck Rail Trail Brochure," contact: "Daily Hampshire Gazette," 15 Conz Street, Northampton, MA 01060; phone (413) 584-5000.

Massachusetts Contacts

Boston Area Bicycle Coalition (B.A.B.C.), P.O. Box 1015, Cambridge, MA 02142; phone (617) 491-RIDE.

Falmouth Chamber of Commerce, P.O. Box 582AA, Falmouth, MA 02541; phone (508) 548-8500 or 1-800-526-8532.

Martha's Vineyard Chamber of Commerce; phone (508) 693-0085.

Massachusetts Office of Travel and Tourism, 100 Cambridge Street, 13th Floor, Boston, MA 02202; phone (617) 727-3201 or 1-800-447-MASS.

Metropolitan District Commission, Public Information, 20 Somerset Street, Boston, MA 02108 (with information available on bicycle paths and trails).

Nantucket Island, Box 1016, Department A, Nantucket, MA 02554; phone (508) 228-1894.

Plymouth Area Chamber of Commerce, 91 Somoset Street, Plymouth, MA; phone (508) 746-3377.

Provincetown, Box 815, Department A, Provincetown, Cape Cod, MA 02657

State Bicycle Coordinator, 10 Park Plaza, Rm. 4150, Boston MA 02116; phone (617) 973-7329.

New Hampshire
• **The White Mountains of New Hampshire**
Distance: 130 miles/217 kilometers
Duration: 3–5 days
Rating: Strenuous
Type: Loop Tour
Access: North Conway is in east central New Hampshire, near the Maine border (on No. 302).
Accommodations: Full services are available in this White Mountain resort area. For more information, contact: The Mount Washington Valley Chamber of Commerce, Main Street, North Conway, NH; phone (603) 356-3171.
Route Description: The White Mountains of New Hampshire present the cyclist with a full table: challenging terrain, spectacular scenery and a wealth of cultural and historic stops.

Begin this loop tour in the resort town of Conway. You won't go far before tempting detours begin. The first: Echo Lake State Park with its scenic outlook and hiking trails high above the river valley. Other possibilities: journey by tramway to the top of Mount Cranmore, or take the Conway Scenic Railroad on an excursion through the rural Mount Washington Valley.

Cycle north from North Conway on No. 302 to Glen, riding through the Mount Washington Valley. Then continue north on No. 16 to Jackson, and climb Pinkham Notch, one of the easternmost of the major White Mountain passes. The twisting road threads through the pass, surrounded by mountain peaks. As you cycle along, you will see the Presidential Range, with Mount Washington towering above the others. On the south side of Pinkham Notch, the road parallels the Ellis River and offers access to such points of interest as Glen Ellis Falls and Crystal Cascades. You can also ride the Wildcat Mountain Gondola Tramway from a base at Pinkham Notch to the summit of Wildcat Mountain, where a view of the White Mountains spreads in all directions. At Glen House, you will see the Mount Washington Auto Road, which leads to the summit of Mount Washington (a very tough climb!). Continuing on No. 16, you will bike to Gorham, and then you will ride west on No. 2 to Randolph, Jefferson Highlands, Star King, and Jefferson. As you enter Jefferson, you can hear Christmas music, even during a summer heat wave, because year-round tourist attraction "Santa's Village" is here. Leave Jefferson by cycling southwest on No. 116 to Whitefield, and then bike south on No. 3 to Twin Mountain.

The easy way to reach the summit of Mount Washington? Ride on No. 302 to Bretton Woods, and then follow the signs to the famous, mountain-climbing cog railway that takes you to the top of the highest mountain in the northeast. Be prepared for a much cooler temperature at the summit. The normal summer high temperature is less than 50 degrees.

Continue the loop tour from Twin Mountain by cycling southwest on No. 3 to Franconia Notch. Another possible side trip is to poet Robert Frost's New Hampshire home (near Franconia).

Franconia Notch has some of the most spectacular scenery in the White Mountains, including tumbling waterfalls, covered bridges, and

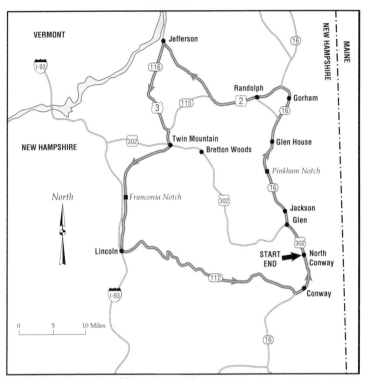

The White Mountains of New Hampshire

tree-lined hiking trails. Franconia State Park offers 8 miles (14 kilometers) of twisting bicycle paths that pass several natural attractions, including "The Old Man of the Mountain" (a stone "face" cut into the rock above Profile Lake) and "The Flume" (an 800 foot chasm with sheer walls that rise as high as 70 feet).

Cycle south on No. 3 from Franconia Notch and Franconia State Park to Lincoln, another resort area. Then turn east on No. 112, the Kancamagus Highway, one of the most scenic routes in the state. Just 2 miles (4 kilometers) east of Lincoln, on the Kancamagus Highway, is the Loon Mountain Gondola Skyride, offering views of the White Mountains from the summit of Loon Mountain. You will cycle through the Pemigewasset Valley before climbing the Kancamagus Pass and descending into the Swift River Valley, passing Sabbaday Falls, Passaconaway (settled in about 1790 and once a logging village), and the Rocky Gorge Scenic Area. This route offers several interesting hiking trails, including those at Passaconaway Historic Site and near the Covered Bridge Campground.

Challenging No. 112 ends at Conway. You will then cycle north on No. 302 to North Conway, your destination on this loop tour of New Hampshire's White Mountains.

Other Tours

• **Gorham Loop Tour**

Do a circle tour around a portion of the White Mountain National Forest by cycling northwest on No. 2 from Gorham to Lancaster, north on No. 3 to Groveton, southeast on No. 110 to Berlin, and south on No. 16 back to Gorham (a distance of about 75 miles or 125 kilometers).

• **Southern New Hampshire**

Cycle from Winchester, in the southwestern corner of the state, to Laconia (105 miles or 175 kilometers), the headquarters of the White Mountain National Forest. Several old covered bridges grace the side roads of this scenic route.

Ride northeast on No. 10, No. 9, and No. 202 to Concord, the state capital. Then ride northeast to Shaker Village, which preserves the Shaker way of life. A restaurant that serves Shaker food and a museum displaying Shaker crafts are in Shaker Village.

Continue north to Belmont, northwest on No. 140 to Franklin (the birthplace of Daniel Webster), and northeast on No. 3 to Laconia, a popular recreation area near several beautiful lakes.

New Hampshire Contacts

Appalachian Mountain Club, Pinkham Notch Camp, Box 298, Gorham, NH 03581; phone (603) 466-2725.

Franconia-Easton-Sugar Hill Chamber of Commerce, Box A, Franconia, NH 03580; phone (603) 823-5661. Franconia Notch State Park; phone (603) 823-5563.

New Hampshire Division of Economic Development, 105 London Road, Prescott Park, P.O. Box 856, Concord, NH 03301; Request a "New Hampshire Bicycle Map."

New Hampshire Office of Travel and Tourism Development, P.O. Box 856, Concord, NH 03302-1856; phone (603) 271-2343 or 1-800-386-4664.

State Bicycle Coordinator, Department of Public Works, Hazen Drive, Concord, NH 03301; phone (603) 271-3734. Ask for a state bicycle map.

Supervisor, White Mountain National Forest, P.O. Box 638, Laconia, NH 03246; phone (603) 524-6450.

White Mountains Visitor Center, Box 10 M G North Woodstock, NH 03262.

New Jersey
• **Atlantic City and the Southern Seashore**
Distance: 120 miles/200 kilometers
Duration: 3–5 days
Rating: Easy
Type: Loop Tour
Access: Airlines servicing the International Airport in Pomona include Northwest Airbank (1-800-225-2525) and USAir (1-800-428-4322). The bus terminal services include Greyhound Lines Inc. (1-800-582-5946) and New Jersey Transit ([609]-343-7876). Amtrak offers daily rail service (1-800-872-7245). Atlantic City's Boardwalk is accessible by bicycle.
Accommodations: Full facilities are found in this gambling resort area.
Route Description: This tour begins and ends in Atlantic City, where the lavish casinos, the Boardwalk, and the sandy beach all contribute to the city's reputation as one of the East Coast's major tourist areas.

After exploring Atlantic City, follow the coast south as you ride to Ventnor City, Margate City—where you can tour an interesting building in the shape of an elephant: Lucy, the Margate Elephant—and Ocean City. Ocean City was established, in 1879, as a Christian summer resort, and no liquor was served; this injunction is still in effect here. Popular with families, Ocean Beach boasts excellent sport fishing and yachting and a beautiful 8-mile (14-kilometer) beach.

Continue south, along the coast, to Strathmere, Sea Isle City, Avalon, Stone Harbor, and Cape May. Self-guiding tours of Cape May's historic sites are available. If you wish, you can take a ferry from Cape May, New Jersey, to Lewes, Delaware (the address has been given elsewhere). Cape May State Park, southwest of town, offers bicycle trails and is the site of the Cape May Lighthouse, built in 1859. The lighthouse's spiral staircase affords a beautiful view of the Delaware Bay and the Atlantic Ocean.

Cycle north to Rio Grande and then northwest (on No. 47) to Green Creek, Dias Creek, and the Dennis Creek Wildlife Area. Ride east on No. 83 to Clermont and north on No. 9 to Ocean View and Seaville. Then bike northwest on No. 50, through the Tuckahoe Corbin City Fish and Wildlife Management Area, to May's Landing. Take No. 40 northwest from May's Landing back to Atlantic City.

This loop tour has taken you on relatively flat terrain as you have cycled around the southern tip of New Jersey.

Other Tours
• **Delaware**
A ferry will take you from Cape May, New Jersey to Lewes, Delaware. For information, contact: Lewes Terminal, Lewes, Delaware 19958; phone (302) 645-6346.
• **Delaware and Raritan Canal State Park**
A rail trail of crushed rock takes you along 68 miles (113 kilometers) of the D&R Canal, from Frenchtown, through Stockton, Washington Crossing State Park, Trenton, and on to New Brunswick. For more information, contact: D&R Canal, 625 Canal Road, Somerset, NJ 08873; phone (908) 873-3050.

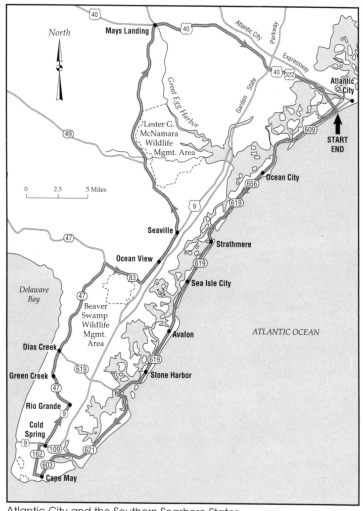

Atlantic City and the Southern Seashore States

• Along the Coastal Beaches

New Jersey is blessed with many beautiful beaches and opportunities for ocean recreation along its eastern coastline. Cycle south from Asbury Park, a popular resort area, to Ocean Grove, a family-oriented seaside resort. Then continue to ride along the beautiful coast to Bradley Beach, Avon by the Sea, Belmar, Point Pleasant Beach, Bay Head, Mantoloking, Normandy Beach, Chadwick, Lavallette, and Ortley Beach. Cycle west on No. 37 to Winding River Park, with a canoe route and nature, hiking, bridle, and bicycle trails. Continue your trip to Lakehurst, and then cycle northeast on No. 70 to Brick and on No. 36 to Belmar. You will then complete this 63-mile (105 kilometer) loop tour by returning to Asbury Park.

• **Morristown to Princeton**
    Northwest of Jersey City, Morristown was selected as winter quarters for George Washington's army in the late 1770s. Morristown National Historical Park contains Washington's headquarters, a museum, and reconstructed housing for troops.
    Cycle southwest on No. 202 to Far Hills and then south to Somerville, where the Wallace House State Historic Site and the Old Dutch Parsonage Site are. Complete this 36-mile (60-kilometer) route by continuing to ride south to Princeton, where Princeton University spreads over 2,500 acres.

• **Across New Jersey–High Point to Cape May**
    "The High Point to Cape May Bike Trail" is a series of linked roads that form a route from the northwest corner of the state (at High Point) to the southernmost point in the state (at Cape May), taking you from the hilly terrain of the state's north to the flat terrain of the southern coastline. For specific details on this 225-mile (375-kilometer) route, contact the State Bicycle Coordinator (address previously given).

New Jersey Contacts

Atlantic City Chamber of Commerce, 1301 Atlantic Avenue, Atlantic
    City, NJ; phone (609) 345-5600.
Atlantic City Convention and Visitors Bureau, 2314 Pacific Avenue,
    Atlantic City, NJ; phone (609) 348-7100.
Bicycle Touring Club of North Jersey, P.O. Box 865, Montclair,
    NJ 07042; phone (201) 284-0404.
Ferry Information, P.O. Box 827, North Cape May , NJ 08204; phone
    (609) 886-2718.
New Jersey Division of Travel and Tourism, 20 West State Street,
    CN 826, Trenton, NJ 08625; phone (609) 292-2470 or 1-800-JERSEY-7;
    FAX (609) 633-7418.
Ocean City Chamber of Commerce, Ocean City, NJ; phone
    (609) 399-6344 or 1-800-624-3746 in New Jersey or 1-800-225-0252
    outside the state.
Pedestrian/Bicycle Coordinator, New Jersey Department of
    Transportation, 1035 Parkway Avenue, CN600, Trenton, NJ 08625;
    phone (609) 530-4578. A free bicycle information package is
    available, including a state map and tour guides.

New York
• **New York's Adirondacks**
Distance: 159 miles/265 kilometers
Duration: 3–6 days
Rating: Strenuous
Type: One-way Tour
Access: The resort town of Tupper Lake is about 96 miles (160 kilometers) east of Watertown, at the intersection of No. 3 and No. 30; this area offers cycling, hiking, climbing, and skiing. The resort town of Lake George is at the south tip of Lake George, in the southeastern section of Adirondack Park.
Accommodations: Several facilities are available in this resort area, including camping in Adirondack Park. Full facilities are available in Saranac Lake, Lake Placid, and Lake George.
Route Description: Begin your trip in Tupper Lake. Cycle east on No. 3 to Saranac Lake, another picturesque resort town in "Upstate" New York. Known as a major tuberculosis treatment center during the late 19th and early 20th centuries, several historic clinics still stand along Saranac Lake's winding roads. Author Robert Louis Stevenson lived in a cottage in this town during the winter of 1887–88; tours of the preserved cottage are available.

Complete your trip through this lakes region by cycling to Lake Placid, the site of the 1980 Winter Olympics. Actually situated on two lakes—Lake Placid and Mirror Lake—Lake Placid offers a great variety of seasonal activities, including cycling, hiking, swimming, fishing, golfing, tennis, skiing, snowmobiling, snowshoe walking, dog-sled rides, skating, and a toboggan chute. You can even try the Olympic luge and bobsled runs or watch ski jumpers train on the ski jump.

Follow the Ausable River as you cycle northeast from Lake Placid to High Falls Gorge (a deep ravine at the base of Whiteface Mountain) and Wilmington. Near Wilmington, an aerial chairlift will take you to the summit of Whiteface Mountain. There you'll see a spectacular view of the St. Lawrence River, Lake Placid, Lake Champlain, and the surrounding area. A road also leads to the summit of Whiteface Mountain.

Ride east on No. 86 from Wilmington to Jay. Then cycle southeast on No. 9N to Keene and Elizabethtown. The Adirondack Center Museum and Colonial Garden, which offers both a formal garden and a history of the Champlain Valley, is in Elizabethtown.

You will enjoy a very scenic ride through the Boquet River Valley as you cycle on No. 9 to New Russia and Severance. Turn east at Severance, taking No. 74 to Ticonderoga. Nearby is Fort Ticonderoga, on Lake Champlain, a fort built by the French in 1755. Now restored, you can tour the area of the original fort. You will also find an informative museum and a scenic overlook, at Mount Defiance, of the Green Mountains, Lake Champlain, and the valley.

Cycle south on Lake Shore Drive (No. 9N) to Silver Bay, Sabbath Day Point, Bolton, and Lake George. The resort town of Lake George is this tour's destination, and it is a great base for a variety of activities, including factory outlets for shopping and cruises on Lake George. Points of interest include Lake George Battlefield Park, Gaslight Village, and Fort William Henry Museum.

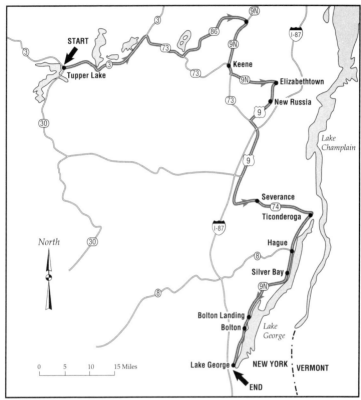

New York's Adirondacks

This trip has taken you on a magnificent tour of New York's Adirondacks as you have traveled from Tupper Lake to Lake George on several pleasant roads with paved shoulders.

Other Tours
• The Finger Lakes Region
Several wineries lie along scenic No. 89 as you cycle south from Seneca Falls to Ithaca (hugging the shore of Cayuga Lake). Cycle west on No. 79 (to Mecklenburg), southwest on No. 228 (to Odessa), northwest on No. 224 (to Montour Falls), and north on No. 14 to Watkins Glen (famous for auto racing). Continue north on No. 14, passing several more wineries, along Seneca Lake to Geneva. Complete this 116 miles (194 kilometers) loop tour by riding east on No. 20 back to Seneca Falls.

• Niagara Falls Loop Tour
One of North America's most famous tourist sites, Niagara Falls offers a great variety of attractions and scenic splendors. You can cycle a loop, visiting both Niagara Falls, Canada and Niagara Falls, New York—by crossing the Rainbow Bridge and the bridge at Lewiston. You

can also explore a 65-mile (108-kilometer) loop of the area within the U.S.A. by cycling north to the Lake Ontario shore; then take No. 18 through Four Mile Creek State Park and Wilson-Tuscarora State Park to Olcott; cycle south on No. 78 to Lockport and west on No. 31 back to Niagara Falls. For more information, contact Niagara County Tourism, 139 Niagara Street, Lockport, NY 14094; phone 1-800-338-7890.

• The Canal Way Trail

When completed, "The Canal Way Trail" will provide a cross-state route that follows New York's canal system. Portions of the trail are now open, and you can ride this route, from Buffalo to Albany, by using No. 5 for the uncompleted sections. For more information, contact the state bicycle coordinator.

• The Catskills

In southeast New York, the Catskills are the highest part of the Appalachian plateau. Here the cyclist faces challenging routes through rugged, mountainous terrain.

You will have a wide, paved shoulder as you cycle west from Kingston on No. 28, following the shore of the Ashokan Reservoir, which provides New York City with millions of gallons of water daily. You will pass near the site of the famous Woodstock concert. At Phoenicia, cycle northeast on No. 214 to Lanesville and southeast on No. 23A to Tannersville, Haines Falls, Palenville, and Catskill. Follow the Hudson River as you cycle south from Catskill to Kingston, completing this 72-mile (120-kilometer) loop.

You will face some tough climbs as you ride through the Catskills, including one over East Windham Mountain, but the route described here avoids the really tough climb you would face if you cycled from Haines Falls to Tannersville.

• Ride to Cooperstown

Instead of doing the described loop tour in the Catskills (above), you could stay on the wide, paved shoulder of No. 28 from Kingston to Cooperstown, the site of the Baseball Hall of Fame. Cooperstown is on the southern tip of Otsego Lake.

• New York's Long Island

This relatively flat trip (96 miles or 160 kilometers) on the south fork of Long Island takes you along the coast and to Shelter Island.

The traffic can be heavy as you cycle east on No. 27 from Southampton, along the peninsula, to Montauk, but you will find a nice paved shoulder. The "cod ledge" off the banks of Montauk is one of the best known fishing areas in North America.

Cycle west on No. 27 to East Harbor and northeast on No. 114 to Sag Harbor. Then take the ferry to Shelter Island, where you can explore miles of quiet country roads that wind along the shore, past several almost deserted beaches. Returning to the mainland, follow the shoreline of Little Peconic Bay as you ride to your destination, Southampton, one of the oldest towns on Long Island, and now a famous resort area.

• **Explore Block Island, Rhode Island**

A ferry will take you from Montauk, New York (on Long Island) to Block Island, Rhode Island, where you can explore this summer home of many artists. An excellent view of the area is available from Mohegan Bluffs, on the southeast shore. Phone (401) 789-3502 for ferry information.

• **New York City to Montreal, Canada**

"Bike Route 9" is a 345-mile (575-kilometer) route that takes you across the George Washington Bridge from New York City and takes you along the west side of the Hudson River to Bear Mountain, where you cross the Bear Mountain Bridge (and the Appalachian Trail). You

Ausable Canyon, in upper New York state.

follow the east side of the Hudson River Valley through Poukeepsie to Albany. Continue north on No. 9 through the Champlain Valley and the eastern Adirondacks to the Canadian border. The route joins Quebec route No. 223 north of Rousses' Point and follows the Richellieu Valley and the Chambly Canal Towpath to Montreal. For more information about "Bike Route 9," contact the state bicycle coordinator.

New York Contacts

Department of Economic Development, Division of Tourism, One Commerce Plaza, Albany, NY 12245; phone 1-800-225-5697.

Lake Placid Commerce and Visitors' Bureau, Lake Placid, NY; phone (518) 523-2445.

New York State Office of Parks, Recreation and Historic Preservation, Agency Bldg. No. 1, Empire State Plaza, Albany, NY 12238; phone (518) 474-0456.

Saranac Lake Chamber of Commerce, 30 Main Street, Saranac Lake, NY; phone (518) 891-1990.

State Bicycle Coordinator, New York DOT, 1220 Washington Avenue, Albany, NY 12232.

Transportation Alternatives, 494 Broadway, Room 300, New York, NY 10012; phone (212) 941-4600.

Tupper Lake Chamber of Commerce, 55 Park Street, Tupper Lake, NY; phone (518) 891-1990.

Pennsylvania

• **Pennsylvania Dutch Country**

Distance: 65 miles/108 kilometers
Duration: 2–3 days
Rating: Moderate
Type: Loop Tour
Access: Lancaster is southeast of Harrisburg and southwest of Reading, in the heart of Lancaster County.
Accommodations: Full facilities available in Lancaster and at several of the towns along this route.
Route Description: The Pennsylvania Dutch Country, in the southern part of the state, is rich farmland. The Plain People, as the inhabitants are often called, include members of the Amish, Mennonite, and Brethren faiths; most dress in plain colors and clothes; some use only horses and do not use electricity or modern plumbing. Members of the sect work together cooperatively, and their farms are very productive.

This loop tour begins in Lancaster, which boasts a large number of factory outlets and heavy traffic. But this is a historic town where you can visit such points of interest as the Heritage Center Museum of Lancaster County, Hans Herr House (the oldest Mennonite meeting house in the U.S.A. and the oldest building in Lancaster County), Lancaster County Winery (tours of the wine cellar are available), the Amish Farm and House, and the Amish Homestead. After exploring the Lancaster area, cycle east on No. 340 through the heart of Pennsylvania Dutch Country. You will arrive at Bird-in-Hand, where you can visit Old Village Store, one of the oldest hardware stores in the country, and Pearl's House of Dolls. Continuing east, you will ride to the Weaverton One-Room Schoolhouse and Plain and Fancy Farm, a village of craft and gift shops, before arriving at Intercourse.

Intercourse supposedly received its name from the old racehorse near town, the Entercourse, or from the joining (intercourse) of the Old King's Highway and the Wilmington-Erie Road here. Intercourse was used as a setting in the film, *Witness,* in which a police officer, played by Harrison Ford, investigates a murder that has entangled a young Amish boy. Kitchen Kettle Village, in Intercourse, has a number of old shops, including Bratton's Woodcraft, Susquehanna Decoy Shop, and Jim Garrahy's Fudge Kitchen. You watch candles being made at the nearby Candle Shop. The People's Place is the center for Amish and Mennonite arts and crafts, and it interprets the story of the Plain People; it includes the Old Country Store, Old Road Furniture Company, Village Pottery, the People's Place Quilt Museum, and the People's Place Gallery.

Leaving Intercourse, cycle east on No. 340 to White Horse, and then ride northeast to Honey Brook. Take No. 322 northwest to Beartown, Blue Ball, Hinkletown, and Ephrata. Continue northwest to Clay, and then ride southwest to Lititz, where you can watch hand-dipped candies being made at Candy American Museum and Candy Outlet, and where you can also twist a pretzel and watch it bake at Sturgis Pretzel House. It's thought to be the oldest pretzel bakery in the U.S. From Lititz, ride south on No. 501 and then east to the Landis Valley Museum, where pioneer life in Pennsylvania is interpreted.

Cycle southwest from the Landis Valley Museum back to Lancaster, completing the loop.

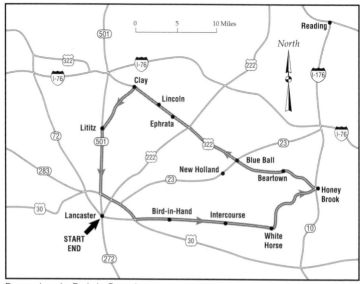

Pennsylvania Dutch Country

As you ride through Pennsylvania Dutch Country, you will be sharing the road with horse-drawn buggies. The terrain will be hilly as you pass the rich farmland and many craft shops and fresh food outlets. Pennsylvania Dutch Country is famous for its great food, so be sure to stop at a local hall for a delicious buffet.

Other Tours

• Harrisburg Loop Tour

You will cycle on relatively quiet roads in the Lebanon Valley as you travel from Harrisburg (the state capital) to Hershey (where you can tour Hershey's Chocolate World, one of the world's largest cocoa and chocolate factories), Palmyra (where tours of Seltzer's Lebanon Bologna Company are available), Lebanon (with several historic churches), Bunker Hill, Ono, and Paxtonia. Take No. 422 east to Lebanon, No. 72 northwest to Bunker Hill, and No. 22 west back to Harrisburg, completing the 70-mile (116-kilometer) loop. For more information, contact: Lebanon Valley Tourist and Visitors Bureau, P.O. Box 329, Lebanon, PA 17042; maps of bicycle trails are available; phone (717) 272-8555.

• Gettysburg Loop Tour

There are more than 1,000 monuments, statues, and markers in Gettysburg National Military Park. Your cycling trip through the park can include stops at the Battlefield Tower, the Eternal Light Peace Memorial, the National Cemetery, and the Visitor Center.

After your tour of this famous battlefield, cycle east on No. 30 to York, which served as the national capital in 1777-78, while the British occupied Philadelphia. Then head southeast on No. 24 to Winterstown, southeast on No. 216 to Codorus State Park and Hanover, and finally back to Gettysburg on No. 116, completing the 66-mile (110-kilometer) loop tour.

• **Valley Forge**

Valley Forge National Historical Park is the site of the famed 1777–78 winter encampment of George Washington and his army. There is a 5-mile (8-kilometer) biking and hiking trail within the park. The 22-mile (37-kilometer) Valley Forge to Philadelphia bike path begins near Betzwood Bridge; it runs along the Schuylkill River and the Manayunk Canal.

• **The Pocono Mountains**

The Poconos offer many recreational opportunities in a landscape of wooded hills and valleys, with many lakes, waterfalls, and beautiful mountain views. Begin your 88-mile (147-kilometer) loop tour in Stroudsburg, and cycle northeast on No. 209 to Bushkill, site of scenic Bushkill Falls and the Pocono Indian Museum, depicting the life of the Delaware Indians. Follow the Delaware River along the New Jersey border as you cycle through the Delaware National Recreation Area to Dingmans Ferry. Take No. 739 northwest to Lords Valley, No. 6 northwest and No. 507 southeast (along Lake Wallenpaupack) to Angels, and No. 196 south, through a section of Tobyhanna State Park, to Mount Pocono. Pocono Knob is one of the most scenic outlooks in this area. From there, you can see the Pocono Mountains, New Jersey, and New York. Take No. 940 east from Mount Pocono to Paradise Valley, and then cycle southeast on No. 191 back to Stroudsburg.

• **Western Pennsylvania Rails/Trails**

Several sections of a proposed system linking Erie, Pennsylvania, with Washington, D.C., via the C & O Canal Trail are open. They include 30 miles (50 kilometers) from Titusville to Kennerdell; 52 miles (87 kilometers) of the Armstrong Trail, northeast of Pittsburgh; a 28-mile (47-kilometer) section that winds through Ohiopyle State Park, and the 14-mile (23 kilometer) Allegheny Highlands Trail from Markleton into Garrett, Maryland. For more information, contact: Pennsylvania Rails-to-Trails Conservancy, 105 Locust Street, Harrisburg, PA 17101; phone (717) 238-1717.

Pennsylvania Contacts

Bicycle Federation of Pennsylvania, 413 Appletree Road, Camp Hill, PA 17011; phone (717) 761-3388.

Bicycle Information Coordinator, Pennsylvania Department of Transportation, Bureau for Highway Safety and Traffic Engineering, P.O. Box 2047, Harrisburg, PA 17105; phone (717) 783-8444.

Kitchen Kettle Village, Route No. 340, Intercourse, PA 17534; phone (717) 768-8261 or 1-800-732-3538.

"Pennsylvania Bicycling Guide," phone (717) 787-6746.

Pennsylvania Dutch Convention and Visitors Bureau, 501 Greenfield Road, Lancaster, PA 17601; phone (717) 299-8901.

Pennsylvania Office of Travel and Tourism, 453 Forum Bldg., Harrisburg, PA 17120; phone 1-800-847-4872.

"Pennsylvania Rail-Trail Guide" is available through American Youth Hostels, Pittsburgh Council, 5604 Solway Street, Room 202, Pittsburgh, PA 15217; phone (412) 422-2282.

The People's Place, Main Street, Intercourse, PA 17534; phone (717) 768-7171.

Rhode Island
• **Rhode Island Sound**
Distance: 36 miles/60 kilometers
Duration: 2–4 days
Rating: Easy to Moderate
Type: Loop Tour
Access: Providence, the state capital, is at the north tip of Narragansett Bay, about 27 miles (45 kilometers) from the sea.
Accommodations: Full facilities are available on this relatively short route.
Route Description: This tour will take you from Providence, the state capital, along Narragansett Bay, to Newport, on Rhode Island Sound, and out to Block Island, off the southern coast.

Rhode Island's industrial and commercial center, Providence, was named by founder Roger Williams in gratitude "for God's merciful providence unto me in my duties" in 1636. Williams was banished from Massachusetts for his religious views; a monument and his grave are found at Providence, as well as the Roger Williams National Memorial and Roger Williams Park.

Cycle south from Providence, along the east coast of Narragansett Bay (on No. 114). You will ride to Barrington, Warren, Colt State Park (with bicycle paths), and Bristol. Then take the ferry to Prudence and Hog Islands. After doing some exploring on these islands, return to the mainland.

Continue south on No. 114 from Bristol to Newport, where you'll find beautiful beaches and magnificent estates. Newport is home to the Naval War College Museum and the Naval Education and Training Center. Narragansett Bay was the principal anchorage for the Atlantic fleet in the early 1900s, protected by Fort Adams, the guardian of the bay; the fortifications can still be seen in Fort Adams State Park. Other points of interest in Newport include Touro Synagogue National Historic Site (the oldest synagogue in the nation), Rochambeau Statue and Monument (which commemorates the landing of the French allies in 1780), the Museum of Yachting, and the International Tennis Hall of Fame and Museum.

While in the Newport area, consider a tour of Jamestown, on Conanicut Island. Jamestown is the site of several historic homes and forts (the forts guard the entrance to Narragansett Bay). One of the oldest lighthouse locations in the country is found at the southern tip of Conanicut Island (the original Beavertail Lighthouse was established in 1749).

After exploring the area, take the ferry from Newport to Block Island, a summer resort area and artists' haven. You can get an excellent view of the area by cycling to Mohegan Bluffs, rising high above the southeast shore. Other points of interest worth visiting include Dickens Point, where you'll see the Palatine Graves, where a shipwrecked group from Germany's Palatinate are buried. Other sites to see: Cow Cove, where Settlers Rock is inscribed with the names of the first settlers, and Block Island State Beach. Return by ferry from Block Island to Providence, completing this loop tour.

The Rhode Island Sound-Block Island area is known for excellent fishing. Hooked here are cod, flounder, mackerel, marlin, tuna, and swordfish.

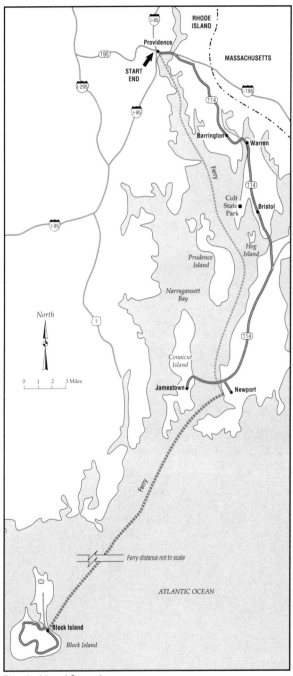

Rhode Island Sound

Other Tours
• By Ferry to Montauk, New York
You can take a ferry from Block Island, Rhode Island to Montauk, New York, where you can cycle on Long Island (previously described under tours of New York). For ferry information, phone (401) 789-3502.

• By Ferry to New London, Connecticut
Take a ferry from Block Island, Rhode Island to New London, Connecticut, where you can ride along Connecticut's southeastern shore and through the Connecticut River Valley (as described under tours of Connecticut). For New London reservations, write to Nelseco Navigation Company, P.O. Box 428, New London, CT 06320.

• By Ferry to Galilee
Take a ferry from Block Island, Rhode Island, to Galilee, where you can join the New England Heritage Trail (described next). Write to Interstate Navigation Company, Galilee State Pier, Point Judith, RI 02882.

• The New England Heritage Trail
This 50-mile (83-kilometer) tour of southwestern Rhode Island will take you past many of the state's historic and scenic attractions. You will cycle from Westerly, in the southwest corner of the state, to Haversham, and then you will bike on the New England Trail (No. 1) to Charlestown and Narragansett Pier. Cycle north on No. 1A to Saunderstown, where you can take a side trip to historic Jamestown on Conanicut Island (previously described). Continue riding north, through Hamilton, rejoin No. 1, and ride along the west coast of Narragansett Bay to Goddard Memorial State Park and Warwick, the route's destination. Warwick has several beautiful beaches and resorts. Beachcombers search for quahogs (a clam) at low tide. For more information about Warwick, phone 1-800-333-9035.

Rhode Island Contacts
Ferry service to Block Island; phone (401) 789-3502.
Ferry trips from Bristol to Prudence and Hog Islands; phone (401) 253-9808.
Greater Providence Convention and Visitors Bureau, 30 Exchange Terrace, Providence, RI; phone (401) 274-1636.
Newport County Convention and Visitors Bureau, 23 America's Cup Avenue, Newport, RI; phone (401) 849-8098 or 1-800-326-6030.
Rhode Island Tourism Division, 7 Jackson Walkway, Providence, RI 02903; phone (401) 277-2601 or 1-800-556-2484.
State Bicycle Coordinator, Rhode Island DOT/Planning, Two Capitol Hill, Providence, RI 02903; phone (401) 277-2694.

Vermont
• **Vermont's Green Mountains**
Distance: 112 miles/187 kilometers
Duration: 2–4 days
Rating: Strenuous
Type: Loop Tour
Access: Rutland is situated in the Otter Creek Valley, in southwestern Vermont.
Accommodations: Full services are available in Rutland, Killington, and Ludlow.
Route Description: This loop tour takes you from Rutland, in southwestern Vermont, through a section of the scenic Green Mountains. You will face some tough climbs on this mountainous route, but the traffic should be relatively light on the quiet country roads.

Known as "Marble City" because of its quarries and finishing industries, Rutland is in the Otter Creek Valley, with the Taconic Mountains to the west and the Green Mountains to the east. Rutland is the headquarters for the Green Mountain National Forest and is the site of the Vermont State Fair each year. *The Rutland Herald,* founded in 1794, is the state's oldest continuously published newspaper.

Take No. 4 east from Rutland, and cycle through the Sherburne Pass to Killington, a popular recreational area throughout the year. Killington is best known for its excellent winter skiing facilities, but in summer Killington Peak affords a scenic view of the area; the panorama embraces part of Canada and five states.

Continue cycling on No. 4 to West Bridgewater, and then ride south on No. 100 to the small town of Plymouth, birthplace of Calvin Coolidge. His home and grave are in Plymouth Notch. Continue south on No. 100 to Tyson, near Lake Rescue, and then ride southeast on No. 103 to Ludlow, a resort town in the Black River Valley.

Continue on No. 103 to Proctorsville and Chester, where several of the structures are built from locally quarried stone. Bike south on No. 35 to Grafton, which was once home to Henry David Thoreau, Ulysses S. Grant, and Theodore Roosevelt. Cycle northwest on No. 121 and No. 11 to Londonderry; then ride north on No. 100 to Weston and Ludlow. Ride northeast on No. 103 to Okemo State Park, Bowlsville, Cuttingsville, and Pierces Corner. Finally, head north on No. 7 back to Rutland.

This challenging route will take you past orchards, farmland, mountain valleys, and tiny villages in the Green Mountains of Vermont.

Other Tours
• **Northern Vermont—From Jay to Stowe and Montpelier**
The resort town of Jay is best known for its skiing facilities; Jay Peak towers over the town. There are, however, year-round recreational activities in this area, particularly in Jay Peak State Park. You can take an aerial tram to the summit of Jay Peak for a view of part of Canada and the states of Vermont, New Hampshire, and New York.

Take No. 101 from Jay to Troy, and then cycle southwest on No. 100 to Stowe. This beautiful resort town can be explored on its paved bicycle path to Mount Mansfield, the loftiest peak in the Green Mountains and the highest summit in Vermont. The Stowe Gondola will take you

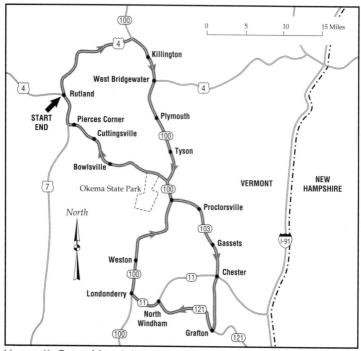

Vermont's Green Mountains

to the summit for a spectacular view. For more information about the Stowe area, contact the Stowe Area Association, Main Street, Stowe, VT; phone (802) 253-7321 (in Canada and Vermont) or 1-800-24-STOWE.

Continue south on No. 100 from Stowe to Waterbury, where you can visit Ben and Jerry's Ice Cream Factory; Waitsfield, site of an old covered bridge, and Warren, near Granville Gulf State Park. Cycle east from Warren on No. 12A and No. 64 to Williamstown. Then ride northeast on No. 14 to Barre, which is sometimes referred to as "The Granite Center of the World" (you can take a tour of Rock of Ages Quarry, thought to be the largest quarry in the world). Bike northwest on No. 302 to Montpelier, another area with important granite quarries, and the destination of this 129-mile (215-kilometer) tour. Montpelier is the capital of Vermont and the site of the Vermont Museum.

• The Champlain Valley

Lying between New York's Adirondacks and Vermont's Green Mountains, the fertile Champlain Valley is a biker's delight. Your wheels roll over gently rolling terrain along the shore of Lake Champlain. The roads and paths will take you past fragrant apple orchards, historic villages, and traditional dairy farms.

Begin this trip in Alburg, and ride south (on No. 2) on the Lake Champlain Islands. You will bike past South Alburg, North Hero,

Knight Point State Park, Grand Isle, and South Hero before joining the mainland and cycling through Sand Bar State Park to Chimney Corner, Winooski, and Burlington. Continue south on No. 7 to Shelburne, Vergennes, and on to the final destination, Middlebury.

This 72-mile (120-kilometer) scenic tour along the shore of Lake Champlain will be a much easier ride than the other tours described for Vermont.

Vermont Contacts

State Bicycle Coordinator, Agency of Transportation, 133 State Street, Montpelier, VT 05602; phone (802) 828-2711.

Summer Mountains, 559A Killington Road, Killington, VT 05751.

Supervisor, Green Mountain National Forest, Box 519, Rutland, VT 05701; phone (802) 775-2579.

Vermont Attractions, Box 1284A, Montpelier, VT 05602; phone (802) 229-4581.

Vermont Travel Division, 134 State Street, Montpelier, VT 05602; phone (802) 828-3237.

A bike path awaits the cyclist in Stowe, Vermont.

Chapter 5

Midwestern States

The eastern states of this region (Illinois, Indiana, Michigan, Minnesota, Ohio and Wisconsin) border four of the five Great Lakes, which comprise one of the main passages west for early explorers and settlers. The western section of this region (Iowa, Kansas, Missouri, Nebraska, North Dakota, and South Dakota) is part of the Great Plains, where much of America's wheat, corn and livestock is raised.

Often referred to as "the Heartland of America," the Midwestern States are relatively flat. There are, however, exceptions. This area includes the Black Hills in South Dakota (where Harney Peak reaches 7,242 feet into the sky) and the moonscape of the Badlands, sections of which straddle the western part of both Dakotas. In Missouri, the Ozarks offer hilly, thickly forested terrain. In the eastern part of this region, Ohio is known for its beautiful hill country.

Weather and wind more than make up for the lack of hills in presenting the cyclist with challenges. In Nebraska, Kansas, and Missouri, humidity combined with highs that often reach 100 degrees in summer can test the strongest rider. To the north, the Dakotas are usually cooler, but if you're riding into a head wind, you'll work up a sweat anyway. Be prepared for precipitation and cooler temperatures near the Great Lakes. Throughout the region, intense thunder and hail storms can cause problems: For example, the world's largest hailstones were recorded in Coffeyville, Kansas on Sept. 3, 1979. Wear your helmet!

Illinois
• **Rock River Country**
Distance: 165 miles/275 kilometers
Duration: 3–4 days
Rating: Easy
Type: Loop Tour
Access: Rockford is in north-central Illinois and is accessible by road and air.
Accommodations: Some facilities are available in Rockford, Dixon, and Freeport. Camping is available in Lowden State Park and Rock Cut State Park.
Route Description: You begin this trip in Rockford, bisected by the Rock River. Since the streets were originally designed to accommodate the winding river, they can be a bit confusing. While in Rockford, check out the Midway Village and Museum Center, The Time Museum, Burpee Museum of Natural History, Tinker Swiss Cottage, Inc.,

and the Sinnissippi Gardens, Greenhouse, and Lagoon, which contains a bicycle trail.

Cycle southwest on No. 2 from Rockford, following the Rock River through Byron, Oregon, Castle Rock State Park, Grand Detour, and Dixon (where former President Ronald Reagan grew up; his boyhood home has been restored and is open to the public). Continue your ride to Sterling (noted as a producer of builders' hardware). Cycle northeast on No. 88, No. 9, No. 12, and No. 7 to Polo, and then bike on No. 26 north to Forreston and Freeport.

Take No. 75 northeast from Freeport to Rockton, crossing the Rock River. Continue east to No. 251, and then ride southwest on No. 251, back to Rockford.

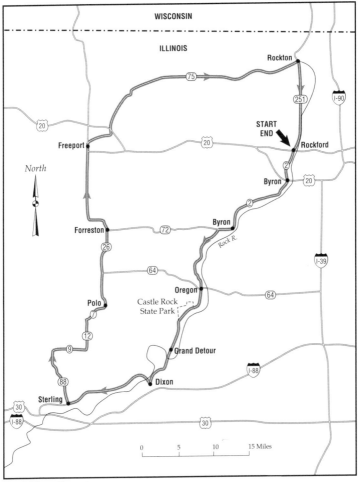

Rock River Country

The cycling has been relatively easy, as Illinois is one of the levelest of the prairie states. You have followed a section of the picturesque Rock River on this loop tour.

Other Tours

• **The Shawnee National Forest Loop**

In southeastern Illinois, the hilly terrain of Shawnee National Forest serves as a contrast to the level farmland of central Illinois. Several country roads provide access to campgrounds, hiking trails, and unusual rock formations as you cycle through this forested area. Begin this 130-mile (217-kilometer) tour in Marion, and travel south on No. 37 to Goreville and Ferne Clyffe State Park. Ride east on No. 12 by the Lake of Egypt Recreation Area to Tunnel Hill. Then take No. 45 north, No. 8 east, and No. 15 south to the Bell Springs Recreation Area. The trail here features caves and a natural bridge. Cycle southeast on No. 5 to Golconda and northeast on No. 146 to Elizabethtown and Tower Rock Recreation Area. Then take No. 1 south to Cave-in-Rock. If you wish, a ferry will take you across the Wabash River into Kentucky; however, you can continue the Illinois tour by cycling north on No. 1, past Cave-in-Rock State Park and Pounds Hollow Recreation Area. Turn west on No. 13 to Harrisburg, and complete the loop tour by cycling on No. 13 back to Marion.

For more information about the Shawnee National Forest area, contact the Forest Supervisor, Shawnee National Forest, 901 South Commercial Street, Harrisburg, IL 62946; phone (618) 253-7114.

• **From Marion, Illinois, to Marion, Kentucky**

On the Shawnee National Forest Loop (previously described), instead of completing the loop from Cave-in-Rock, take the ferry across the Wabash River into Kentucky, and ride southeast on No. 91 to Marion, Kentucky.

You can complete a loop by cycling north on No. 60 to Sturgis. Then ride northwest on No. 109. Cross the state border line back into Illinois, and cycle west on No. 13 back to Marion, Illinois.

• **Jacksonville Loop**

Cycle south from Jacksonville to Greenfield (on No. 67). Then ride west on No. 108 (taking the ferry across the Illinois River) and north on No. 96 to Kinderhook. Cycle on scenic No. 106 to Woodson, and then travel north on No. 67 back to Jacksonville, completing the 165-mile (275-kilometer) loop tour.

• **The Grand Illinois Trail**

Sections of this 475-mile (792-kilometer) planned trail that are now usable include 55 miles (92 kilometers) of the Illinois Prairie Path through suburban west Chicago, tied in with the 33-mile (55-kilometer) Fox River Trail to the west and a 66-mile (110-kilometer) section of the Illinois and Michigan Canal State Trail from LaSalle to Joliet. For further information, contact: Illinois Department of Natural Resources, 524 S. Second Street, Springfield, IL 62701; phone (217) 782-3715.

Illinois Contacts

Illinois Office of Tourism, 2209 W. Main Street, Marion, IL 62959;
    phone 1-800-223-0121.
Illinois Tourist Information Center, Office of Tourism,
    310 S. Michigan Avenue, Chicago, IL 60604; phone (312) 793-2094.
Midwest Organized Ride Information Service (MORIS); phone
    (708) 848-BIKE.
State Bicycle Coordinator, Illinois Department of Transportation,
    2300 S. Dirksen Parkway, Springfield, IL 62764; phone
    (217) 782-3194.

Indiana

• **Indiana Limestone and Architecture Tour**
Distance: 180 miles/300 kilometers
Duration: 3–5 days
Rating: Moderate
Type: Loop Tour
Access: Columbus is in south-central Indiana (southeast of Indianapolis); routes No. 31, No. 46, No. 9, No. 7, and No. 65 are all in this area.
Accommodations: A variety of lodging is available in Columbus, Scottsburg, Bedford, Bloomington, and Nashville. Camping facilities are also available in Clifty Falls State Park and Spring Mill State Park.
Route Description: This scenic tour passes sharp ridges, deep valleys, mineral springs, and caves in the great limestone belt. You will cycle on several scenic back roads curving through hilly terrain as you journey to several architecturally important areas.

You begin this tour in Columbus. Buildings of advanced architectural design have been fashioned here by such famous architects as Weese, Saarinen, Jones, and Girard; these master architects were attracted by a local foundation that donated the architectural fees for several buildings.

After exploring Columbus, cycle southeast on No. 7, through Elizabethtown, Selmier State Forest, Vernon, Dupont, and Wirt, then on to Madison (near the Kentucky border), where several nineteenth century Federal, Classic Revival, and Italianate style buildings are found. Then ride west on No. 56 to Clifty Falls State Park, Hanover, Scottsburg, and Salem. Ride northwest on No. 60 and north on No. 37 to Bedford, which is an important area for limestone. Some of the nation's most famous buildings have been partially constructed with Bedford limestone, including the Washington Cathedral in Washington, D.C. and the Empire State Building in New York.

Continue north on No. 37 from Bedford, past the Fairfox State Recreation Area and Lake Monroe (Indiana's largest lake), to Bloomington. With about 30 quarries in the Bloomington area, this is another important region for the production of Indiana limestone. Some of the quarries and stone mills are open to visitors.

Cycle east on No. 46 from Bloomington to Belmont Brown County State Park (Indiana's largest state park), Nashville (in the foothills of the Cumberland Mountains, in an area that has attracted many artists), and then back to Columbus.

Other Tours

• **Hoosier National Forest Loop**

The Hoosier National Forest offers many hiking and bridle trails in south-central Indiana. This 63-mile (105-kilometer) tour begins in Bedford (described earlier), at the forest headquarters. You will ride south on No. 37 to Paoli. Just south of Paoli is Pioneer Mothers' Memorial Forest, which is renowned for its big, old trees and is used in ecological studies. Cycle northwest on No. 150 from Paoli to Shoals, and then northeast on No. 50 back to Bedford For more information about the Hoosier National Forest area, phone (812) 275-5987.

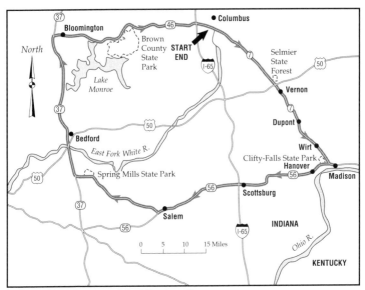

Indiana Limestone and Architecture Tour

• Wabash Valley

Terre Haute, a popular recreational area, is in the fertile Wabash Valley. Blessed with several lovely parks, two of which have 18-hole golf courses, Terre Haute also has more than 800 historic buildings in the Farrington's Grove Historical District. After exploring this area, cycle north on No. 41, following the Wabash River; then turn northeast to Rockville (near Rockville is Billie Creek Village, a re-created early 20th century village). Rockville hosts the Parke County Covered Bridge Festival each year— it has more than Madison County, Iowa. Continue on No. 41 to Annapolis, and then head northeast on No. 47 to Turkey Run State Park, with its deep canyons, spectacular gorges, and bicycle trails; for more information about this beautiful state park, phone (317) 597-2635.

Ride northeast from Turkey Run State Park to Crawfordsville. Then travel south on No. 231, through Greencastle, and take No. 40 west, through Knightsville and Staunton, to the destination of Terre Haute, completing the loop tour of 126 miles (210 kilometers).

• Whitewater Valley

Begin this tour of southeastern Indiana at Versailles State Park, where bike trails are available. Cycle northeast on No. 129 to Batesville. Continue riding northeast, and cross the Whitewater River to Brookville. Bike east to Palestine and north on No. 101 to Liberty. Ride east on No. 44 and north on No. 227 to Richmond, the destination. The Whitewater River Gorge is bordered by a 3.5-mile (6-kilometer) trail that passes several of Richmond's natural and historic attractions.

Indiana Contacts

Brown County Convention and Visitors Bureau, P.O. Box 840, Nashville, IN 47448; phone 1-800-753-3255.

Columbus Visitors Center, 506 Fifth Street, Columbus, IN; phone (812) 372-1954.

Indiana Department of Natural Resources, 402 W. Washington Street, Room 298, Indianapolis, IN 46204; phone (317) 232-4200; guidebooks are available for the Hoosier Bikeway System, with several routes throughout the state.

Madison Chamber of Commerce Visitor Center, Main and Jefferson Streets, Madison, IN; phone (812) 265-2956.

State Bicycle Coordinator, Indiana Department of Transportation, 100 N. Senate Avenue, Room N755, Indianapolis, IN 46204; phone (317) 232-5653.

Tourism Development Division, One N. Capitol, Suite 700, Indianapolis, IN 46204-2288; phone (317) 232-8860 or 1-800-289-6646.

Iowa

• **Across Iowa**

Distance: 441 miles/735 kilometers
Duration: 7–12 days
Rating: Moderate
Type: One-way Tour
Access: Missouri Valley, at the junction of No. 30 and No. 183, is northeast of Omaha, Nebraska, and borders the Willow River, just below a rim of high bluffs. Just to the west is the De Soto National Wildlife Refuge and the Missouri River. Bellevue is situated on the bank of the Mississippi River and is southeast of Dubuque.
Accommodations: This route passes through many small communities, so it's most suitable for the camper; there are, however, some lodgings to be found in some of the small towns. Bellevue State Park, near the destination, has camping facilities.
Route Description: Sponsored by the *Des Moines Register,* the "Register's Annual Great Bike Ride Across Iowa" (RAGBRAI) takes place each summer. Participants in the ride are chosen through a drawing. If you wish to participate in this event, you can register for the draw by mailing an entry and a self-addressed stamped envelope to the address given above. Rides across Iowa vary in length, as do the towns included in the year's RAGBRAI. The ride takes seven days, however, and crosses Iowa from its western border, where you can dip your bicycle wheels in the Missouri River, to the eastern border, where you can jump into the Mississippi. You can, of course, decide to ride across Iowa at your own convenient pace and time, and one particular route across the state is given here.

Begin your tour across Iowa at Missouri Valley, and cycle east to Beebeetown and south to Underwood. Then take No. G30 east to Bentley, Hancock, and Atlantic. This is a hilly route, so be prepared for some good climbs.

Cycle northeast on No. 83 to Wiota, Anita, and Adair (site of Jesse James' first robbery). Continue east to Casey, Stuart, Dexter, and Earlham. Then ride on No. P57 south and No. 92 east to Winterset, in Madison County, setting of the best-seller *The Bridges of Madison County.* Winterset hosts a Covered Bridge Festival, and there are several of them in the area. Donahue Bridge, in City Park, is the oldest of these covered bridges. John Wayne was born in Winterset, and two rooms of his birthplace have been restored to their 1907 appearance (the year of his birth).

Bike southeast on No. G50 to Hanley, St. Charles, and St. Marys. Then cycle south on No. R45 to New Virginia. Head east on No. G76 to Medora, Lacona, and Melcher, and then ride northeast to Knoxville and Pella. Pella is known as the childhood home of Wyatt Earp, and is a well-known center for Dutch heritage. Pella has many tulip gardens and an annual Tulip Festival. The Pella Historical Village Museum displays an early Dutch settlement and the history of this town. The Klockenspel, the town clock, features figures from town history.

Bike north on No. T14 to Galesburg and on No. F62 and No. T22 to Kilduff. Then ride northeast on No. 6 to Oakland Acres, Grinnell, Victor, and Marengo. Cycle northeast from Marengo to the seven

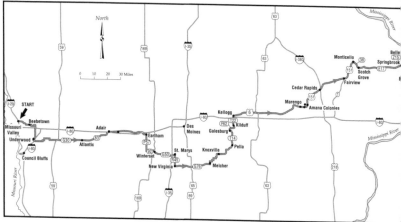

Across Iowa

closely united villages of the Amana Colonies. There are a number of shops and points of interest to visit in this area, including the Amana Woolen Mill, Krauss Furniture Shop, the Museum of Amana History, Barn Museum, and the Communal Kitchen and Coopership Museum. The first houses in the Amana Colonies were large but did not contain kitchens, so central village kitchens were used for the community meals.

Continue northeast on No. 151 to Walford, Cedar Rapids, Marion, Springville, Fairview, Langworthy, and Monticello. Ride on No. 38 southeast to Scotch Grove and No. E17 east to Canton and Springbrook. Finally, bike northeast on No. Z15 to Bellevue, the destination of this trip.

This route takes you on relatively quiet roads through the small towns of central Iowa as you ride from Missouri Valley to Bellevue, across the state from west to east.

Other Tours
• Studying Immigrants and Colonies

Begin this tour in Des Moines, at the fork of the Raccoon and Des Moines Rivers. Cycle southeast (on No. 163) to Pella (detailed in above tour) and Oskaloosa (which was settled by Quakers in 1843). Ride east on No. 92 to Sigourney, and then cycle north on No. 149 to Williamsburg. Continue north on No. V77, doing a loop tour of the Amana Colonies (detailed in above tour). Complete this 158-mile (263-kilometer) trip by cycling on No. 151 to Cedar Rapids, a center of Czech heritage with the nicely preserved, historic Czech Village.

This educational and relatively easy cycling tour presents an interesting cross-section of ethnic Iowa, from the Dutch of Pella to the Amana Colonies, to the Quakers in Oskaloosa and finally to the Czechs in Cedar Rapids.

• **Along the Mississippi River**

This scenic route of 105 miles (175 kilometers) follows the Mississippi River from Dubuque, the oldest city in Iowa, to Davenport. Dubuque is connected by bridges to two other states: Wisconsin and Illinois. Take No. 61 south and No. 52 southeast from Dubuque to Clinton. Head southwest on No. 67 to Folletts, and then bike west on No. F33 to McCausland. Near that tiny village is the Buffalo Bill Homestead, the childhood home of Buffalo Bill Cody (built by his dad in 1847). Cycle south on No. Z16 to the destination of Davenport, which is cradled in a loop of the Mississippi River and is one of the (weirdly enough) five communities known as Quad Cities (the others are Bettendorf, Iowa; East Moline; Moline, and Rock Island all in Illinois); these communities link the states of Iowa and Illinois at this point on the Mississippi River.

• **Wabash Trace Nature Trail**

This 63-mile (105 kilometer) rails-trails route runs from Council Bluffs to Blanchard, in southwestern Iowa. The crushed limestone path even has some bike racks and pop machines along the way. Some portions of this trail extend through open countryside while others are shaded by trees that seem to form an arch over the path. There are daily or annual fees. For more information, contact Depot Deli, 101 Railroad Road, Box 581, Shenandoah, IA 51601; phone (712) 246-4444.

• **Heritage Trail**

This 26-mile (43-kilometer) trail of crushed limestone follows a former railway corridor from Dyersville (setting for the film, *Field of Dreams*) to Segeville (just north of Dubuque). A fossil collecting site is near the halfway point of this relatively easy ride.

Iowa Contacts

Amana Colonies Convention and Visitors Bureau; phone (319) 622-3828 or 1-800-245-5465.

RAGBRAI, P.O. Box 622, Des Moines, IA 50303-0622; phone (515) 284-8282; for information about the "Register's Annual Great Bike Ride Across Iowa."

State Bicycle Coordinator, Iowa Department of Transportation, 800 Lincoln Way, Ames, IA 50010; phone (515) 239-1621.

Tourism Division, Iowa Department of Economic Development, 200 E. Grand, Des Moines, IA 50309; phone (515) 242-4705 or 1-800-345-IOWA.

Kansas
• **Along The Santa Fe Trail**
Distance: 140 miles/233 kilometers
Duration: 2–3 days
Rating: Easy
Type: One-way Tour
Access: Great Bend, the starting point, is in central Kansas, at the junction of No. 96, No. 156, No. 56, and No. 281. Garden City, the destination, is in western Kansas and on the Arkansas River.
Accommodations: Facilities are to be found in Great Bend, Dodge City, and Garden City.
Route Description: Wagon-wheel ruts are still visible in spots, reminders of the pioneers who crossed the Great Plains on the Santa Fe Trail, looking for a more prosperous future. You will cycle near part of the original trail on this route from Great Bend to Garden City.

Great Bend grew up around Fort Zorah, built to protect travelers on the Santa Fe Trail. Fort Zorah Park, 3 miles (5 kilometers) east of town, is the site of the old fort. As the pioneers did, you will head west from Great Bend. Take No. 56, parallel to the original trail. You will pass Pawnee Rock, a large landmark and a dangerous place on the Santa Fe Trail (Indians sometimes waited here for the wagon trains). Next you will arrive at Larned, midway along the Santa Fe Trail. Nearby is Fort Larned National Historic Site, an important post, also built to protect travelers on the trail. Nearby, the Santa Fe Trail Center Museum and Cultural Center depicts the trail's history.

Continue west on No. 56 through Kinsley and Spearville to Dodge City, at one time known as the "Wickedest Little City in America." Dodge City was a stopover on the Santa Fe Trail, and by the late 1800s it was home to many criminals and the site of many gunfights. Boot Hill became the famous cemetery of gunmen and friendless unfortunates. Lawmen such as Bat Masterson and Wyatt Earp were brought in to Dodge City to establish order. Fort Dodge, 5 miles (8 kilometers) to the south, was a vital Army outpost established to protect travelers on the Santa Fe Trail; the fort's history includes such names as Custer, Cody, and Hickock.

Cycle west on No. 50 from Dodge City to Cimarron, Ingalls, and the trip's destination, Garden City. Situated on the Arkansas River, Garden City is in the heart of irrigated lands that produce bumper crops of alfalfa, wheat, and corn.

Other Tours
• **Little House on the Prairie Loop**
Laura Ingalls Wilder, the author *of Little House on the Prairie*, lived in a log cabin near Independence, Kansas, from 1869 to 1871. A reconstructed log cabin, post office, and a one-room schoolhouse are displayed at the original site. To get there, ride southwest on No. 75 from Independence. For more information, phone: Little House on the Prairie at (316) 331-1890.

After visiting this site, complete your 229-mile (382-kilometer) loop tour by riding west on No. 166 to South Haven, north on No. 81 to Wellington, and east on No. 160 back to Independence. It's a relatively flat ride.

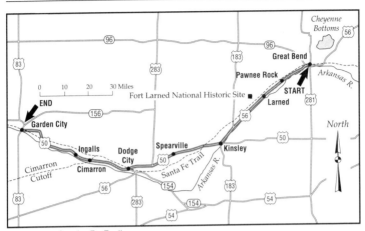

Along the Sante Fe Trail

• **Central Kansas**

To explore central Kansas, ride east on No. 4 from LaCrosse to Hope (a 136-mile or 227-kilometer route) or south on No. 14 from Jewell to Anthony (a 192-mile or 320-kilometer route). These two routes are most suitable for the camper, as you cycle through many small towns.

• **Biking Across Kansas**

Biking Across Kansas (BAK) is an annual 8-day bicycle tour that crosses the Sunflower State in early June, with more than 1,000 participants. Groups of riders ride on three parallel routes, beginning at separate points on the Colorado border; these groups converge in Missouri. One specific route used on this tour is begins at Saunders, near the Colorado border, and goes east to Johnson City, Sublette, Dodge City, St. John, Kingman, Wellington, Howard, Parsons, and on to the Missouri border. Another route begins northwest of Elkhart (on No. 51) and takes you east to Liberal, Ashland, Medicine Lodge, Anthony, Arkansas City, Sedan, Parsons, and on to the Missouri border. The third route has you begin northeast of Elkhart (on No. 51), cycling east to Satanta, Meade, Coldwater, Harper, Winfield, Sedan, Parsons, and on to the Missouri border. I would recommend yet another west to east route, from St. Francis to Elwood (on No. 36). If you prefer a north-south route, cycle south on No. 23 from Hoxie to Meade.

Kansas Contacts

Dodge City Convention and Visitors Bureau, P.O. Box 1474, Dodge City, KS 67801; phone (316) 227-2176.

Fort Larned National Historic Site; phone (316) 285-6911.

Kansas road conditions hot-line: phone 1-800-585-ROAD.

Kansas Travel and Tourism, 700 S.W. Harrison Street, Suite 1300, Topeka, KS 66603-3755; phone 1-800-2 KANSAS.

State Bicycle Coordinator, Kansas Department of Transportation, 2nd Floor, Thrasher Bldg., 217 S.E. 4th Street, Topeka, KS 66603; phone (913) 296-7448; a free "Bicycle Guide" with recommended routes is available.

Michigan
• **Upper Peninsula Tour**
Distance: 205 miles/342 kilometers
Duration: 3–6 days
Rating: Moderate
Type: Loop Tour
Access: Marquette (at the intersection of No. 41 and No. 28) is on the southern shore of Lake Superior and is surrounded by the rugged Laurentian Uplands.
Accommodations: Services are available at Marquette and at several locations along this route.
Route Description: Begin this trip in Marquette, where a bicycle trail will help you to avoid the heavy city traffic. You will ride east on No. 28 from Marquette to Harvey, Au Train, Christmas (where you can do "Christmas shopping" or mail a "Christmas letter" year-round), and Munising. This route has many scenic outlooks as you cycle along the shore of Lake Superior, passing miles of rocky cliffs and sandy beaches.

At Munising, you should cruise by Pictured Rocks National Lakeshore. You will then follow the lakeshore by cycling northeast on No. H58 (partially gravel) to Grand Marais, passing high cliffs and beautiful sand dunes along this fascinating route (referred to in Longfellow's poem, *The Song of Hiawatha*).

You will leave the Lake Superior shoreline and cycle south on No. 77 to Seney (where you might explore the Seney Wildlife Refuge) and Blaney Park. Turn west on No. 2, and ride along the north shore of Lake Michigan, through Gulliver, Manistique (which provides access to Lake Superior State Forest, with its many lakes and streams), Thompson, Cooks, Isabella, Nahma Junction, and Ensign to Rapid River. Then bike northwest on No. 41, through the Hiawatha National Forest, back to Marquette.

You will find a good, paved shoulder for most of this hilly, pretty route.

Other Tours
• **The Keweenaw Peninsula**
The Keweenaw Peninsula is the northernmost point on Michigan's Upper Peninsula and is the spectacular setting for this cycling tour. For more information about the peninsula, phone Keweenaw Tourism at 1-800-338-7982.

Cycle northeast from Hancock to Calumet on No. 203. Then take No. 41 to Ahmeek. Pedal west to Five Mile Point Road, which skirts the shoreline and the bluffs. Take No. 26 from Eagle River to Copper Harbor (near Fort Wilkins State Park). Cycle southwest on No. 41 past Mandan and take the road that follows around the peninsula to Gay. Cycle west to Lake Linden, and then ride southwest on No. 26 back to Hancock, completing the 102-mile (170-kilometer) loop tour.

• **Tahquamenon Falls Loop Tour**
Begin this trip in Newberry, in northeast Michigan, on Michigan's Upper Peninsula. Cycle east on No. 28 to Soo Junction (where you can take a narrow gauge railroad and boat trip to the rapids above the Upper Tahquamenon Falls) and Hulbert (where you can take a riverboat

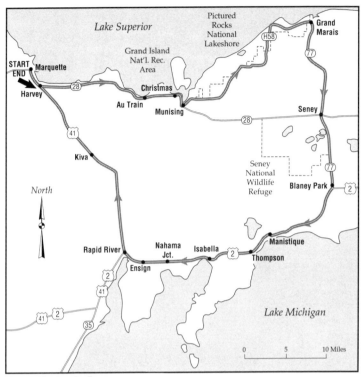

Upper Peninsula Tour

cruise and a timber train to the Upper Falls). Leave No. 28, and cycle north on No. 123 to Paradise (really!) on Whitefish Bay. Continue north to Whitefish Point, site of the Great Lakes Shipwreck Historical Museum, which features the ore carrier *Edmund Fitzgerald,* which sank in a November gale and is immortalized in song by Gordon Lightfoot. After exploring this area, return to Paradise, and then bike southwest on No. 123, completing your tour of Tahquamenon Falls State Park. Lower Tahquamenon Falls is divided by an island. The Upper Falls is nearly 50 feet high and 200 feet wide, making it Michigan's largest. Continue cycling through Lake Superior State Forest, passing Four Mile Corner, and return to Newberry.

This 205-mile (342-kilometer) loop tour in northern Michigan takes you through a densely forested region as you cycle on relatively quiet roads and in rather hilly terrain.

• **Lake Michigan Shoreline**
    This 96-mile (160-kilometer) trip takes you along a picturesque section of Lake Michigan's shoreline, past sand dunes, lighthouses, and several state parks (with camping facilities), as you cycle from Ludington to Holland (on Michigan's west coast).

Leaving Ludington, cycle around Pere Marquette Lake, hugging the shoreline as you ride south to Charles Mears State Park, Pentwater, Silver Lake State Park, Sand Dunes Little Point Sable, Stony Lake, Duck Lake State Park, Muskegon State Park, and Muskegon. Continue south, on the quieter shoreline roads, to P. J. Hoffmaster State Park, Little Black Lake, and Grand Haven (at the mouth of the Grand River). Bike along the shoreline from Grand Haven to Holland State Park, and complete the route by riding to Holland, which (did you guess from the name?) was settled by Dutch immigrants. Holland's roots are still in evidence in Dutch Village (with its gardens, klompen dances, carvings, and windmills), the Wooden Shoe Factory, Netherlands Museum, Veldheer Tulip Gardens, the DeKlomp Wooden Shoe and Delftware Factory, and Windmill Island.

• **Pedal Across Lower Michigan**
Begin this route at Benton Harbor, near the southeastern tip of Lake Michigan. Ride east on No. 62 to Cassopolis and No. 60 to Homer. Go southeast on No. 99 and northeast on No. 12 to Cambridge Junction. Head southeast on No. 50 to your destination, Monroe (on Lake Erie). This 163-mile (272-kilometer) route is most suitable for campers, and you ride on relatively quiet roads on your journey across Lower Michigan.

For more information about P.A.L.M. (Pedal Across Lower Michigan), contact: PALM, P.O. Box 7161, Ann Arbor, MI 48107; phone (313) 665-6327.

Michigan Contacts

League of Michigan Bicyclists, P.O. Box 16201, Lansing, MI 48901; phone (313) 379-BIKE.

Michigan Mountain Biking Association, P.O. Box 274, Detroit, MI 48231.

Non-motorized Coordinator, Statewide Planning Section, Michigan Department of Transportation, P.O. Box 30050, Lansing, MI 48909; phone (517) 335-2823.

Three Oaks Spokes, Bicycle Museum and Information Center, 110 N. Elm, Three Oaks, MI 49128; phone (616) 756-3361.

Travel Bureau, Michigan Department of Commerce, P.O. Box 30226, Lansing, MI 48909; phone 1-800-5432-YES.

Upper Peninsula Travel and Recreation, 600 Stephenson Avenue, P.O. Box 400, Iron Mountain, MI 49801; phone 1-800-562-7134.

Minnesota
• **Paul Bunyan Country**
Distance: 166 miles/277 kilometers
Duration: 3–5 days
Rating: Moderate
Type: One-way Tour
Access: In northwestern Minnesota, on the shore of Bemidji Lake, Bemidji is at the junction of No. 2 and No. 71. Brainerd is about 17 miles (28 kilometers) west of Mille Lacs Lake (on No. 18).
Accommodations: Several services are available in this recreation area, with full services available in both Bemidji and Brainerd.
Route Description: According to legend (actually a publicity campaign for an early lumber company), the thousands of lakes across Minnesota were formed when melting snow filled in the hoof prints left by Babe, Paul Bunyan's blue ox. As you begin this trip at Bemidji, south of Red Lake, you will see a massive statue of Babe and Paul Bunyan, on the waterfront.

Leaving the statue behind, cycle southwest on No. 71 from Bemidji (which means "lake with river flowing through it" to the Ojibwe tribe) to Itasca State Park (where you can see the source of the Mississippi River). There are 17 miles (28 kilometers) of paved bicycle trails in Itasca State Park, so this is a great place for an enjoyable, traffic-free exploration. You will also find bike rentals, cabins, and lake cruises within this park.

Continue south on No. 71, passing several more of Babe's "hoof prints" before you arrive at Park Rapids, a fishing and recreation resort town. Ride northeast on No. 34 to Walker, another fishing resort town. Bike south on No. 37 from Walker to Hackensack, Pine River, and Nisswa, and then cycle southeast to Brainerd, site of the Paul Bunyan Amusement Center (yet another town that banks on the legend of Paul Bunyan and Babe).

Other Tours
• **North Shore of Lake Superior Route**
The ride along Highway 61, following the North Shore of Lake Superior in northeast Minnesota, is possibly one of the prettiest in the country. Highway 61 crops up again and again in Top 10 lists of the nation's most scenic roads. Start in Duluth and head northeast to Grand Portage, near the Canadian Border. This route is hilly in places, and the shoreline is often rugged. The 150-mile (250-kilometer) route offers many opportunities for camping and hiking, but it's also a popular resort area, with lots of motels and lodges.

Cycle on North Shore Drive (No. 61) as you ride northeast along the North Shore of Lake Superior. You will pass many parks and waterfalls on this magnificent route, including Gooseberry Falls State Park (camping and hiking, several waterfalls, rugged lakeshore), Split Rock Lighthouse State Park (which has access to the Superior Hiking Trail), Tettegouche State Park (which has one of the highest waterfalls in Minnesota), Caribou Falls State Park, Temperance River State Park, and Judge C. R. Magney State Park, before you reach your destination of Grand Portage. If you wish, you could continue your cycling trip to Thunder Bay, Ontario, Canada. Simply cross the border and continue north on No. 61.

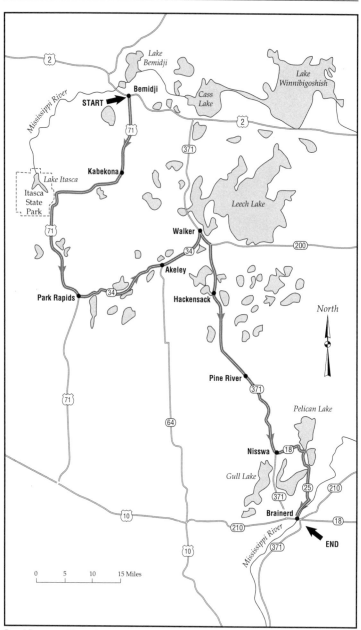

Paul Bunyan Country

Grand Portage was the earliest European settlement in Minnesota. The site has been partially reconstructed at Grand Portage National Monument, where you can learn about the voyageurs, who used the portage routes originally developed for transit and trade by the tribes in the region. An 8.5-mile (14-kilometer) trail follows part of a portage route to Fort Charlotte. For more information, contact: Superintendent, Grand Portage National Monument, Box 666, Grand Marais, MN 55604; phone (218) 387-2788.

• From Manitoba to Wisconsin

For an enjoyable 270-mile (450-kilometer) route across Minnesota, cycle from Warroad (near the Manitoba border) to Duluth, where you can cross a bridge to Superior, Wisconsin. Ride southwest on No. 11 from Warroad (known as "Hockeytown, U.S.A.") to Baudette ("Walleye Capital of the World") and International Falls ("Icebox of the Nation").

A slightly shorter alternative takes you through a section of Canada—from Rainy River (near Baudette) to Fort Frances (just across the border from International Falls). Cycle south on No. 53 from International Falls, through Kabetogama State Forest and Superior National Forest. With its wide shoulders, this is an excellent road for cycling—you'll feel as if you have an entire lane to yourself. As you ride through scenic, forested northern Minnesota, you will see deer and maybe even a moose; however, you are even more likely to see a few lumber trucks along the way.

As you near the end of this trip, you will travel on a 4-lane highway (from Virginia to Duluth).

At Duluth, visit the Enger Memorial Tower on Skyline Parkway, the highest point in Duluth. Enjoy the view of the Twin Ports (Duluth and Superior) before descending (on a 9 percent grade) on your way to the No. 2 bridge to Superior. Take note that you must leave No. 53 at Duluth. Do not cross the Blatnik Bridge on No. 53; it's far too dangerous for bicycles.

• Across Southern Minnesota

This quiet, 260-mile (433-kilometer) route will take you across southern Minnesota, from Pipestone (stop at the National Monument where tribes from all over the Great Plains quarried stone to make sacred pipes) to the Mississippi River town of Winona. Ride east on No. 30 from Pipestone to Hayfield. Ride north on No. 56 to Dodge Center and east on No. 14, through Rochester, to your destination, Winona (on the Mississippi River). Winona serves as the headquarters for the Upper Mississippi River National Wildlife and Fish Refuge, an area of almost 200,000 acres.

Minnesota Contacts

Explore Minnesota Bikeways, Minnesota Department of
   Transportation, Room G-19, M.S. 260, St. Paul, MN 55155; phone
   (612) 296-2216.
Itasca State Park, phone (218) 266-3654.
Minnesota Travel Information Center, 250 Skyway Level, 375 Jackson
   Street, St. Paul, MN 55101; phone (612) 296-5029 or 1-800-657-3700.
State Bicycle Safety Coordinator, 340 Coffey Hall, University of
   Minnesota, St. Paul, MN 55108; phone (612) 625-9719.

Missouri
• **Mark Twain Country**
Distance: 130 miles/217 kilometers
Duration: 2–4 days
Rating: Easy
Type: One-way tour
Access: Hannibal is in the northeast part of the state, on the Mississippi River, which marks the border with Illinois. St. Louis, further south, and still along the Mississippi River, is accessible by roads, river, air, and rail.
Accommodations: Full services are available at both Hannibal and St. Louis, with some services also along the route.
Route Description: This tour will take you from Mark Twain's childhood home in Hannibal, south along the Mississippi River, to St. Louis. The cycling will be relatively easy as you bike through Mark Twain Country.

Hannibal is the southern migration destination for many bald eagles; they live here along the high bluffs above the Mississippi River. Hannibal is also known as the home of Samuel Clemens (Mark Twain), author of classics such as *The Adventures of Tom Sawyer* and *Huckleberry Finn*. Twain used the Hannibal area as the setting for several of his stories. Hannibal plays host to Tom Sawyer Days each summer, a festival that includes a fence-painting contest. A Tom-and-Huck Monument is at the foot of Cardiff Hill. You might also like to visit Mark Twain's Boyhood Home and Museum, Riverview Park (with a statue of Mark Twain), Adventures of Tom Sawyer Dioramas, and Mark Twain Excursion Boat tours on the Mississippi River.

When you leave Hannibal on No. 79 south, ride 2 miles (3 kilometers) before arriving at Mark Twain Cave, the cave where Tom and Becky get lost in *The Adventures of Tom Sawyer*; guided tours are available.

Continue southeast on No. 79, traveling through Louisiana and Clarksville (an apple-growing area), and down to St. Peters. Ride northeast to Kempville, Orchard Farm, and West Alton. Take No. 111 south to St. Louis, the destination.

St. Louis is most famous for the Gateway Arch, but other points of interest include the National Museum of Transport, the National Bowling Hall of Fame and Museum, St. Louis Science Center, St. Louis Zoological Park, Missouri Botanical Garden, Forest Park, Laumeier Sculpture Park, Lone Elk Park, Soldiers' Memorial Military Museum and, of course, the Anheuser-Busch Brewery.

Other Tours
• **Jefferson City Loop Tour**
Jefferson City, the state capital, overlooks the Missouri River. This 275-mile (458-kilometer) loop tour takes you west on No. 50 from Jefferson City to Otterville and north on No. 135 and No. 41 to historic Arrow Rock State Park, where the Santa Fe Trail met the Missouri River. Continue on No. 41 and then on No. 240 and No. 40 east to Columbia, home of the University of Missouri as well as Columbia and Stephens colleges. Ride on quiet rural roads southeast from Columbia to Fulton and Readsville. Then cross the Missouri River to Hermann (in wine

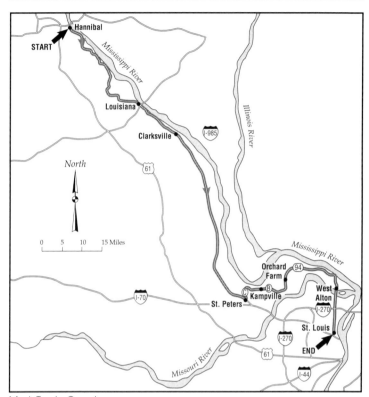

Mark Twain Country

country). Ride south on No. 19 to Drake and west on No. 50 back to Jefferson City.

• The Ozarks

The Ozark Mountains stretch across southern Missouri. In earlier times, the area gained a reputation as an isolated region in which farmers could hide moonshine stills. The hardwood forests covering the hills hide many caves (in what is sometimes referred to as "The Cave State"). You will cycle through a rather remote area, so be prepared. Your route will be quite hilly and wooded, and you will pass several caves and large springs on this 120-mile (200-kilometer) trip.

Begin this tour in Van Buren, in southeastern Missouri, at park headquarters for Ozark National Scenic Riverways. For more information, contact: Ozark National Scenic Riverways, P.O. Box 490, Van Buren, MO 63965; phone 314-323-4236.

Travel west on No. 80 to Winona. Then cycle north on No. 19 to Eminence and Round Spring (near Round Spring you can take a lantern tour of the Round Spring Cavern). Continue north to Timber, and then cycle east on No. 72 and south on No. 21 to Ellington, Deer Run State Forest, and back to Van Buren.

• **The Katy Trail**

This rails-to-trails conversion route, known as the Katy Trail or as the Missouri River State Trail, stretches for about 200 miles (350 kilometers) along the Missouri River from Boonville to St. Charles (near St. Louis), passing close to several small towns (handy for camping and supplies). At Defiance, near the end of the route, you can visit the house that Daniel Boone lived in during his last years (after he had left Kentucky in debt). For more information about this crushed-limestone trail, contact: Katy Trail State Park, Missouri Department of Natural Resources, P.O. Box 176, Jefferson City, MO 65102; phone 1-800-334-6946.

Missouri Contacts

Mark Twain Cave, Hannibal, MO; phone 1-800-527-0304.

Missouri Division of Tourism, P.O. Box 1055, Jefferson City, MO 65102; phone (314) 751-2781.

State Bicycle Coordinator, Missouri Highway Department, P.O. Box 270, Jefferson City, MO 65102; a bicycle map of the state is available.

St. Louis Convention and Visitors Commission's Office, 10 S. Broadway, St. Louis, MO 63102; phone (314) 421-1023 or 1-800-247-9791.

Mickey Gilley's tour bus is often found parked near his restaurant in the renowned country music town of Branson, Missouri.

Nebraska

• Scottsbluff to Grand Island

Distance: 344 miles/573 kilometers
Duration: 5–8 days
Rating: Easy/Moderate
Type: One-way tour
Access: Scottsbluff is in the fertile valley of the North Platte River, in western Nebraska, near the Wyoming border. It's accessible by motor vehicle, boat, and airplane. Grand Island, the destination, is accessible by air, rail, and road.
Accommodations: Facilities are found in both Scottsbluff and Grand Island. This route is most suitable for the camper, however, because it's a rural area, and because it goes past several recreation areas with camping facilities.
Route Description: This scenic tour will take you across central Nebraska from Scottsbluff to Grand Island. Much of this route traverses less-traveled state roadways and roads with wide, paved shoulders.

Scotts Bluff (it's two words; the town is one), 5 miles (8 kilometers) southwest of town, is a national monument now. During the 1800s, it was a prominent landmark on the Oregon Trail. At that point, pioneers quit following the river and cut through the Mitchell Pass to avoid rough terrain. Scotts Bluff was named after a trapper who died in the area in about 1828. A 1.5-mile (3-kilometer) paved road passes through three tunnels to the summit, and from here you can get a panoramic view of the North Platte Valley. Biking and hiking trails are plentiful in this area.

Leaving Scotts Bluff, cycle east on No. 92 to Chimney Rock, an Oregon Trail landmark that signaled the end of the prairies for the pioneers heading west. Chimney Rock rises high above the south bank of the North Platte River.

Continue riding east on No. 92 through the Bridgeport State Recreation Area, past such pioneer landmarks as Courthouse Rock and Jail Rock. Cross the river to Northport, and then bike north on No. 385 to Alliance where, nearby, you can see Carhenge, a spoof of Stonehenge

Scottsbluff to Grand Island

where 26 cars have been buried trunk down and 7 more cars have been placed atop them, forming arches.

From Alliance, cycle east on No. 2 to Broken Bow, the Ravenna State Recreation Area, and on to your destination, Grand Island, where you can learn more about prairie life in Nebraska by visiting the Stuhr Museum of the Prairie Pioneer.

Other Tours
• Around Lake McConaughy

Begin this 69-mile (115-kilometer) tour of the lake at Ogallala, named for the Oglala band of the Lakota tribe. Although now a quiet resort town, Ogallala was once known as the "Gomorrah of the Plains" because of the violence and rowdy behavior of the cowboys who liked to "let off steam" after bringing cattle here for shipping.

Head northwest on No. 26, which has a wide, paved shoulder. Climb Windlass Hill, the place where pioneers' wagons had to be lowered from a hill crest by windlass; ruts carved by wagon trains are still in evidence at this famous spot on the Oregon Trail. As you continue on this route, you will pass Ash Hollow State Park and stretches of fertile cropland on your way to Lewellen. Turn east on No. 92, cycling through the Lake McConaughy State Recreation Area to the Lake Ogallala State Recreation Area. Complete your journey by continuing to ride around the lake (the largest in Nebraska) and back to Ogallala.

• Lincoln Loop

Lincoln, the state capital, is in southeastern Nebraska. Ride east on No. 2 to Nebraska City, where Arbor Lodge State Historical Park is found on the edge of town. The homestead of J. Sterling Morton, founder of Arbor Day is in the park. Head south on No. 75 to Auburn and west on No. 136 to Beatrice. Just northwest of Beatrice (on No. 4) is Homestead National Monument, which contains displays about pioneer life and the evolving of the Homestead Act of 1862, which opened a vast area of the West to settlers. Returning to Beatrice, ride north on No. 77 back to Lincoln.

• Cowboy Trail

A planned 320-mile (533-kilometer) rails-to-trails route between Chadron and Norfolk, across northern Nebraska, is well under way. For information about this wide gravel trail, contact: Nebraska Game and Parks Commission, P.O. Box 30370, Lincoln, NE 68503; phone (402) 471-5425.

Nebraska Contacts

Nebraska National Forest; phone (308) 432-3367.
Nebraska Travel and Tourism Division, P.O. Box 94666, Lincoln, NE 68509; phone 1-800-742-7595 (in Nebraska) or 1-800-228-4307.
State Bicycle Coordinator, Nebraska Department of Roads, Transportation Planning Division, P.O. Box 94759, Lincoln, NE 68509; phone (402) 479-4519; a free "Suggested Bicycle Route Guide Map" is available.
Superintendent, Scotts Bluff National Monument, NE; phone (308) 436-4340.

North Dakota
• **Theodore Roosevelt National Park**
Distance: 296 miles/493 kilometers
Duration: 5–8 days
Rating: Easy to Moderate
Type: Loop tour
Access: Williston is in the northwestern part of the state, near the Montana border (at the junction of No. 85 and No. 2). Williston is also accessible by rail and air.
Accommodations: Facilities are available in Williston, but this route is best suited to the camper (campsites available near Watford City, in Theodore Roosevelt National Park, and in Little Missouri Bay Primitive State Park).
Route Description: Theodore Roosevelt first came to North Dakota's Badlands in 1883 to hunt bison and other game. Theodore Roosevelt National Park is so named to pay tribute to his contributions to the conservation of the area's natural resources. Bison, pronghorn antelope, mule deer, white-tailed deer, elk, and buffalo are among the wildlife found in this park.

This tour begins and ends in Williston, in northwestern North Dakota. It was near here that Chief Sitting Bull surrendered in 1881 (Fort Buford State Historic Site). Cycle south from Williston to Rawson on No. 85. Then

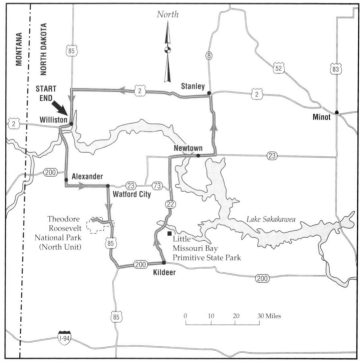

Theodore Roosevelt National Park

bike east on No. 23 to Watford City and south on No. 85 to the entrance to the North Section of Theodore Roosevelt National Park (the park is divided into three units: North, South, and the Elkhorn Ranch Site).

Once in the park, take the 14-mile (23-kilometer) route to Oxbow Overlook, and then return. You'll see geological layers of history in the exposed rock walls of the buttes and ridges.

After exploring the park, continue south on No. 85 past Grassy Butte. Cycle east on No. 200 to Kildeer. Ride north on No. 22, past Little Missouri Bay Primitive State Park and on to the Fort Berthold Indian Reservation. Cycle east on No. 23 through New Town. Bike north on No. 8 to Stanley, and then ride west on No. 2 back to Williston.

The grades have been relatively easy on this loop tour, which has included a section of Theodore Roosevelt National Park. Be mindful of the weather; sudden storms can come up, and finding shelter in this remote area can be difficult.

Other Tours
• **The International Peace Garden**

Set among the lakes and streams of the Turtle Mountains, the International Peace Garden commemorates the friendship between the United States and Canada, which share the world's largest unfortified border. With acreage in both countries, be prepared to go through customs. Then ride south on No. 281 for 45 miles (75 kilometers) through Dunseith to Rugby, "the Geographical Center of North America."

• **Wildlife Refuge Loop**

This loop begins in Minot, in northwestern North Dakota. Cycle northwest on No. 92 to the first of the wildlife refuges on this tour, the Des Lacs National Wildlife Refuge (sharp-tailed grouse and Baird's sparrows are among the bird species found in this river valley). Cycle east on No. 5, riding through a part of the Upper Souris Wildlife Refuge, which extends along the Souris River and is a resting and feeding area for shore birds during migration (partridge, ring-necked pheasants, sharp-tailed grouse, and tundra swans are commonly seen). Travel south on No. 14 to another waterfowl sanctuary along the Souris River, the J. Clark Sayer National Wildlife Refuge, which extends all the way north to the Canadian border (a sanctuary where mallards, blue-winged teal, and Canada geese are commonly seen). Continue southwest on No. 14 to Towner. Then bike west on No. 2 back to Minot, your destination on this 210-mile (350-kilometer) loop tour. For more information, contact: Des Lacs National Wildlife Refuge by phoning (701) 385-4046; Upper Souris National Wildlife Refuge by phoning (701) 468-5467; J. Clark Sayer National Wildlife Refuge by phoning (701) 768-2548.

North Dakota Contacts
North Dakota Tourism, 604 E. Boulevard Avenue, Bismarck, ND 58505; phone 1-800-435-5663.

State Bicycle Coordinator, State Highway Department, 600 E. Boulevard Avenue, Bismarck, ND 58501; phone (701) 328-4463.

Superintendent, Theodore Roosevelt National Park, Medora, ND 58645; phone (701) 623-4466.

Ohio
• The Lake Erie Islands

Distance: 57 miles/95 kilometers
Duration: 3–4 days
Rating: Easy
Type: One-way Tour
Access: Port Clinton is 40 miles (67 kilometers) east of Toledo on the shore of Lake Erie. Vermilion, the destination, is 20 miles (33 kilometers) east of Sandusky and also on the shore of Lake Erie.
Accommodations: The small resort town of Port Clinton offers a variety of facilities, as do several of the islands and towns on this tour. Excellent camping opportunities abound.
Route Description: Off the Marblehead Peninsula in northern Ohio is a group of islands in Lake Erie that is renowned as a vacation area. This relatively easy bicycle trip will take you to these islands and along the shore of beautiful Lake Erie.

Begin this trip at Port Clinton, and ride northeast on No. 53, past Catawba Island State Park, to Catawba Point (riding on a very nice bike lane). Take the ferry to Put-in-Bay, on South Bass Island. This area is known for its fish hatcheries, caves, and wineries. For example, you might visit Crystal Cave, with one of the world's largest geodes, or Heineman Winery, with a tour and explanation of the wine-making process. South Bass Island is also the site of South Bass State Park, which offers fishing, camping, boating, and hiking.

If you have time, take a ferry from South Bass Island to Middle Bass Island and explore it before you return to the mainland at Catawba Point. Then ride south on No. 53 and east on No. 163 to East Harbor State Park (with nature programs and hiking trails), Lakeside (a resort with large summer conference facilities), and Marblehead (at the top of Marblehead Peninsula); this section of the peninsula is noted for its orchards (peaches and apples) and vineyards.

Take the ferry from Marblehead to Kelleys Island. This summer resort is at the center of a grape-growing region. At the southern tip of the island is Kelleys Island State Park, where the Glacial Grooves tell part of the area's geological story. These scars in rock were made by the glaciers of the Ice Age, and where they stripped away stone, you can see fossilized marine life is embedded in the limestone bedrock. Human history can be seen in the pictographs at Inscription Rock State Memorial.

After exploring Kelleys Island, take the ferry back to the mainland, to Sandusky, which is on Sandusky Bay, a natural harbor on Lake Erie formed by the Cedar Point and Marblehead Peninsulas. While in this area, visit Cedar Point, an amusement park well-known for its water slides and roller coasters.

Complete your tour by cycling east on No. 6 from Sandusky to Huron, Ruggles Beach, Mitiwanga Park, and Vermilion (the destination). Vermilion is a fishing village and popular resort on the banks of the Vermilion River and Lake Erie, and it celebrates its heritage through an annual Boat Regatta and the Festival of the Fish. Guided tours of the old downtown area, Harbour Town, are available. You can also learn more about the history of the area in the Great Lakes Historical Society Museum.

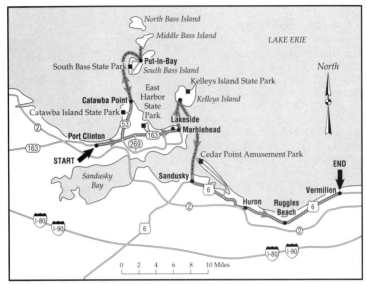

The Lake Erie Islands

Other Tours
• Southern Ohio

The Ohio and Scioto Rivers meet at Portsmouth, where you begin this relatively easy 177-mile (295-kilometer) loop tour. Cycle west on No. 52, following the Ohio River to Friendship, Buena Vista, Rome, Wrightsville, and Aberdeen. Leave the banks of the Ohio River at Aberdeen, cycling northeast on No. 41 to Bentonville, Adams Lake State Park, Fort Hill State Memorial (site of a prehistoric earthwork thought to have been built by the Hopewell Indians), and Bainbridge (called the "Cradle of American Dentistry" after the first school of dentistry was established here in 1826). Just west of Bainbridge is Seven Caves, where a tour guides you underground; above ground, you can see fascinating waterfalls, cliffs, and canyons.

Ride northwest on No. 50 from Bainbridge to Seip Mound State Memorial, which contains the great central mound of the Hopewell Indians. Continue your journey by cycling to Chillicothe, and then bike south on No. 23, past Scioto Trail State Park, and through a section of the Wayne National Forest (with more than 100 miles or 160 kilometers of hiking trails and several scenic covered bridges) before completing the loop by returning to Portsmouth.

• Amish Country

Begin this 45-mile (75-kilometer) loop tour in Berlin, about 36 miles (60 kilometers) southwest of Canton. Berlin is in the heart of Amish Country and provides you with an opportunity to view the Amish lifestyle. You will cycle on quiet country roads, perhaps accompanied by families in horse-drawn buggies, as you ride through this area, visiting such towns as Charm, New Bedford, Baltic, Ragersville, and Sugarcreek.

Ride northwest on No. 39 from Sugarcreek (known as the "Little Switzerland of Ohio" because of its Swiss architecture) to Walnut Grove, and then bike north on No. 515 to Winesburg (setting for Sherwood Anderson's ground-breaking novel, *Winesburg, Ohio*). Ride southwest from Winesburg back to Berlin.

• **Richland County Bikeway**
This 18-mile (30-kilometer) blacktop bikeway follows the former B&O Railroad right of way through the Clear Fork River Valley and connects Mansfield, Lexington, Bellville, and Butler. By cycling south, you will notice a slightly downhill grade on this route. For more information, phone the Gorman Nature Center at (419) 884-3764.

• **Ohio to Erie Trail**
A planned 325-mile (542-kilometer) rails-to-trails route, from Cleveland to Cincinnati, has begun. A 72-mile (120-kilometer) section of this trail is already open north of Cincinnati; included is the 25-mile (42-kilometer) Little Miami River Gorge section, where bluffs tower above the crushed limestone and asphalt path. For more information, contact: Ohio to Erie Trail Fund, P.O. Box 21246, Columbus, OH 43221; phone (614) 538-0607.

Ohio Contacts
Friends of Harbour Town 1837, Old Jib's Corner, 5741 Liberty Avenue, Vermilion, OH; phone (216) 967-4262.
Miller Ferry from Catawba to Put-in-Bay, South Bass Island; phone (419) 285-2421.
Ohio Bicycle Federation, Dayton Chamber of Commerce, Chamber Plaza, 5th and Main Streets, Dayton, OH 45402; phone (513) 226-1444.
Ohio Division of Travel and Tourism, P.O. Box 1001, Columbus, OH 43216; phone 1-800-BUCKEYE.
State Bicycle Coordinator, Ohio Department of Transportation, Room 308, P.O. Box 899, Columbus, OH 43216; phone (614) 644-7095.

South Dakota
• **The Black Hills of South Dakota**
Distance: 134 miles/223 kilometers
Duration: 2–4 days
Rating: Strenuous
Type: Loop Tour
Access: Rapid City is in southwestern South Dakota and is the tourist headquarters for the Black Hills area. Several routes meet at Rapid City (including No. 16, No. 79, No. 44, and No. 90). The town is also accessible by air.
Accommodations: Full facilities at Rapid City. The Black Hills offer many motel, hotel and camping opportunities, though facilities can be full during peak season (June-August).
Route Description: The Black Hills, an ancient, eroding mountain chain, was named for its dark appearance; from a distance, the thick pine forests make them look black. This tour of the Black Hills of South Dakota will include Mount Rushmore, Crazy Horse Memorial, Custer State Park, and Wind Cave National Park.

Begin this loop tour in Rapid City, which boasts a 9-mile (15-kilometer) bikeway along Rapid Creek. One of Rapid City's unusual features is a large sculpture called TOTH (Tower On The Hill), which symbolizes the role of gold mines in the history of the area.

Cycle south from Rapid City on scenic No. 16, passing Marine Life Aquarium, Reptile Gardens, Bear Country U.S.A. (where bears, wolves, bighorn sheep, elk, and antelope roam freely in a drive-through wildlife park), and Sitting Bull Crystal Cave (one of the few caves to have triangular calcite crystals called "dogtooth spar").

When you arrive at Keystone, consider a visit to the Rushmore-Borglum Story (which chronicles the story of the mountain carving), Big Thunder Gold Mine (a tour takes you underground in the 1800s-era mine), and beautiful Rushmore Cave (limestone caverns with stalagmites and stalactites). Mount Rushmore National Monument is just 2 miles (4 kilometers) southwest of Keystone, and here you can photograph the four colossal sculpted heads of George Washington, Thomas Jefferson, Theodore Roosevelt, and Abraham Lincoln.

After viewing Mount Rushmore, head southeast on No. 16A to the Norbeck Overlook and on to Custer State Park (habitat of one of the world's largest free-roaming bison herds). Turn south on No. 87, and ride part of the Wildlife Loop Road. Then continue on No. 87 into Wind Cave National Park (where cave tours and spelunking opportunities are available); take a walk to the summit of Rankin Ridge for a panoramic view of the Black Hills of South Dakota.

Bike northwest (on No. 385) to Pringle and north to Custer and the Crazy Horse Memorial (which will be the largest rock sculpture in the world when it's completed); this enormous sculpture of Lakota holy man Crazy Horse on his horse was begun in 1947 by sculptor Korczak Ziolkowski, and the work is being continued by his family.

Continue north on No. 385 and then east on No. 44 (Rim Rock Drive). You will pass Black Hills Caverns and Crystal Cave Park (a well-lit cavern with almost every type of cave formation found in the Black Hills) as you ride back to Rapid City.

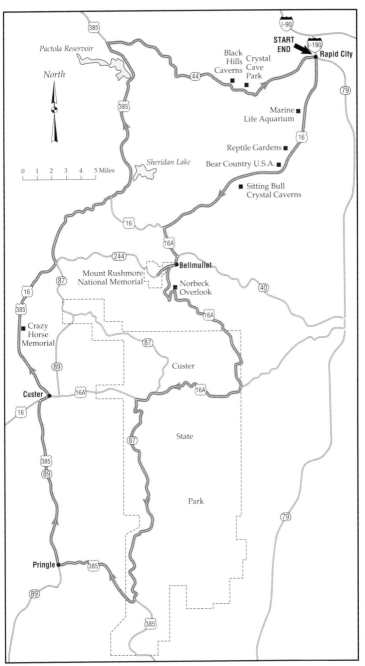

The Black Hills of South Dakota

Other Tours
• Needles Highway Loop
Ride north on No. 16 from Custer (past the Crazy Horse Memorial, previously discussed), and take the spectacular Needles Highway (No. 87), which winds through narrow tunnels and around hairpin turns. You will pedal past towering granite spires, including the Needle's Eye. Return to Custer on No. 16, completing this 33-mile (55-kilometer) loop tour.

• Spearfish Canyon Loop
Spearfish is nestled in a picturesque valley in the northern Black Hills with Lookout Mountain visible in the distance. "The Black Hills Passion Play," portraying Christ's last days, is performed at Spearfish each summer.

Cycle on the scenic Spearfish Canyon Highway (No. 14) south to Cheyenne Crossing. Then climb to Lead, site of the Homestake Gold Mine (one of the largest producing mines) and descend into Deadwood (on the narrow floor of Deadwood Gulch). Ride north on No. 85 and then cycle west back to Spearfish, completing this challenging, scenic 48-mile (80-kilometer) loop tour of the northern corner of the Black Hills area.

• George S. Mickelson Trail
This rails-to-trails route in the Black Hills will eventually span 110 miles (183 kilometers) between Deadwood and Edgemont. At present, a 15-mile (25-kilometer) section runs from Custer to Pringle and a 9-mile (15-kilometer) section runs west from Deadwood. For more information, contact: George S. Mickelson Trail Office, P.O. Box 1065, Hill City, SD 57745; phone (605) 574-4927.

• Badlands National Park Loop
Begin this loop tour in Wall, the northern gateway to the park, and home of well-advertised, block-long Wall Drug Store. Ride east on No. 14 to Cottonwood and south on No. 127 (a gravel road) to Cactus Flat. Then ride south to Cedar Pass, the eastern entrance to Badlands National Park, where a prairie homestead will greet you. A registered national historic site, this sod dwelling was built in 1919. Many hiking trails are available in the park, but no rock or fossil collecting is allowed. Wildlife in the park include deer, buffalo, coyote, pronghorn antelope, eagle, and prairie dog.

Cycle between the rock walls of Badlands National Park, and then bike north on No. 240 back to Wall, completing this 62-mile (104-kilometer) loop tour.

South Dakota Contacts
Black Hills, Badlands and Lakes Association, 900 Jackson Blvd., Rapid City, SD 57701; phone (605) 341-1462.

Black Hills Bicycling, P.O. Box 3361, Rapid City, SD 57709.

Custer State Park, HC 83, Box 70, Custer, SD 57730; phone (605) 255-4515.

Department of Tourism, Capitol Lake Plaza, Pierre, SD 57501; phone 1-800-952-2217 (in South Dakota); 1-800-843-1930.

Keystone, P.O. Box 653, Keystone, SD 57751; phone 1-800-843-1300.

State Bicycle Coordinator, South Dakota Department of
 Transportation-Planning and Programs, 700 Broadway Avenue E.,
 Pierre, SD 57501-2586; phone (605) 773-3155.
Superintendent, Wind Cave National Park, Hot Springs, SD 57747;
 phone (605) 745-4600.

Spearfish Canyon, in the Black Hills of South Dakota. *Photo courtesy of South Dakota Department of Tourism*

Wisconsin
• **The Dells of the Wisconsin River**
Distance: 174 miles/290 kilometers
Duration: 3–5 days
Rating: Easy
Type: Loop Tour
Access: A dam separates the Wisconsin River into the Upper and Lower Dells at Wisconsin Dells, northwest of Madison. The area is especially spectacular for autumn colors. Flights are available at Wisconsin Rapids.
Accommodations: Wisconsin's premier natural attraction offers the cyclist a great variety of facilities.
Route Description: The Wisconsin River has carved the soft sandstone rock into fantastic shapes, making this a very popular tourist area. Your trip will take you on relatively quiet country roads and a bicycle trail as you explore the dells of the Wisconsin River.

Begin this tour in Wisconsin Dells, where you can visit such points of interest as the Chapel Museum (including thousands of Norman Rockwell illustrations), Park Lane Model Railroad Museum, Storybook Gardens, Biblical Gardens, and the Wisconsin Opry. You can also tour the unique sandstone formations of the area by taking a boat trip on the

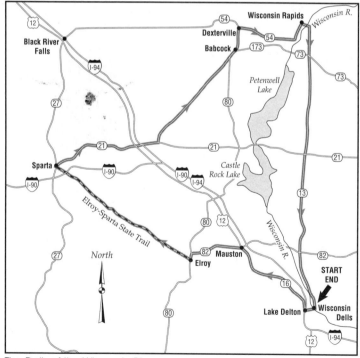

The Dells of the Wisconsin River

Wisconsin River or by touring Lost Canyon (near Wisconsin Dells) by horse-drawn wagon.

Ride northwest on No. 16 and No. 12 from Wisconsin Dells to Mauston, and then west on No. 82 to Elroy. Take the 32.5-mile (54-kilometer) Elroy-Sparta State Trail, which includes passage through three tunnels. At Sparta, return to road cycling, riding east on No. 21 and northeast on No. 173 to Babcock, and then bike north on No. 80 to Dexterville. Ride northeast on No. 54 to Wisconsin Rapids, which is the center of a cranberry-producing area and also has several important paper mills. While in Wisconsin Rapids, you might decide to take a tour of Consolidated Papers Inc. or Port Edwards Mill of Georgia-Pacific/Wisconsin.

Cross the Wisconsin River at Wisconsin Rapids, and pedal south on No. 13, passing through several small towns and enjoying magnificent views of the dells on your return to Wisconsin Dells. Some of the area landmarks include Sugar Bowl, Grotto Island, Twin Ink Stand, Lone Pine, Stand Rock, and Witches Gulch.

Other Tours

• **Milwaukee Triangle Tour**

This tour, which features both on- and off-road cycling, will take you from Wisconsin's largest city, Milwaukee, to its capital, Madison, and to the city at the "fond" or "farther end" of Lake Winnebago, Fond Du Lac.

Milwaukee has a beautiful 76-mile (127-kilometer) bicycle trail encircling the city. After exploring the city, cycle west on No. 18 to Waukesha. Then enjoy off-road cycling on the Glacial Drumlin State Trail as you ride to Cottage Grove. Return to road cycling by riding on No. 18 to Madison. Head to Picnic Point, a narrow peninsula jutting into Lake Mendota, for a nice view of the town.

The Military Ridge Trail is a 39.6-mile (66-kilometer) state trail that takes you from Madison to Dodgeville. Head north on No. 23, east on No. 60 (to Columbus), north on No. 73, and northeast on No. 68 to Fond Du Lac. Bike southeast on No. 175 back to Milwaukee, where you once again can pick up the bicycle trail.

• **Madison Area**

Because of the dairy industry's need to get tank trucks to farms, there is a great network of country roads near Madison. The only Midwestern representative in *Bicycling* magazine's recent list of "Best Cities for Cycling," Madison's network of trails includes the Military Ridge Trail (previously described) and the Isthmus Bike Path, along a rail corridor. For more information, contact the Bicycle Safety Program Manager (address previously given).

• **Lake Superior Loop**

Cycle east on No. 2 from Superior (on the border of Minnesota and on the southwest tip of Lake Superior) almost to Ashland. Although this route can have heavy traffic, the paved shoulder helps. Bike north and then east on No. 13 as you cycle around the Bayfield Peninsula, enjoying the spectacular views of Lake Superior. You will return to Superior to complete this scenic 150-mile (250-kilometer) loop tour.

Bear signs are common as you cycle through northern Wisconsin.

• Rhinelander Loop

Rhinelander is in a lake-rich area (more than 200 within a 12-mile radius). Head west on Swamp Lake Road to just north of Heafford Junction, where you can enjoy the tranquillity of off-road cycling on the Bearskin State Trail. You ride through a forested area to Minocqua. Then cycle south on No. 47, back to Rhinelander, completing this 55-mile (92-kilometer) loop tour.

• The La Crosse River State Trail

This 21-mile (35-kilometer) off-road trail takes you from La Crosse (on the Minnesota border and on the banks of the Mississippi River) northeast to Sparta (where you can link up with the previously described Elroy-Sparta State Trail). You can also hook up with the 22.5-mile (38-kilometer) Great River State Recreational Trail, which goes from La Crosse, along the Mississippi River.

Wisconsin Contacts

Bicycle Safety Program Manager, Wisconsin Department of Transportation, P.O. Box 7910, Madison, WI 53707; phone (608) 267-3154. "Wisconsin Bicycle Maps" available.

Wisconsin Bicycle Campers, 3267 S. Illinois Avenue, Milwaukee, WI 53207.

Wisconsin Dells Visitor and Convention Bureau, 701 Superior Street, Wisconsin Dells, WI; phone (608) 254-8088 or 1-800-22-DELLS.

Wisconsin Tourism Development, Box 7606, Madison, WI 53707; phone (608) 267-7474; 1-800-372-2737 (Wisconsin and neighboring states); 1-800-432-TRIP (all other states).

Chapter 6

Southern States

The Mason-Dixon line, an east-west boundary line separating Pennsylvania from Maryland, came to be considered the dividing line between the North and the South. Before the Civil War (1861–1865), the southern border of Pennsylvania was also the boundary between the anti-slavery states to the north and the pro-slavery states to the south.

The South embraces a wide range of terrain, including rolling hills, mountains, and plains; it's bordered by broad beaches along the Atlantic Ocean and the Gulf of Mexico. The flat or gently rolling plains areas along the coasts and into parts of Kentucky and Tennessee are forested or farmed (cotton was once "king" in the Deep South). The Piedmont, which begins in New York, widens in Virginia, and extends south into Alabama. The Appalachian range extends from the North into the South as the Blue Ridge Mountains and the Great Smoky Mountains.

The northern states of this region have a greater variety of temperatures, with seasonal changes (and, yes, snow), making cycling seasonal, but the Deep South could be ridden year round (but be wary of "hurricane season"). The southern states (Alabama; Florida; Georgia; Louisiana; Mississippi; South Carolina) have generally mild winters and hot summers. Florida has the highest annual normal temperature of the region at 78.2 Fahrenheit (25.7 Celsius).

Alabama
• **Bellingrath Gardens and the Gulf Shore**
Distance: 78 miles/130 kilometers
Duration: 2–4 days
Rating: Easy
Type: One-way Tour
Access: Alabama's seaport, Mobile, is in the southwestern part of the state, not far from the Mississippi border. It's easily accessible by road, water, and air. Orange Beach, the destination, is in the state's southeast corner (near the Florida border).
Accommodations: Accommodations are plentiful along this resort-rich route. Camping is available in Gulf State Park.
Route Description: This route takes you to one of the world's most beautiful year-round gardens and, by ferry, to the sandy shoreline of the Gulf of Mexico.

This trip begins in Mobile where, in early spring you can enjoy a spectacular tour along the Azalea Trail. Points of interest in Mobile include the Fine Arts Museum of the South, the Museum of the City of

Mobile, Fort Conde, and U.S.S. *Alabama* Battleship Memorial Park. The city also hosts Mobile's Mardis Gras, the Senior College All-Star Football Classic, and the Mobile Historic Homes Tour.

Cycle south on No. 59 to Bellingrath Gardens, where you will see a spectacular floral display, including daffodils, poinsettias, lilies, dogwood, roses, spirea, and camellias (the state flower). The gardens are patterned after the formal gardens of Italy, France, and England. The visitor lounge houses one of the world's largest displays of Boehm porcelain.

Continue south on No. 59 and No. 193 out onto the peninsula and Dauphin Island. Take the ferry from Fort Gaines to Fort Morgan (both were of strategic importance during the Civil War). Then cycle east on No. 180 along the Gulf of Mexico, through Fort Morgan State Historic Park, to Gulf State Park (where you will find some nice bicycle trails), and Orange Beach.

Having reached your destination, relax on the sandy beach. If you've got energy to burn, try sport fishing. If you don't, take the easy way— head to a restaurant to enjoy some of the fabulous seafood.

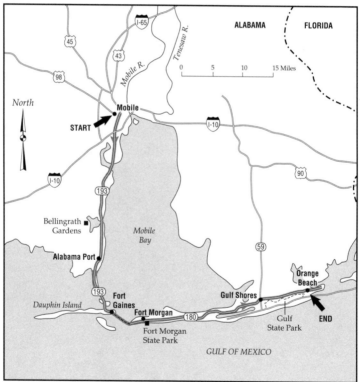

Bellingrath Gardens and the Gulf Shore

Other Tours
• Muscle Shoals Area Loop
This easy to moderate 140-miles (234-kilometer) loop tour begins and ends in Huntsville, considered the birthplace of the nation's space program, where you can visit such points of interest as Huntsville's Space and Rocket Center and NASA's Marshall Space Flight Center.

Cycle west on No. 72 to Athens, south on No. 31 to Decatur, and then west on No. 72, along the Tennessee River, to the Quad Cities of Muscle Shoals, Florence (the largest of the four), Sheffield, and Tuscumbia. You will cross the Tennessee River to reach Florence and then bike east on No. 72 to Joe Wheeler State Park (which contains bicycle trails), Rogersville, and back to Huntsville.

• Russell Cave National Monument
Cycle northeast on No. 72 from Huntsville to Bridgeport. Then bike northwest to this national monument (near the Tennessee border), where a visitor center portrays the various cultures that have lived in this cave area for more than 8,000 years. Nature trails wind through the site.

• Natural Bridge
Cycle south from Muscle Shoals (on No. 43 and No. 13) to Natural Bridge, a 148-foot bridge that towers above winding pathways. Camping facilities are available.

• Natchez Trace Parkway
Cycle the Alabama section of this scenic parkway, which is in the northwest corner of the state. The entire parkway extends 500 miles (833 kilometers) from Nashville, Tennessee, to Natchez, Mississippi.

Alabama Contacts
Alabama's Beautiful Beaches; phone (205) 968-7511 (Gulf Shores); (205) 981-8000 (Orange Beach); 1-800-662-6282.

Bureau of Tourism and Travel, 401 Adams Avenue, P.O. Box 4927, Montgomery, AL 36103-4927; phone (334) 242-4169 or 1-800-ALA-BAMA.

Mobile Convention and Visitors Corporation, One St. Louis Center, Suite 2002, Mobile, AL 36602; phone 1-800-662-6282.

State Bicycle Coordinator, Bureau of Multimodal Transportation, Alabama Department of Transportation, 1409 Coliseum Blvd., Montgomery, AL 36130; phone (334) 242-6085.

Arkansas
• The Ozarks
Distance: 300 miles/500 kilometers
Duration: 5–8 days
Rating: Strenuous
Type: Loop Tour
Access: Fort Smith is in northwestern Arkansas, near the Oklahoma border. It's accessible by both water and air, too.
Accommodations: Full facilities are available at Fort Smith. Several facilities (including camping) are also found along this route, including at Fayetteville, Eureka Springs, and Harrison.
Route Description: This loop tour begins in Fort Smith and takes you through mountainous terrain to a famous health spa at Eureka Springs, on to a picturesque valley and the town of Harrison, through the scenic Ozark National Forest, and back to Fort Smith.

Fort Smith is the site of Clayton House and Darby House, two historically significant restored buildings, and Fort Smith National Historic Site, the location of "Hanging Judge" Parker's courtroom and gallows; during Judge Parker's 21 years on the bench here, he gained his reputation as "the hanging judge." You might also choose to visit the Old Fort Museum, which depicts the development of Fort Smith.

Ride north on No. 59 and northeast on No. 62 to Fayetteville. Then cycle northeast on No. 45, No. 303, and No. 23 to Eureka Springs (where the alleged medicinal powers of the local water made the town a popular health resort). Other points of interest in the Eureka Springs area include Miles Musical Museum, Hammond Museum of Bells, Eureka Springs Historical Museum, Onyx Cave, and one of the largest natural springs in the Ozark Mountains (at Blue Spring). There are also a number of religiously significant places in this area, including Bible Museum, Thorncrown Chapel, St. Elizabeth Church, Sacred Arts Center, Inspirational Wood Carving Gallery, *The Great Passion Play* (Christ's last days on earth are depicted in this theatrical presentation), and *The Christ of the Ozarks* (a statue that weighs more than one million pounds and towers above Magnetic Mountain).

After exploring the Eureka Springs area, bike east on No. 62 to Berryville (the "Turkey Capital of Arkansas") and Harrison. Known as the "Crossroads of the Ozarks," Harrison is a beautiful resort town in Crooked Creek Valley.

Turn south on No. 7 and take this very scenic route through Ozark National Forest. You will pass Mystic Caverns (with guided tours of two Ozark caverns), Dogpatch, Jasper (where you will face a very strenuous climb to Scenic Point!) and Cowell as you ride through the Ozarks and enjoy several breathtaking mountain vistas.

At Pelsor, take No. 215 west, No. 123 south, No. 292 west, No. 21 north, No. 164 southwest, No. 352 west, No. 219 south, and No. 64 west to Mulberry. Continue southwest on No. 64 through Dyer and Alma, and return to Fort Smith. If you wish, a 70-mile (117-kilometer) round trip train excursion is available through the Ozarks from Van Buren (near Fort Smith).

This enchanting loop tour offers several scenic spots for photography, but you are cycling through the Ozark Mountains, so be prepared for some challenging climbs.

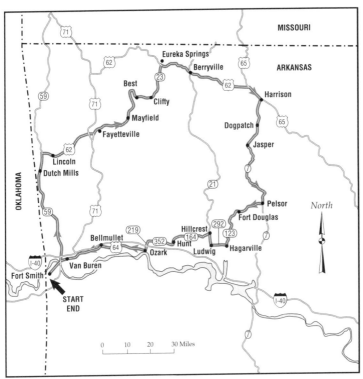

The Ozarks

Other Tours
• To Branson, Missouri
You could combine the detailed trip (above) with a ride to the famous country music town of Branson, Missouri, by cycling north from Harrison on No. 65.

• Hot Springs National Park/Little Rock Loop
Begin this tour by exploring the state capital, Little Rock. Then cycle southwest on No. 5 to Benton and on to Hot Springs National Park (where you can get a scenic view of the park from Hot Springs Mountain Observation Tower). The supposed medicinal power of the hot springs attracts many visitors to Hot Springs National Park; the thermal water that flows from the springs is naturally sterile. The park also offers several good hiking trails and mountain roads for biking and hiking.

Cycle through Hot Springs National Park by heading north on No. 7, through the Ouachita Mountains. Once through the park, continue riding north, to Mountain Valley, Hot Springs Village, Jessieville, Hollis and Fourche Junction. Bike east on No. 60 to Perryville and southeast on No. 10, descending Pinnacle Mountain, and then complete this 175-mile (292-kilometer) loop tour by returning to Little Rock.

- **The Ozark and Ouachita Mountains Loop Tour**

Another exploration of the Ozark and Ouachita Mountains (Hot Springs National Park) area has you ride from Little Rock to Heber Springs by cycling northeast on No. 107, east on No. 64, north on No. 5, east on No. 16, and north on No. 25 (descending into Heber Springs). Then proceed north on No. 16 to Shirley and on No. 9 to Mountain View, (across some very hilly terrain), where you'll find the Ozark Folk Center, dedicated to preserving and interpreting the rich heritage of Ozark life. Ride north on No. 5 to Mountain Home and then west on No. 62 and north on No. 65 to Harrison. Ride south on No. 7 to Jasper (where you will face a very tough climb to Scenic Point!). You will experience several breathtaking mountain vistas into the Arkansas Grand Canyon as you cycle through the heart of the Ozark Highlands and arrive at Russellville.

The terrain of the river valley is quite flat until Ola, and then you begin to climb again, this time into the Ouachita Mountains, as you ride to Hot Springs, where you can take a bath and have a relaxing massage in one of the bathhouses along "Bathhouse Row" on Central Avenue. Continue riding to Hot Springs National Park (previously described), and then take No. 5 (northeast) back to the state capital of Little Rock, completing this 460-mile (767-kilometer) loop tour.

- **Old Washington Area Loop**

Old Washington, in southwestern Arkansas, was the Confederate capital of Arkansas from 1863 to 1865 and was an important stop on the Southwest Trail into Texas and the Mexican Territory. The state park is dedicated to Old Washington's role in that memorable period.

Cycle north on No. 4 from Hope, through the rolling hills of rural Arkansas, and east on No. 332 to Tollette. Turn south on No. 365 to Saratoga, and southeast on No. 73 back to Hope, completing this relatively easy 48-mile (80-kilometer) loop.

Arkansas Contacts

Arkansas Department of Parks and Tourism, 1 Capitol Mall, Little Rock, AR 72203; phone (501) 682-7777 or 1-800-643-8383.

Eureka Springs Chamber of Commerce, P.O. Box 551, Eureka Springs, AR 72632-0551; phone (501) 253-8737.

Fort Smith Convention and Visitors Bureau, 55 South 7th, Fort Smith, AR 72901; phone 1-800-637-1477.

Harrison Chamber of Commerce, P.O. Box 939, Harrison, AR 72602-0393.

Ozark National Forest, P.O. Box 1008, 605 W. Main, Russellville, AR 72801; phone (501) 968-2354.

State Bicycle Coordinator, Arkansas Highway and Transportation Department, P.O. Box 2261, Little Rock, AR 72203; phone (501) 569-2115; ask for "Bike Arkansas" maps/routes.

State Trails Coordinator, Arkansas State Park, One Capitol Mall, Little Rock, AR 72201; phone (501) 569-2115.

Delaware
• **Northern Delaware—Wilmington to Delaware City**

Distance: 81 miles/135 kilometers
Duration: 2–4 days
Rating: Moderate
Type: Loop Tour
Access: Wilmington is in the northeast corner of Delaware, on the Delaware River. The river divides the states of Delaware and New Jersey.
Accommodations: There are several state parks on this route. Facilities are also available in New Castle, Newark, and Wilmington.
Route Description: Wilmington, named and administered by Quakers, has undergone a downtown renewal program, which has led to the restoration of such historic sites as the 1871 Grand Opera House, the Custom House, and Hendrickson House. Other points of interest in the Wilmington area include Brandywine River Museum (a 19th century gristmill), Brandywine Park, Hagley Museum, Nemours Mansion and Gardens (a 102-room Louis XVI-style chateau), Rockwood Museum (an example of Rural Gothic architecture), Old Town Hall Museum (with exhibits pertaining to the history of Delaware), Longwood Gardens, Winterthur Museum and Gardens, and Holy Trinity Church (thought to be the oldest active Protestant Church in North America).

After exploring the Wilmington area, travel southwest on No. 9 to New Castle, where William Penn first set foot on his vast colonial lands. The town prospered under Penn's Quaker administration; however, a fire leveled part of the town in 1812. The New Castle Heritage Tour takes you to many of the remaining historic buildings, including Dutch House (built in the late 17th century), Old Presbyterian Church (built in 1707), New Castle Court House (built in 1732), Amstel House (built in the 1730s), and a number of townhouses on the Strand that survived the fire.

Cycle from New Castle, around Hamburg Cove (on No. 9), to Wrangle Hill and Delaware City. Battery Park, in Delaware City, offers a view of the Delaware River, Sea Patch Island, and the New Jersey shoreline. Sea Patch Island is the location of Fort Delaware State Park (accessible only by water); the fort served as a federal prison during the Civil War.

Bike from Delaware City, through the Augustine Wildlife Area, to Port Penn. Then ride west to Mount Pleasant and north on No. 896, through part of Lums Pond State Park (with camping facilities and several nature trails), to Newark (which began as a crossroads of two well-traveled Indian trails). Cycle northeast on No. 2 and north on No. 100 to the turnoff for Brandywine Creek State Park (which offers both hiking and bicycle trails).

After exploring Brandywine Creek State Park, continue your ride to the town of Brandywine, and then head east on No. 92 and south on No. 261 until you reach the turnoff for Bellevue State Park (another park in northern Delaware with both hiking and bicycle trails). Complete the loop tour by riding southwest from Bellevue State Park to Wilmington.

The cycling will be hilly on this tour of northern Delaware. You will travel on relatively lightly traveled roads, for most of this trip. The many state parks on this route make it an excellent area for the cycling camper.

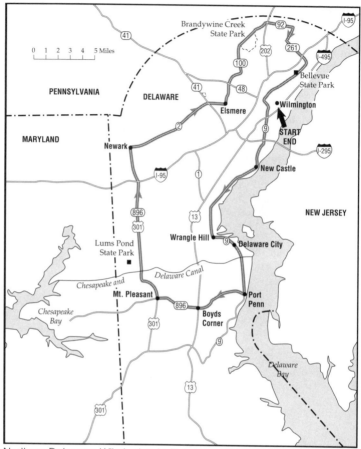

Northern Delaware-Wilmington to Delaware City

Other Tours
• Delaware's Eastern Coast

This beautiful shoreline tour takes you to several coastal state parks as you cycle from Cape Henlopen State Park to Fenwick Island State Park. Several nature trails and bicycle trails are found within Cape Henlopen State Park, which is a good area for whale and dolphin watching. You will cycle on No. 1A and No. 1 to Rehoboth Beach which holds an annual Sand Castle Building Contest, Dewey Beach, through Delaware Seashore State Park (on a strip of land between the Atlantic Ocean and the Rehoboth and Indian River Bays), and past Bethany Beach to the destination, Fenwick Island State Park. You will find many opportunities for swimming, sailing, fishing, wind surfing, and sunbathing as you cycle along this relatively easy 21-mile (35-kilometer) coastal route.

• Delaware's North-South Bicycle Route

A signed 147-mile (245-kilometer) route takes you from Brandywine Creek State Park (in the north) to Fenwick Island State Park (in the southeast corner of the state). Free maps of the route are available from the Delaware Bicycle Coordinator (address previously given). You travel primarily on quiet rural roads as you ride to Lums Pond State Park, Middletown, Smyrna, Dover (the state capital), Killen Pond State Park, Milton, and Cape Henlopen State Park. You then ride along the coast (as described in Delaware's East Coast Tour, above) to the destination of Fenwick Island State Park.

• From Delaware to New Jersey

You can take a ferry from Lewes, Delaware, to Cape May, New Jersey, to cycle in both states. Since the Delaware Memorial Bridge does not permit cycling, this ferry is a popular access point. For more information, contact: Lewes Terminal, Lewes, DE 19958; phone (302) 645-6346; for schedule information, phone (302) 645-6313.

Delaware Contacts

Bicycle Coalition of the Delaware Valley, P. O. Box 8194, Philadelphia, PA 19101; phone (215) BIC-YCLE.

Delaware Bicycle Coordinator, Delaware Department of Transportation, P.O. Box 778, Dover, DE 19903; phone (302) 739-2453; FAX (302) 739-2251; free "Delaware Maps for Bicycle Users" are available.

Delaware State Travel Service, Delaware Tourism Office, 99 Kings Highway, P.O. Box 1401, Dover, DE 19903; phone 1-800-282-8667 (in Delaware); 1-800-441-8846.

New Castle Court House (for information about the New Castle Heritage Tour); phone (302) 323-4453 or 1-800-441-8846.

District of Columbia
• **Washington, D.C. Area**
Distance: 42 miles/70 kilometers
Duration: 1–3 days
Rating: Easy Route
Type: One-way Tour
Access: Washington, D.C., is notched out of the state of Maryland at the point where the Anacostia and Potomac Rivers meet. Visitors arriving by plane can land at Washington National Airport, just across the Potomac River, at Washington Dulles International Airport (near Herndon, Virginia), or at Baltimore-Washington International Airport (BWI); frequent ground transportation is available from all three airports. Trains also run to and from BWI; phone 1-800-USA-RAIL. For information on Greyhound Bus Service, phone (301) 565-2662. Metrorail provides subway access to most of the city's attractions; phone (202) 637-7000.
Accommodations: Full facilities are available in Washington, D.C., the capital of the United States.
Route Description: Washington, D.C., is home to many federal offices and national organizations. You will find dense traffic, but bicycling can be enjoyed along the C & O Canal Towpath, on Rock Creek Park trails, and on other area bike paths. A specific route is suggested here, but "Getting Around Washington By Bicycle" can be purchased from the Office of Documents, Room 19, District Building, 14th Street and Pennsylvania Avenue, NW, Washington, D.C. 20004 (phone (202) 727-5090).

Your tour begins northwest of Washington, D.C., in Potomac, Maryland. Ride southeast on the River Road and the Capital Crescent Trail to K Street, where this trail ends. Head east on K Street to the Rock Creek Trail, which takes you south to the Lincoln Memorial. Explore the city center before biking north to Rock Creek Park (on the Rock Creek Trail), which is your destination. Rock Creek Park contains bridle paths, footpaths, jogging trails, and bicycle trails.

Washington's many attractions include the Anacostia Museum, Ansel Adams Collection, Chinatown Friendship Archway, Congressional Cemetery, Arlington National Cemetery (with the grave of John F. Kennedy, the tomb of the Unknown Soldier, and the Robert E. Lee Memorial), Library of Congress, John. F. Kennedy Center for the Performing Arts, Ford's Theatre (where Lincoln was fatally shot by John Wilkes Booth), Jefferson Memorial, Washington Monument, Washington National Cathedral, the Basilica of the National Shrine of the Immaculate Conception, National Archives, National Air and Space Museum, National Gallery of Art, United States Capitol, Smithsonian Institution, U.S. Botanical Garden, Vietnam Veterans Memorial, Potomac Park, Rock Creek Park, and the White House.

Other Tours
• **Arlington County**
Arlington County provides many opportunities for on- and off-road cycling near Washington, D.C. A map is available by contacting the Arlington County Bicycle Coordinator (address given above).

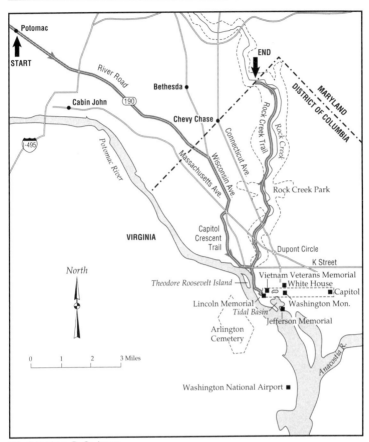

Washington, D.C. Area

• The Washington and Old Dominion Railroad Regional Park

A guide detailing trails in the park (nature trails, and trails for jogging, hiking, biking, and horseback riding) can be purchased from: Northern Virginia Regional Park Authority, 5400 Ox Road, Fairfax Station, VA 22039; phone (703) 352-5900.

• From Washington, D.C., to Cumberland, Maryland

This rails-to-trails route of 185 miles (308 kilometers) of mostly packed dirt offers the cyclist a relatively flat and uncrowded journey. Several amenities are found along this pathway, including restaurants, groceries, water, rest rooms, sleeping accommodations, campsites, and bicycle rentals. "A Guide to Food and Lodging Along the C&O Canal" can be purchased from: the C&O Canal Association, P.O. Box 366, Glen Echo, MD 20812.

• From Washington, D.C., to Pittsburgh, Pennsylvania

By the turn of the century, it should be possible to cycle for more than 300 miles (500 kilometers) of traffic-free pathways from Washington, D.C., to Pittsburgh, Pennsylvania. You will begin this route on the C&O Towpath and climb to Cumberland, Maryland. Then take the Allegheny Highlands Trail, climbing to Frostburg and then up the eastern flank of Big Savage Mountain. You will take a tunnel to cross the crest of the mountain and then descend to Meyersdale. You will eventually descend along the Youghiogheny River to your destination.

District of Columbia Contacts

Arlington County Bicycle Coordinator, 2100 Clarendon Blvd., Suite 717, Arlington, VA 22201; phone (703) 358-3699. Ask for the "Virginia Bikeway and Guide Map," which describes more than 84 miles (140 kilometers) of on- and off-street bicycle routes.

Bicycle Coordinator, DC-DPW, 2000 14th Street, NW, Washington, D.C. 20009; phone (202) 939-8016.

Smithsonian Information Center, Smithsonian Institution, Washington, D.C. 20560; phone (202) 357-2700.

Washington Area Bicyclist Association, 1819 H Street, NW, Suite 640, Washington, D.C. 20006; phone (202) 872-9830.

Washington, D.C. Convention and Visitors Association, 1212 New York Avenue, NW, Washington, D.C. 20005; phone (202) 789-7000.

Washington Visitor Information Center, 1455 Pennsylvania Avenue, NW, Washington, D.C. 20004; phone (202) 789-7038.

Florida
• Everglades National Park
Distance: 99 miles/165 kilometers
Duration: 2–4 days
Rating: Easy
Type: Return Trip
Access: Homestead, which serves as the gateway to Everglades National Park, is southwest of Miami, near the eastern entrance to the park. Homestead is accessible by air and road.
Accommodations: Several facilities are available in the Homestead area and in Flamingo. Camping is available in Everglades National Park.
Route Description: This return trip will take you through the largest subtropical wilderness in the United States, a sanctuary for a number of interesting birds and animals, including the great white heron, Cable Sable sparrow, snowy egret, water turkey, manatee, American crocodile, alligator, sea turtle, and a variety of snakes.

It's best not to take this cycling trip during the summer because the heat and insects can make the journey rather uncomfortable. During our summer trip to the park, a ranger we met wore a head-netting to raise and lower the park flag. We ended up building a smoky campfire to try to keep the mosquitoes away.

Begin this trip at Homestead, the gateway to the park. In the center of Florida's fruit and nursery region, the Homestead area is also the site of Orchid Jungle and Coral Castle of Florida (built of massive blocks of coral). You will cycle south from Homestead, on No. 997, to Florida City, through prime agricultural land; you will pass fields of strawberries, avocados, cucumbers, potatoes, corn, and beans.

Leave Dade County's fruit and vegetable farms behind as you cycle southwest on No. 9336 to the park, where you will enter a subtropical wilderness. You can stop for information on the park at the Parachute Key Visitor Center. As you explore the park, there are many boardwalk or blacktop nature trails to assist you; these trails help you to view the vegetation and the wildlife of Everglades National Park. You will pass Ashinga Trail, Gumbo Limbo Trail, Pinelands Trail, Long Pine Key Nature Trail, Pa-hay-okee Overlook, Mahogany Hammock, and Mangrove Trail as you bike to Flamingo, at the western tip of the park. Boat tours, canoe trips, tram tours, and self-guided bicycle trips are available at Flamingo.

After exploring fascinating Everglades National Park, return to Homestead by the same flat route (you're cycling almost at sea level).

Other Tours
• Florida's Eastern Coast
Florida's magnificent coastline offers miles of sandy beaches and opportunities for a great variety of water activities. This trip begins in St. Augustine, taking you southeast for 321 miles (535-kilometers) to Fort Lauderdale. Although this area is often crowded with tourists, you will bypass freeways for picturesque coastal roads.

Cycle southeast on No. A1A from St. Augustine to Daytona Beach, and then continue southeast on No. 1 to Titusville (across the Indian River from the Kennedy Space Center) and Cocoa Island. Take No. 520

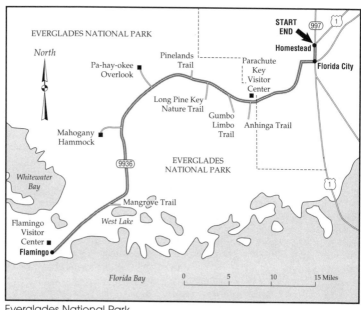

Everglades National Park

east to Merritt Island, and then cycle on No. A1A southeast to Cocoa Beach (where Canaveral Pier extends out into the Atlantic Ocean, offering opportunities for fishing, surfing, dining, and dancing), and on to the Pelican Island Wilderness. Cross west on No. 1 to Wabasso, and then ride southeast to Vero Beach and Fort Pierce. Cycle east on No. A1A to Jensen Beach (where sea turtles can be seen making their annual journey from ocean to shore and back during June and July). Return to No. 1, and bike to Stuart (at the eastern terminus of the Okeechobee Waterway, which crosses the state to the Gulf of Mexico), Jupiter, and Palm Beach. Take No. A1A from Palm Beach to your destination, Fort Lauderdale.

This route takes you to some of North America's most popular beaches along Florida's East Coast. For more information about your starting point, contact: the St. Augustine Visitor Information and Preview Center, 10 Castillo Drive, St. Augustine, FL 32805; phone (904) 825-1000. For more information about this tour's destination, contact: the Greater Fort Lauderdale Convention and Visitors Bureau, 200 E. Las Olas Blvd., Fort Lauderdale, FL; phone (305) 765-4466.

• The Northwestern Shoreline

Follow along the magnificent shoreline of the Gulf of Mexico as you ride 36 miles (60 kilometers) from Santa Rosa Beach to St. Andrews State Park (3 miles or 5 kilometers east of Panama City), passing several beautiful beaches, including Laguna Beach and Panama City Beach (a very popular resort area).

• **The Florida Keys**

This fascinating 111-mile (185-kilometer) tour of the Florida Keys will take you on a flat, picturesque cycling trip south of the Florida mainland, where you travel through a series of islands that are linked together by bridges. ("Keys" is from the Spanish word "cayos," meaning "small isles.")

Key West is the southernmost town in the continental United States and the southernmost terminus of the scenic Overseas Highway. As you travel from Key West to Key Largo, the Overseas Highway on which you travel will separate the Straits of Florida from the Gulf of Mexico. You will ride to such enchanting islands as Big Pine Key (which has a wildlife refuge to protect an endangered type of deer), Pigeon Key (after crossing Seven-Mile Bridge), Marathon Key, Key Vaca, Key Colony Beach, Grassy Key, Duck Key, Long Key, and Fiesta Key before you reach your destination of Key Largo, the largest of the Florida Keys (just south of the Florida mainland). While on Key Largo, you might visit John Pennekamp Coral Reef State Park, which offers a mangrove area, aquarium displays, boardwalks, and boat, snorkel, and scuba tours.

• **Across Florida**

Begin this cross-state tour in Homosassa, on the Gulf of Mexico, near Homosassa Springs State Wildlife Park (where the freshwater spring emits millions of gallons of water each hour at a constant temperature—and where the native wildlife of Florida can be observed). Cycle northeast on No. 490, No. 491, and No. 41 to Williston. Ride east on No. 318 to Orange Springs. Cycle northeast on No. 315, No. 310, and No. 19 to Palatkan (where you will find the Ravine State Gardens). Cross the St. Johns River and bike on No. 207 to Hastings. Cycle east on No. 206 to the coast, and then cycle north on No. A1A to the destination of St. Augustine, where you can relax on the Atlantic Ocean beach. This relatively flat route has taken you on generally quiet roads as you have cycled from Florida's West Coast (on the Gulf of Mexico) to its East Coast (on the Atlantic Ocean).

Florida Contacts

Florida Bicycle Association, Inc., P.O. Box 16652, Tampa, FL 33687; phone 1-800-FOR-BIKE.

Florida Division of Tourism, 126 W. Van Buren Street, Tallahassee, FL 32399-2000; phone (904) 487-1462.

State Bicycle Coordinator, Florida Department of Transportation, 605 Suwanee Street, Mail Station 82, Tallahassee, FL 32399-0450; phone (904) 487-1200.

Superintendent, Everglades National Park, P.O. Box 279, Homestead, FL 33090.

Tropical Everglades Visitor Association's Visitor Center, 160 U.S. Highway 1, Homestead, FL 33034; phone (305) 245-9180 or 1-800-388-9669.

Georgia
• **Old Southern Culture and Indian Mounds**
Distance: 164 miles/273 kilometers
Duration: 3–5 days
Rating: Easy
Type: Loop Tour
Access: Macon is in central Georgia, on the west side of the Ocmulgee River. There is an airport.
Accommodations: Lodging is available in Macon and Milledgeville. Camping is available in Eatonton and Dublin.
Route Description: Macon is a blend of Old Southern culture and New South progress. The older residential sections of Macon are lined with antebellum mansions, several of which are open to the public. Macon's historical buildings include the birthplace of Sidney Lanier (a famous Georgia poet), Wesleyan College (the first college chartered specifically to grant degrees to women), Hay House, and Grand Opera House. Macon is also a very progressive city, attracting several industries. Located in an area known for its Yoshino cherry trees, Macon plays host to an annual Cherry Blossom Festival each March.

After exploring Macon, cycle northeast on No. 44, riding through a section of the Oconee National Forest, important to the state's timber industry. Campsites and trails are to be found in Oconee National Forest. Continue cycling on No. 44 to Eatonton, the birthplace of Joel Chandler Harris, the creator of such popular children's characters as Uncle Remus (commemorated in a town marker), Br'er Rabbit, and Br'er Fox. Eatonton was also the home of another notable writer—Alice Walker, author of *The Color Purple*.

Cycle southeast, on No. 441, from Eatonton to Milledgeville, which has maintained its Southern gentility, a legacy from the days when it was Georgia's capital. Its historical buildings include the Old Governor's Mansion, John Marlor House, Stetson-Sanford House, and St. Stephen's Episcopal Church. Guided trolley tours are available. Writer Flannery O'Connor was a famous resident of Milledgeville; she is now honored by a room in Georgia College's Dillard Russell Library.

Continue riding southeast on No. 441 to Irwinton and Dublin. Then cycle northeast on No. 80 to Dudley, Montrose, Danville, Jeffersonville, Dry Branch, and the Ocmulgee National Monument (which contains impressive Indian mounds and archeological remains). *People of the Macon Plateau* is a film shown at the Visitor Center at Ocmulgee National Monument, near Macon's eastern limits. The many trails at the Monument take you to explore the Indian mounds and the Walnut Creek area.

Complete this loop tour through central Georgia by returning to Macon.

Other Tours
• **The Golden Isles of Georgia**
Located along the southeastern coast of Georgia, the Golden Isles provide a beautiful resort area for riding on miles of level bicycle trails. Swimming, fishing, tennis, golf, hiking, horseback riding, and boating are other popular activities. Begin this tour in Brunswick, on a peninsula in southeastern Georgia. Cycle southeast on No. 17 and No. 520 (Jekyll Island Road) to Jekyll Island; here you can enjoy miles

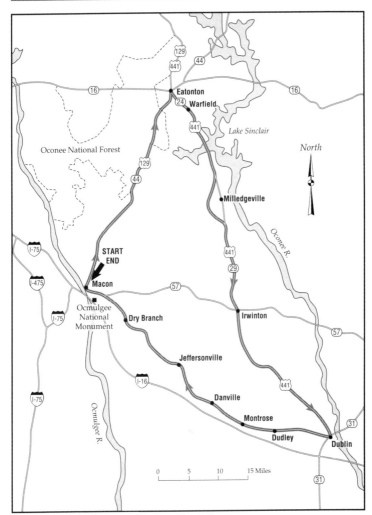

Old Southern Culture and Indian Mounds

of beautiful bicycle trails, and camping is available on this popular is-land in the Atlantic Ocean. Returning to Brunswick, take the causeway to St. Simons Island, where bicycle trails parallel many of the island's roads, making it an excellent, relaxing area for cycling. Accessible from St. Simons Island by causeway is yet another resort island: Sea Island, a lush garden setting of flowering shrubs, oaks, pines, and palms lying between the marshes of Glynn County and the Atlantic Ocean. After ex-ploring these exquisite Golden Isles of Georgia, return to Brunswick. For more information about this area, contact: Brunswick and the Gold-en Isles of Georgia Visitors Bureau, 4 Glynn Avenue, Brunswick, GA 31520; phone 1-800-933-COAST.

• **Georgia's Eastern Coast**

This route through Georgia is described in chapter 11, as part of the "The Atlantic Coast Tour-Maine to Florida."

• **The Chattahoochee Trail**

Begin this cross-state trip of about 427 miles (715 kilometers) at Ringold, in the northeast corner of the state, near the Tennessee border. Ride through the Chattahoochee National Forest (on No. 201) to Gore, and then take No. 27 south to Rome and No. 101 south to Villa Rica. Bike on No. 166 to Carrolton and Franklin. Take No. 34 west and No. 219 south to La Grange. Continue south on No. 219 to Columbus, and then cycle on No. 27 to Lumpkin. Ride west on No. 27 to Georgetown, and then follow the Chattahoochee River south (on No. 39) to Fort Gaines. Continue cycling on No. 39 to the destination: Seminole State Park, on Lake Seminole and near the southern border of the state.

• **Bike Ride Across Georgia**

For more information about this yearly, organized trip, contact: BRAG, P.O. Box 871111, Stone Mountain, GE 30087-0028; phone (770) 921-6166.

One suggested route across the state begins at Rome, near the northwest corner of the state. Cycle east on No. 293 and 320 to Buford, No. 324 to Bethlehem, and No. 53 to Watkinsville (just south of Athens). Cycle southeast on No. 15 to Wrightsville, No. 57 to Stillmore, and then complete the 310-mile (517-kilometer) ride by traveling on No. 46 and No. 80 into Savannah (on the east coast of Georgia, near the border of South Carolina). This route takes you through many small towns and is well suited for camping.

Georgia Contacts

Bicycle Coordinator, Georgia Department of Transportation, 2 Capitol Square, Room 343, Atlanta, GA 30334; phone (404) 656-5336; ask for a copy of "The Georgia Bicycle Touring Guide."

Department of Industry, Trade, and Tourism, P.O. Box 1776, Atlanta, GA 30367; phone (404) 347-2384.

Macon-Bibb Convention and Visitors Bureau, Terminal Station, 200 Cherry Street, Macon, GA 31208; phone (912) 743-3401.

Milledgeville-Baldwin County Department of Tourism, 200 W. Hancock Street, Milledgeville, GA 31061; phone (912) 452-4687.

Supervisor's Office, Chattahoochee and Oconee National Forests, 508 Oak Street, Gainesville, GA 30501.

U.S. Forest Service, 1720 Peachtree Road, NW, Atlanta, GA 30367; phone (404) 347-2384.

Kentucky
• **Bluegrass Country**
Distance: 252 miles/420 kilometers
Duration: 4–6 days
Rating: Moderate
Type: Loop Tour
Access: Lexington, Kentucky, is in the north-central part of the state, east of Louisville. You can arrive at the Blue Grass Airport or by one of several major highways (including No. 64 and No. 75).
Accommodations: Full facilities are found in Lexington. Some facilities are also available at many of the towns along this route.
Route Description: North-central Kentucky is known as "Bluegrass Country." Horse breeding is an important business in the rolling farmland of the area.

Begin your trip in Lexington, the "Heart of the Bluegrass," and the country's chief producer of bluegrass seed and white barley. Many celebrated horse farms dot the area. Kentucky Horse Park traces the importance of horses to the region; it includes the International Museum of the Horse and The Man O'War Monument, which is the burial site of the famous racehorse. Other points of interest in the Lexington area include Mary Todd Lincoln House (the girlhood home of the wife of Abraham Lincoln), Waveland State Historic Site, Red Mile Harness Track, and Keeneland Race Course (site of the Bluegrass Stakes).

Leave Lexington by cycling southwest on No. 68 to Pleasant Hill (Shakertown), said to contain America's largest restored Shaker Village. The village was founded in 1805 by members of a celibate, communal religious sect. Shaker crafts are demonstrated in the original buildings, but the Shaker community officially ended here in 1910. The Shaker way of life is explained, and Shaker furniture and memorabilia are displayed.

Continue biking to Harrodsburg, the first permanent English settlement west of the Allegheny Mountains. Old Fort Harrod State Park, in Harrodsburg, includes replicas of the pioneer cabins and Kentucky's first school house; the Mansion Museum, the Lincoln Marriage Temple (the cabin in which Abraham Lincoln's parents were wed), and the oldest cemetery west of the Alleghenies are also included. *The Legend of Daniel Boone* is performed in the park's amphitheater each summer.

Cycle southwest on No. 68 to Perryville, where Kentucky's bloodiest Civil War battle occurred (the Perryville Battlefield State Historic Site is just 2 miles or 4 kilometers north of town). Ride northwest on No. 150 to Springfield, site of Lincoln Homestead State Park, which includes a replica of the log cabin home of Abraham Lincoln's father, Thomas.

As you continue on this route, you will arrive at Bardstown, Kentucky's second oldest city and site of some of Kentucky's largest distilleries (including Heaven Hill, Makers Mark, and Jim Beam); tours are available. Bardstown is also the location of Bardstown Historical Museum, St. Joseph's Proto Cathedral, and the Oscar Getz Museum of Whiskey History. It's believed that Stephen Foster wrote "My Old Kentucky Home" in this area in 1852; the family cemetery and a musical presentation entitled *The Stephen Foster Story* are found in My Old Kentucky Home State Park.

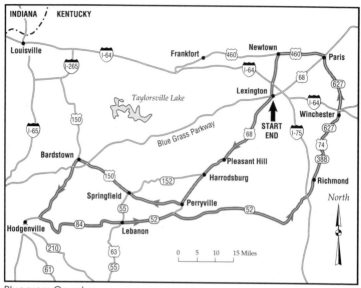

Bluegrass Country

Ride southwest on No. 31E to Hodgenville, where you will find a Lincoln Statue and the Lincoln Museum. Nearby is the former president's boyhood home, at Abraham Lincoln Birthplace National Historic Site.

Cycle east on No. 84 to Lebanon and northeast on No. 52 to Richmond, site of the first Confederate victory in Kentucky during the Civil War. Ride north on No. 388 and No. 627 to Winchester (considered the marketing center of the inner Bluegrass region) and Paris (with several important horse farms in the area). Complete this loop tour by cycling west on No. 460 to Newtown and south on No. 922 back to Lexington.

Other Tours
• Mammoth Cave National Park

In south-central Kentucky, Mammoth Cave is one of the longest cave systems anywhere. It has more than 300 miles (500 kilometers) of underground passages; tours of varying length are available.

Begin this trip in Bowling Green, in south-central Kentucky (where tours of the General Motors Corvette Assembly Plant are offered). Cycle northwest on No. 31W to Park City (where you can visit Kentucky Diamond Caverns, with stalactite and stalagmite formations and peaks of onyx) and Cave City, considered the center of Kentucky's cave area (where you can visit Crystal Onyx Cave and the Mammoth Cave Wildlife Museum).

Cycle northwest on No. 7 into Mammoth Cave National Park. The scenic Green River traverses much of this forested, rugged terrain. Several miles of back country trails exist within the park; camping is available. After visiting Mammoth, cycle through the park to Brownsville and Aberdeen. Then bike on No. 79 to Morgantown. Continue southeast on No. 79 and No. 231 back to Bowling Green, completing this 125-mile (208-kilometer) loop tour.

• **Kentucky's Southern Lakes**

This route roughly follows the Tennessee- Kentucky border from west to east, beginning at Hickman, on the mighty Mississippi River. Head east on No. 94 and No. 68 to Hopkinsville and Russellville. Ride southeast on No. 100 to Tomkinsville and across the Cumberland River by ferry. Continue riding northeast to Ida, and then ride east on No. 90 to Monticello and southeast on No. 92 to Williamsburg and Pineville. Ride northeast on No. 119 to Harlan and Cumberland, and then bike south to the border. This magnificent route has taken you past some of the best recreational areas in the eastern United States. Pine Mountain State Resort Park is a great place to relax and enjoy the mountain scenery. You'll also want to view gigantic Cumberland Falls and explore Cumberland Gap National Historical Park.

• **Kentucky's Trans America Bike Trail**

The Kentucky section of this national trail takes you more than 600 miles (1000 kilometers) from west to east as you cycle across the center of the state. The trail begins at Rough River Dam State Resort Park (near the Illinois border) and winds up at the Breaks Interstate Park (on the Virginia border). Bike south on No. 91 to Marion, northeast on No. 120 and No. 132 to Sebree, and east on No. 136 and No. 140 to Pleasant Ridge. Take No. 764 and No. 54 to Litchfield, No. 62 to Bardstown, No. 150 to Springfield, and No. 152 to Burgin. Ride on No. 33 south and No. 52 northeast to Richmond. Continue on No. 52 (southeast) to Beattyville, and then ride on No. 28 to Blue Diamond. Cycle south on No. 15 to Hazard and northeast on No. 60 and No. 1428 to Allen. Bike south on No. 23 and No. 460 to Regina. Continue south to Belcher and Breaks Interstate Park.

This route begins at the Ohio River, and takes you through gently rolling countryside, past Amish roadside stands. You will eventually cycle through a section of the Daniel Boone National Forest and climb the challenging Cumberland Plateau of the Appalachian Mountains. Breaks Interstate Park provides you with a "gorgeous" view of a massive gorge.

Kentucky Contacts

Bardstown-Nelson County Tourist Commission, Bardstown, KY; phone 1-800-626-1563 (during summer) or 1-800-638-4877.

Greater Lexington Convention and Visitors Bureau; phone 1-800-845-3959.

Harrodsburg Tourist Commission, 103 S. Main, Harrodsburg, KY 40330; phone (606) 734-2364.

Historical Heartland of Kentucky; phone 1-800-225-8747.

Kentucky Travel, P.O. Box 2011, Frankfort, KY 40602; phone 1-800-225-TRIP.

Shaker Village of Pleasant Hill, 3500 Lexington Road, Harrodsburg, KY 40330; phone (606) 734-5411.

State Bicycle Coordinator, Transportation Cabinet, 125 Holmes Street, 3rd Floor, Frankfort, KY 40622; phone (502) 564-7433; request a copy of "Kentucky Bicycle Tours."

Louisiana
• **Cajun Loop**
Distance: 351 miles/585 kilometers
Duration: 5–9 days
Rating: Easy
Type: Loop Tour
Access: New Orleans International Airport is a major port of exchange between the U.S., Mexico, and South America. Express buses are available to and from the airport. For information on Greyhound Bus Lines, phone (504)525-9371. For information on Amtrak rail service, phone 1-800-872-7245. New Orleans is by Lakes Pontchartrain and Borgne, in southeastern Louisiana.
Accommodations: Full facilities are available in Louisiana's two largest cities, New Orleans and Baton Rouge. Some lodging is also found in Opelousas and Lafayette. Camping is available in the St. Martinville and Houma areas.
Route Description: French-influenced speech, cuisine, and music add a uniqueness to southern Louisiana, which is inhabited by a large number of Cajuns, descendants of the Acadians who were expelled from Nova Scotia by the British in the 1700s.

Begin this tour in New Orleans, where you can visit the original settlement, now known as the French Quarter (Vieux Carre). Within this historical area is the Arsenal, Beauregard-Keyes House, the Cabilido, Her-

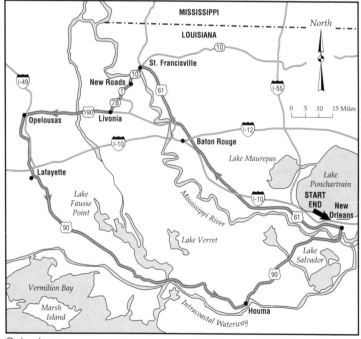

Cajun Loop

mann-Grima House, U.S. Mint, Preservation Hall, Pontalba Buildings, the Historic New Orleans Collection, Gallier House Museum, Jackson Square, New Orleans Pharmacy Museum , Louisiana State Museum, and Washington Artillery Park. Part of the Lafitte National Historical Park and Preserve is also within the French Quarter. Other points of interest in New Orleans include the New Orleans Museum of Art, Louisiana Historical Association Confederate Museum, Louisiana Nature and Science Center, City Park, Aquarium of the Americas, Zoological Garden, Lake Pontchartrain Causeway, New Orleans School of Glass Works, and the Louisiana Superdome. While in this area, you might like to hunt for antiques on Royal Street or listen to jazz on Bourbon Street. You might like to have a boat tour of the swamps and bayous; several trips are offered, including a dinner jazz cruise by a historic plantation and battlefield, or a swamp boat tour past the alligators, snakes, and egrets.

After exploring the fascinating diversity of life in New Orleans, cycle west on No. 61, through plantation country to Baton Rouge, Louisiana's capital and second largest city. The flags of seven nations have flown in Baton Rouge (France, England, Spain, West Florida, the Sovereign State of Louisiana, the Confederacy, and last but not least the United States). Baton Rouge has one of the nation's largest ports. You will find many cypress and magnolia trees and sugar plantations in this area.

Cycle north on No. 61 to St. Francisville. Take the ferry across the Mississippi River, and continue biking southwest on No. 10, No. 1, and No. 78 to Livonia. Then ride west on No. 190 to Opelousas (which is named after its original settlers, the Opelousas Indians). Opelousas was established as a French trading post in 1720. Jim Bowie, namesake of the Bowie knife and legendary American hero, lived here in the early 1800s.

Cycle south on No. 182 to Lafayette, in the heart of Cajun Country. Many French Acadian farmers settled here in the 1700s. For an authentic Cajun experience, attend Lafayette's Cajun Mardis Gras Festival, the Festival International, or the Festivals Acadians. Lafayette is known as the "Capital of French Louisiana," and it's the site of Acadiana Park and the Lafayette Museum. Near Lafayette is Acadian Village, a restored bayou town that depicts the early 19th century lifestyle of the Acadians who settled in southern Louisiana.

Leaving Lafayette, bike southeast on No. 90 on a flat but picturesque ride through Bayou Country. You will cycle to Franklin, Morgan City, and Houma. The delta city of Houma is spanned by 52 bridges. Seven bayous converge here. Houma celebrates its Cajun roots in such annual events as the Blessing of the Shrimp Fleet, the Louisiana Praline Festival, Lagniappe on the Bayou, and the Bayou Blue Food Festival. Many boat tours into the deep swamp country of southern Louisiana begin here.

Continue cycling on No. 90 from Houma to Des Allemands, Boutte, Westwego, and back to New Orleans, completing the loop tour. This flat cycling route will give you a good sampling of life, culture and food on the bayou.

Other Tours
• **Cycle to Mississippi**

Ride through New Orleans, taking No. 90 across the state line into Mississippi. Continue cycling east on No. 90 to Gulfport.

• **Kisatchie National Forest**

This 122-mile (204-kilometer) loop tour will take you through part of Kisatchie National Forest, the only national forest in Louisiana. It offers many recreation areas and an opportunity to explore a variety of terrain, ranging from sandstone hills covered with pine, to swamps of hardwood and cypress trees covered in Spanish moss.

Begin this trip in Alexandria, at the geographical center of Louisiana. Cycle northwest on No. 1 to Zimmerman. Take No. 8 east to Flatwood. Then ride on the Longleaf Scenic Byway (No. 337) through Kisatchie National Forest. This road winds through rugged, forested land. Bike south on No. 117 to Kisatchie and Leesville, named after General Robert E. Lee. Ride north on No. 28 back to Alexandria, the final destination.

• **Wild Azalea National Recreation Trail**

Near Alexandria (on No. 273) is the 31-mile (52-kilometer) Wild Azalea National Recreation Trail, which offers magnificent floral displays in season. From this trail you can reach the Castor Creek Scenic Area.

Louisiana Contacts

Acadiana Tourist Center, Opelousas, LA; phone (318) 948-6263.

Baton Rouge Visitor Information Center; phone 1-800-LA ROUGE or (504) 383-1825.

Convention and Visitors Commission Tourist Information Center, Lafayette, P.O. Box 52066, Lafayette, LA 70505; phone 1-800-346-1958.

Houma-Terrebonne Tourist Commission, P.O. Box 2792A, Houma, LA 70361; phone 1-800-688-2732.

Louisiana Office of Tourism, P.O. Box 94291, Baton Rouge, LA 70804; phone 1-800-33-GUMBO.

State Bicycle Coordinator, Louisiana Department of Transportation, P.O. Box 94245, Capitol Station, Baton Rouge, LA 70804-9245; phone (504) 356-1841.

Maryland
• Chesapeake Bay Area
Distance: 85 miles/142 kilometers
Duration: 2–3 days
Rating: Easy
Type: One-way Tour
Access: St. Michaels, the starting point, is on the Miles River, near the eastern bank of Chesapeake Bay (on No. 33). This small town is accessible by boat, bus, and other motor vehicles. The destination, Chesapeake City, is at the northern end of Chesapeake Bay, in the northeastern corner of the state, near the Delaware border.
Accommodations: Lodging facilities are available in St. Michaels, Easton, Chestertown, and Chesapeake City.
Route Description: The eastern shore of Chesapeake Bay is known for its fine seafood, especially steamed crabs, crab cakes, and fresh oysters. This tour will take you along the eastern shoreline from St. Michaels to Chesapeake City.

Begin this tour in St. Michaels, an excellent yachting center and the site of the Chesapeake Bay Maritime Museum. Cycle east on No. 33 from St. Michaels to Newcomb. Take No. 329 south to Bellevue, where a ferry will take you to Oxford. Bike north on No. 333 to Easton, site of one of the oldest frame buildings of worship in North America. Settled in the late 17th century by Quakers, the Third Haven Friends Meeting House was built by the Society of Friends in 1862.

Ride north from Easton on No. 50 and No. 213 to Centreville, cycling on quiet roads through farmland. Continue on No. 213 to Church Hill, Kings Town, and Chestertown.

You can explore Chestertown's historic district before continuing north on No. 213 to Kennedyville, Locust Grove, Galena, Georgetown, Fredericktown, Ceciltown, and the destination of Chesapeake City, near the north tip of the bay and the Delaware border.

The Chesapeake and Delaware Canal links Chesapeake Bay and Delaware Bay. Of vital importance during World War II, the canal is now a popular avenue for travel from one bay to the other. Chesapeake City became a popular spot because of the canal.

Most of this trip has been on relatively flat, shoreline roads as you have cycled in the Chesapeake Bay area.

Other Tours
• Dorchester County
Begin this 70-mile (117-kilometer) loop tour at Cambridge, on the fertile bank of the Choptank River, near the east side of Chesapeake Bay. Cycle southwest on No. 341, No. 16, and No. 335 to Honga, where you can watch fishermen unload rockfish, oysters, and the famous Maryland blue crabs. Continue on No. 335 to Hopersville, on the south end of Hooper's Island. Retrace your route on No. 335, watching for hermit crabs scurrying along the road. Your only climbs on this very level route are over the Hooper Island Bridge (at Honga). Take No. 335 and No. 536 to Lakesville. You will enter the Blackwater Refuge by cycling through a beautiful marsh by way of a narrow roadway. Follow the signs to Seward, the Refuge Headquarters, and the Visitor Center (for information,

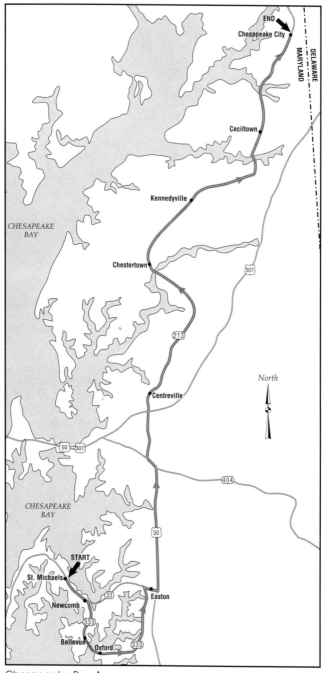

Chesapeake Bay Area

phone (410) 228-2677). Take No. 335 back to Church Creek, and then complete this pleasant, relaxing route by returning to Cambridge.

If you wish to extend your route by 21 miles (35 kilometers), you could ride from Lakesville down the peninsula (on No. 536) and return through Toddsville to Andrews (where you rejoin the described route).

Scenic bike routes of Dorchester County are available through Dorchester County Tourism (phone 1-800-522-8687).

• Worcester County

Enjoy a scenic loop tour of more than 100 miles (167 kilometers) of unspoiled countryside along the Pocomoke River in Worcester County. A brochure is available by contacting: Worcester County Tourism Office, 105 Pearl Street, P.O. Box 208, Snow Hill, MD 21863; phone (410) 632-3110 or 1-800-852-0335.

• Eastern Maryland

This relatively flat 119-mile (195-kilometer) loop tour will take you from the largest city on Maryland's eastern shore, along the Atlantic Ocean, past several state parks, and will include visits to Ocean City and Assateague State Park. Cycle east on No. 346 from Salisbury to St. Martin. Then bike east on No. 50 to Ocean City, a resort town on a barrier island that separates a chain of bays and the Atlantic Ocean (for more information, contact: Ocean City Visitor Information Center, Convention Center, Ocean City, MD; phone (410) 289-2800 or 1-800-62-OCEAN). Take No. 50 west and No. 611 south to Assateague State Park, on Assateague Island National Seashore (for more information, phone (410) 641-1441); this narrow island is a stopover for various waterfowl and the endangered peregrine falcon; it's also home to a number of free-roaming Chincoteague ponies. Return on No. 611 from the Assateague Island National Seashore, and then bike northwest on No. 376 to Berlin. Ride southwest on No. 113 to Snow Hill (on the Pocomoke River), Shad Landing State Park, and Pocomoke City. Then cycle northeast on No. 13 to Princess Anne, at the headwaters of the Manokin River. Bike northwest on No. 362 to Widgeon, and take the ferry across the Wicomico River. Ride east on No. 349 back to Salisbury (for more information about the Salisbury area, including detailed maps of more than 35 rides, contact: Wicomico County Tourism, 500 Glen Avenue, Salisbury, MD 21801; phone (410) 548-4914 or 1-800-332-TOUR).

• Western Maryland

You will gain some insight into the state's history on this 66-mile (110-kilometer) tour of western Maryland as you cycle on relatively quiet, hilly roads from Hagerstown in the northwest to Rockville. Cycle southeast from Hagerstown to Boonsboro (nearby are the Crystal Grottoes Caverns), and then ride northeast on No. 34, through part of Greenbrier State Park to Frederick (which was occupied by both Union and Confederate forces during the Civil War); self-guiding bicycle tours of Frederick County are available from the Visitor Center at Frederick (contact: Frederick Visitor Center, 19E. Church Street, Frederick, MD; phone (301) 663-8703). Bike on No. 355 from Frederick to the destination of Rockville (where the graves of writer F. Scott Fitzgerald and his wife, Zelda, are found in the cemetery of the 1817 St. Mary's Catholic Church).

For more information about the Hagerstown area, contact: Washington County Tourism Office, 1826 Dual Hwy., Hagerstown, MD; phone 301-791-3130. For more information about Rockville, contact: Rockville Chamber of Commerce, 600 E. Jefferson Street, Rockville, MD; phone (301) 424-9300.

- **Cycle to Washington, D.C.**

The Chesapeake and Ohio Canal National Historical Park follows the Maryland shore of the Potomac River from Washington, D.C., to Cumberland in the northwest corner of Maryland. Cyclists are allowed on this 184-mile (307-kilometer) towpath. "A Guide to Food and Lodging Along the C & O Canal" can be purchased from the C & O Canal Association, P.O. Box 366, Glen Echo, MD 20812.

Maryland Contacts

Bicycle Coordinator, Maryland State Highway Administration,
    707 N. Calvert Street, P.O. Box 717, Baltimore, MD 21203-0717;
    phone (410) 333-1145 or 1-800-252-8776 (24 hour bike hot-line); ask
    for a "Bicycling in Maryland Reference Guide" and a "Travel in
    Maryland" package.
Maryland Office of Tourism Development, Redwood Tower,
    9th Floor, 217 E. Redwood Street, Baltimore, MD 21202; phone
    1-800-543-1036.

Crossing the Potomac River, Maryland.

Mississippi
• The Civil War, the Artist, the Writers, and Elvis

Distance: 190 miles/317 kilometers
Duration: 3–5 days
Rating: Moderate
Type: Loop Tour
Access: Tupelo is in northeastern Mississippi. A number of roads go through Tupelo, including the Natchez Trace Parkway. Tupelo is also accessible by air and rail.
Accommodations: Full services available at Tupelo, and some services available at towns along this route. Camping is available in Holly Springs National Forest
Route Description: Begin this tour in Tupelo, where singer Elvis Presley was born on Jan. 8, 1935. The small white house in which he was born is now a part of Elvis Presley Center.

Cycle north on No. 45 to Baldwyn. Then head west on No. 370 to Brices Cross Roads National Battlefield Site, which commemorates the Civil War battle fought here on June 10, 1864.

Returning to No. 45, continue north to Corinth, which was occupied by both Union and Confederate troops during the Civil War. Troops clashed in the Battle of Corinth in 1862. The Corinth Civil War Battlefield, including the Corinth National Cemetery, can be visited, as can Curlee House, a mansion that housed three different Civil War generals (Confederate Generals Braxton Bragg and Earl Van Dorn; Union General Henry Halleck).

Cycle west on No. 72, traveling near the Tennessee border; then take No. 7 southwest to Holly Springs. General Ulysses S. Grant set up a supply depot here in 1862. General Earl Van Dorn recaptured the town and destroyed Grant's supplies. Several raids occurred here during the Civil War, and you can learn about this history by visiting the Marshall County Historical Museum.

Holly Springs is also noted as the birthplace of artist Kate Clark. She signed her early works Freeman Clark so that no one would know that a woman had painted them. After her death in 1957, the Kate Freeman Clark Art Gallery was built; it houses a large collection of her works.

Head south on No. 7 from Holly Springs through part of Holly Springs National Forest, where camping and hiking are available. Then ride southwest to Oxford, where William Faulkner wrote many of his books (such as *The Sound and the Fury*); he fashioned the mythical world of Yoknapatawpha County out of the town and its environs. Faulkner bought, restored, and lived in Rowan Oak, a house that was almost burned down during the Civil War. Less literary but more popular, John Grisham (author of such books as *The Firm* and *The Client*), is Oxford's best known living writer.

Cycle east on No. 6 from Oxford to your destination of Tupelo, the site of an intense battle during the Civil War. Tupelo National Battlefield is at the site of the Battle of Tupelo, the last major Civil War battle fought in Mississippi.

This route is hilly but not overly strenuous.

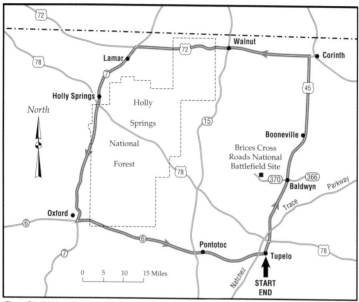

The Civil War, the Artist, the Writers, and Elvis

Other Tours

• **The Natchez Trace Parkway**

The Natchez Trace Parkway evolved from an Indian trail and a pioneer highway; in its current reincarnation it commemorates the Old Natchez Trail. Wayside exhibits and nature trails illustrate the history of the Natchez Trace. The Parkway angles across Mississippi, Alabama, and Tennessee, from Natchez to Nashville. This part of the Natchez Trail Parkway in Mississippi takes you from Natchez (in the southwestern corner of the state), through Jackson (the state capital) and Tupelo (where the Visitor Center relates the story of this route through an audiovisual program), to Tishomingo State Park (in the northeastern corner of the state). You will cycle past fertile lands and on rolling hills as you bike this route of about 297 miles (495 kilometers).

• **From the Mississippi River to the Gulf of Mexico**

This 250 miles (417 kilometers route takes you across the southern section of the state of Mississippi, from Natchez (on the Mississippi River, and near the Louisiana border) to Pascagoula (on the Gulf of Mexico, near the Alabama border). The terrain is relatively flat, particularly along the coast of the Gulf of Mexico.

Leave the Mississippi River behind as you cycle southwest from Natchez to Columbia (on No. 98). Then take No. 43 south, and follow the Pearl River to Picayune (where you can visit the John C. Stennis Space Center). Bike southwest on No. 11 and No. 607, crossing a NASA Test Site, to Bay St. Louis, on the Gulf of Mexico. Cycle east on No. 90, along the Gulf of Mexico, to the resort town of Gulfport (which has miles of beautiful beaches). Then bike to Biloxi, where you can join a shrimping trip into the Gulf of Mexico on a reconditioned shrimp boat to learn about the art of shrimping, and Ocean Springs, where you can view artists at work in their shops. As you bike along, you will see several islands out in the Gulf (Gulf Islands National Seashore). Cycle to Gulf Marine State Park and Shepard State Park on your way to your destination of Pascagoula.

Mississippi Contacts

Division of Tourism, P.O. Box 22825, Jackson, MS 39205; phone (601) 359-3297.

Holly Springs Chamber of Commerce, 154 S. Memphis Street, Holly Springs, MS 38365; phone (601) 252-2943.

Mississippi Bicycle Coordinator, Department of Transportation, 85-01, P.O. Box 1850, Jackson, MS 39215-1850; phone (601) 359-7685.

Tupelo Convention and Visitors Bureau, P.O. Box 1485, Tupelo, MS 38802; phone 1-800-533-0611.

North Carolina
• North Carolina's Blue Ridge Mountains & Great Smoky Mountains
Distance: 189 miles 315 kilometers
Duration: 4–6 days
Rating: Strenuous
Type: One-way Tour
Access: Cherokee is near the southern entrance of Great Smoky Mountains National Park and the Blue Ridge Parkway (at No. 19 and No. 441). Boone is in the northeast corner of the state, at the intersection of two scenic highways (No. 321 and No. 421).
Accommodations: There are lodging facilities at both Cherokee and Boone, but the trip is best suited to the camper (camping is available in designated areas along the Parkway).
Route Description: The Blue Ridge Mountains cut through North Carolina and Virginia. The Great Smoky Mountains span parts of North Carolina and Tennessee. This trip will tour the sections of the mountains that are within the state of North Carolina as you cycle from Cherokee, in the southwest, to Boone, in the northeast.

The Blue Ridge Parkway is a 470-mile (784-kilometer) scenic road that connects Great Smoky Mountains National Park to Shenandoah National Park. You will travel part of this picturesque but physically challenging route through North Carolina. The Parkway offers several panoramic outlooks and hiking trails; however, there will be some very tough climbs as you cycle this twisting road along the crest of the Appalachian Mountains.

Begin this trip in Cherokee, near the entrance to Great Smoky Mountains National Park (described under Tennessee). Cherokee history and culture are displayed in several museums, including the Museum of the Cherokee Indian, and by way of an outdoor drama entitled "Unto These Hills." Ride to the Parkway, and you will soon begin a long climb to Richland Balsam, the highest point on the road. Continue riding the ascents and descents as you pass through the Shining Rock Wilderness Area to Mount Pisgah, Asheville, Mount Mitchell State Park, Little Switzerland (site of the North Carolina Mining Museum and the Gemstone Mine), and Linville Falls (site of a picturesque falls and gorge that is reached by a foot trail just off the Parkway). Exit the Blue Ridge Parkway at Blowing Rock, a resort area, and ride north on No. 321 to Boone, high in the Blue Ridge Mountains.

Named after Daniel Boone, who had a cabin in the area in the 1760s, Boone has a statue of the frontiersman on the campus of Appalachian State University. More than just an image of Boone, the statue includes stones from his original cabin's fireplace. While in the Boone area, consider a visit to the Appalachian Cultural Museum and a showing of *Horn in the West,* a musical about Daniel Boone's struggle to establish freedom in the Southern Appalachian Highlands. You might also like to go white-water rafting on the Nolichucky, Ocee, or Watauga Rivers or Upper and Lower Wilson's Creek. Canoe trips and four-wheel-drive mountain excursions are also offered.

Other Tours
• The Blue Ridge Parkway
     Complete the entire length of this strenuous route by continuing your ride into Virginia.

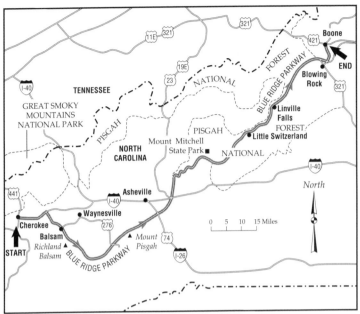

North Carolina's Blue Ridge and Great Smoky Mountains

• **Great Smoky Mountains National Park**

Start in Cherokee and pedal through the park on Newfound Gap Road into Tennessee (described under Tennessee tours).

• **Through North Carolina**

For routes from north to south, refer to chapter No. 11, where two specific routes are given.

• **Quaker Back Country**

You will cycle past gently rolling farmland on relatively quiet roads in this northern section of the state. Begin your 25-mile (42-kilometer) tour in Jamestown, which was first settled by Quakers in 1857. Ride east on No. 62 to Climax and Julian and northeast to Alamance (site of the Battle of Alamance) and Burlington (where many factory outlets attract shoppers).

• **The Outer Banks**

The Outer Banks is a strand of offshore barrier islands just off the northeastern coast of North Carolina. This area of wild beauty, including marshes and sand dunes, is lined with flat roads, perfect for riding. The rather easy cycling takes you to islands that have miles of sandy beaches, where surf fishing, seashell collecting, and scuba diving are popular activities. Some of the nicest beaches are in Cape Lookout National Seashore and Cape Hatteras National Seashore.

Begin this trip in New Bern, in northeastern North Carolina. Cycle southeast to Minnesott Beach and Otway (on No. 306). Then ride northeast along the coast to Atlantic, where a ferry will take you to Cape Lookout National Seashore, with its thousands of acres of undeveloped barrier islands. After exploring this area, return to the mainland, and bike northeast to Cedar Island. Then take the ferry to Ocracoke, a former pirate village on Ocracoke Island. Cycle on No. 12 across the flat island, and then take another ferry to Hatteras Island. Cycle across the bridge to Bodie Island, and continue your ride to Whalebone. Turn west on No. 64, crossing Roanoke Island, and then take the causeway to Manus Harbor, on the mainland. Bike southwest on No. 264, along Pamlico Sound, to Engelhard, Lake Landing (on Mattamuskeet Lake), New Holland (nearby is the Mattamuskeet National Wildlife Refuge, a wintering area for migrating birds), and Belhaven. Ride southwest on No. 99, take the Pamlico River ferry, and then continue cycling south to Aurora. Complete this approximately 300-mile (500-kilometer) loop tour by returning to New Bern.

For more information, contact: Superintendent, Cape Lookout National Seashore, 3601 Bridge Street, Suite F, Morehead City, NC 28557; phone (919) 728-2250; Cape Hatteras National Seashore, Park Headquarters, Rte. 1, Box 675, Manteo, NC 27954; phone (919) 473-2111; Dare County Tourist Bureau, 517 Budleigh Street, Manteo, NC 27954; phone (919) 473-2138; New Bern Chamber of Commerce, P.O. Drawer C, New Bern, NC 28563; phone (919) 637-3111.

North Carolina Contacts

Blue Ridge Parkway, 200 BB&T Building, 1 Pack Square, Asheville, NC 28801; phone (704) 259-0701.

Boone Chamber of Commerce, 112 W. Howard Street, Boone, NC 28607; phone (704) 264-2225 or 1-800-852-9506.

Cherokee Visitors Center, Main Street, Cherokee, NC; phone 1-800-438-1601.

North Carolina Trails Program, North Carolina Division of Parks and Recreation, 12700 Bay Leaf Road, Raleigh, NC 27614; phone (919) 846-9991.

State Bicycle Coordinator, North Carolina Department of Transportation, P.O. Box 25201, Raleigh, NC 27611; phone (919) 733-2804.

Superintendent, Great Smoky Mountains National Park, 107 Park Headquarters Road, Gatlinburg, TN 37738; phone (615) 436-1200.

Travel and Tourism Division, 430 North Salisbury Street, Raleigh, NC 27611; phone (919) 733-4171 or 1-800-VISIT NC.

U.S. Forest Service, P.O. Box 2750, Asheville, NC 28802; phone (704) 257-4200.

South Carolina
• Hilton Head Island Area
Distance: 162 miles/270 kilometers
Duration: 3–5 days
Rating: Easy
Type: Return Trip
Access: Hilton Head Island, off the southeast coast of South Carolina, is the largest island between New Jersey and Florida. A bridge to the mainland was completed in 1956. This popular resort area is also available by air. Several bicycle rental outlets are on the island, with daily and weekly rates.
Accommodations: Full facilities are available in this resort area.
Route Description: Hilton Head Island has become a very popular resort area. The island itself is about 12 miles (20 kilometers) long and up to 5 miles (8 kilometers) wide. With miles of beautiful, sandy beaches, about 30 miles (50 kilometers) of flat, paved bicycle trails (plus miles of beach cycling!), about 300 tennis courts, 25 golf courses, marinas, and riding stables, this area definitely appeals to those looking for outdoor activities and recreation. If you wish, you can take a cruise around the island and also visit Daufuskie Island.

After exploring the island, ride northwest on No. 278 and northeast on No. 170 to Beaufort, a picturesque port town. Mule-drawn carriage tours of historic Beaufort are available. You might enjoy visiting such points of interest as the Beaufort museum, the John Mark Vendier House (built in the 1790s), and St. Helena's Episcopal Church (founded in 1712). Near Beaufort is Parris Island, where the U.S. Marine Corps has a base. Across the Beaufort River is Lady's Island.

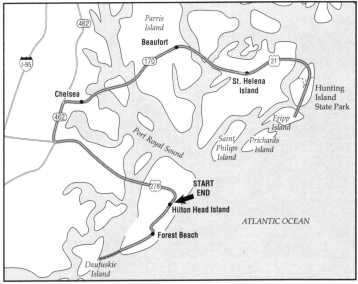

Hilton Head Island Area

Cycle south from Beaufort to St. Helena Island, Hunting Island State Park (a good place to see the state tree, the palmetto or cabbage palm), and Fripp Island.

Be careful on this cycling trip because of the heavy tourist traffic; moreover, sections of this route do not have a paved shoulder. After you have explored this scenic area, retrace your route back to Hilton Head, where you can enjoy more cycling on the beautiful, safer bicycle paths.

Other Tours
• Along the Atlantic Ocean

This tour will take you along the coastline, beginning at Charleston, renowned for its architecture. Charleston is also the site of the Patriots Point Naval and Maritime Museum, the Old Exchange and Provost Dungeon, Magnolia Cemetery, Cypress Gardens, the Audubon Swamp Garden, Magnolia Plantation and Gardens, and Boone Hall Plantation. For more information about the Charleston area, contact: Charleston Visitor Center, 375 Meeting Street, Charleston, SC 29403; phone (803) 853-8000.

After exploring Charleston, cycle northwest on scenic No. 17 through the National Awendaw Forest, and along the coast. You will pass several islands and miles of sandy beaches as you pedal on flat roads to Georgetown, home to a deep water harbor and many historic

Enjoy the beach at Myrtle beach, South Carolina.

plantations. Proceed to Pawleys Island, Huntington Beach State Park, Murrells Inlet (where crabbing and shrimping are popular pastimes), Garden City Beach, Surfside Beach, Myrtle Beach State Park, and Myrtle Beach, which is your destination—and one of South Carolina's most popular resort areas. Be prepared for higher lodging costs and heavy tourist traffic. For more information about the Myrtle Beach area, contact: Myrtle Beach Chamber of Commerce, Myrtle Beach, SC; phone (803) 626-7444 or 1-800-356-3016.

- **Through South Carolina**
  For two specific routes through the state, from north to south, see chapter No. 11.

- **The Northwest Corner**
  The Blue Ridge Mountains come into view in the northwest corner of the state. You will ride through a particularly scenic section of the Sumter National Forest and pass Oconee State Park as you pedal south on No. 107 (from Greenville). Go southeast on No. 28, past Isaqueena Falls, which plunge 200 feet to the valley floor, to Walhalla (named for Valhalla, the legendary garden paradise of the gods, according to Norse mythology). Cycle north on No. 11 to Sunset and on to the junction of No. 253, where you will ride south, past Paris Mountain State Park (encompassing three lakes) and on to the destination of Greenville, a city with more than 60 city parks. This 78-mile (130-kilometer) route will take the cyclist on relatively quiet rural roads through hilly terrain.

- **Columbia Loop**
  The state capital's points of interest include the South Carolina State Museum, the State House, the Hampton-Preston Mansion, Fort Jackson Museum, Riverbanks Zoological Park, and the University of South Carolina. After exploring the city of Columbia, cycle southeast on No. 48 to the Congaree Swamp National Monument, enclosing 22,000 acres of swamp forest along the Congaree River. You can explore the area on boardwalks before continuing your ride to Wateree. Then ride south on No. 601 and southeast on No. 6 to Santee. Cross Lake Marion, and head northeast on No. 15 to Sumter, renowned for its woodworking industry, and Bishopville. Cycle west on No. 34 and No. 1 back to Columbia, completing this 171-mile (285-kilometer) loop in central South Carolina.

South Carolina Contacts

Beaufort Chamber of Commerce, 1006 Bay Street, Beaufort, SC 29902; phone (803) 524-3163.
Coastal Cyclists, P.O. Box 32095, Charleston, SC 29407.
Hilton Head Island Chamber of Commerce, Hilton Head, SC; phone (803) 785-3673.
South Carolina Department of Parks, Recreation and Tourism, 1205 Pendleton Street, Suite 106, Edgar Brown Bldg., Columbia, SC 29201; phone (803) 734-0122.
State Bicycle Coordinator, South Carolina DHPT,1205 Pendleton Street, E.A.Brown Bldg., Columbia, SC 29202; phone (803) 734-0141.

Tennessee
• Great Smoky Mountains National Park
Distance: 190 miles/317 kilometers
Duration: 3–5 days
Rating: Strenuous
Type: Loop Tour
Access: Known as the "Gateway to the Smokies," Knoxville is in eastern Tennessee, north of Great Smoky Mountains National Park. Several major roads go to Knoxville, including No. 75, No. 81, No. 129, and No. 11W.
Accommodations: Full facilities in Knoxville and Gatlinburg. Camping is available at Sieverville, Pigeon Forge, Alcoa, and in the park.
Route Description: A smoky, haze often hangs over the peaks of the Great Smoky Mountains, accounting for the appropriate name. Great Smoky Mountains National Park is partly in Tennessee and partly in North Carolina. This route will take you into both states as you explore this magnificent park.

Begin in Knoxville, which has several bicycle paths for your convenience. Ride southeast on No. 441 to Sevierville (named for Tennessee's first governor, John Sevier). You might enjoy taking a side trip to Forbidden Caverns (12 miles or 20 kilometers east on No. 411), which once were used as a hideaway for moonshine; the caverns contain a stream, a wall of onyx, natural chimneys, and waterfalls.

Continue south from Sevierville (on No. 441) to Dollywood, Pigeon Forge, and Gatlinburg (a popular resort area near the entrance to the park). Gatlinburg has become an important handicraft center; the Great Smoky Mountains Arts and Crafts Community includes more than 60 craft shops. While in the Gatlinburg area, ride the 5-mile (8-kilometer) Roaring Fork Loop, which presents magnificent views as you bike through the mountainous terrain. You can get scenic views of the Gatlinburg area with less sweat by taking the Sky Lift or the Aerial Tramway.

After exploring the Gatlinburg area, cycle into Great Smoky Mountains National Park (the Sugarlands Visitor Center will provide you with information on the park). There are many miles of paved and gravel roads in the park, presenting opportunities for mountain biking, hiking, and horseback riding. The Appalachian Trail runs along the border through the park. Cades Cove Road is a popular loop; this 11-mile (18-kilometer) route circles the cove and contains several restored cabins, a grist mill, and a Visitor Center; this road is closed to all motor vehicles, making it ideal for cyclists.

Ride across the park on Newfound Gap Road, crossing into the state of North Carolina. Exit the park at Cherokee; then head southwest on No. 19 and No. 28. You'll cross back into Tennessee, pedaling along the edge of Great Smoky Mountains National Park. Bike northwest on No. 115 and No. 129 to Maryville, where Sam Houston taught in a log school house; he later became, among other things, commander of the Army of Texas and president of the Republic of Texas.

Cycle north on No. 33 back to Knoxville, completing a challenging loop tour.

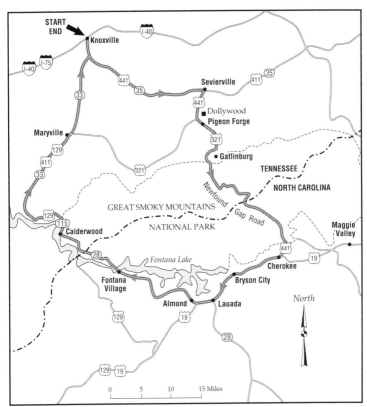

Great Smoky Mountains National Park

Other Tours

• The Blue Ridge Parkway

After riding through Great Smoky Mountains National Park, consider the challenging, scenic Blue Ridge Parkway route that takes you through North Carolina and into Virginia (for more information on this route, consult the specific tours for North Carolina and Virginia).

• The Natchez Trace Parkway

Extending 500 miles (835 kilometers) from Nashville to Natchez (Mississippi), the Natchez Trace Parkway evolved from an old Indian trail and pioneer route. A 90-mile (150-kilometer) section of the Parkway will take you south from Nashville to the Alabama border.

• Country Music and Central Tennessee

Nashville is best known as "Music City, U.S.A." and as the home of the Grand Ole Opry and the Opryland Complex. For more information about this country music hot spot, contact: Grand Ole Opry Tickets, 2808 Opryland Drive, Nashville, TN 37214; phone (615) 889-3060;

Nashville Area Chamber of Commerce, 161 4th Avenue N., Nashville, TN 37219; phone (615) 259-4700.

After exploring the Nashville area, cycle southeast on No. 41 to Smyrna and Murfreesboro. An obelisk 3 miles (5 kilometers) from the public square in Murfreesboro marks the geographic center of Tennessee. About 3 miles (5 kilometers) northwest of town is the Stones River National Battlefield, site of a bloody battle during the Civil War; this battlefield and other area sites are linked by bicycle routes that follow lightly traveled back roads (maps of the routes are available by contacting: Murfreesboro Chamber of Commerce, 302 S. Front Street, Murfreesboro, TN; phone (615) 893-6565).

Cycle northeast on No. 96 and No. 266 to Lebanon. Then complete this 95-mile (158-kilometer) loop tour by riding west on No. 70 back to Nashville.

• From North to South—Reelfoot Lake State Park to Pickwick Landing State Park

Begin this 145-mile (242-kilometer) route in Tennessee's northwest corner, at Reelfoot Lake State Park. Reelfoot Lake is the winter home of thousands of ducks and geese and for a growing number of bald eagles. Ride east on No. 21 and No. 216 to Martin and southeast on No. 22 to Huntingdon, Lexington, and Adamsville. Bike east on No. 64 to Crump and southeast on No. 142 and No. 57, through Shiloh National Military Park (site of one of the bloodiest battles of the Civil War), to the destination, Pickwick Landing State Park, which is on the Tennessee River, near the Alabama and Mississippi borders.

"Graceland" was the home of rock and roll legend Elvis Presley, in Memphis, Tennessee. Tours of this home are available.

Tennessee Contacts

Gatlinburg Chamber of Commerce, P.O. Box 527, Gatlinburg, TN 37738; phone 1-800-568-4748.

State Bicycle Coordinator, Tennessee Department of Transportation, Suite 900, James Polk Bldg., Nashville, TN 37243-0349; phone (615) 741-5310; ask for the free touring maps of Tennessee.

Superintendent, Great Smoky Mountains National Park, 107 Park Headquarters Road, Gatlinburg, TN 37738; phone (615) 436-1200.

Tennessee Department of Tourist Development, P.O. Box 23170, Nashville, TN 37202; phone (615) 741-2158 or 1-800-TENN-200.

One of the waterslide rides available in "Opryland," located in Nashville, Tennessee.

Virginia

• **Historic Virginia–Yorktown to Petersburg**

Distance: 108 miles/180 kilometers
Duration: 3–5 days
Rating: Easy to Moderate
Type: One-way Tour
Access: Yorktown is in southeastern Virginia, on the eastern tip of the Colonial Parkway. It's accessible by water, road, and air (the Patrick-Henry International Airport is nearby). Petersburg is west of Yorktown and south of Richmond.
Accommodations: Full services are available at Williamsburg, Richmond, and Petersburg; some services are available at Yorktown and along the route.
Route Description: This historically significant tour takes you from Colonial National Historical Park, in southeastern Virginia, past several plantations, and to several famous battlefields.

The peninsula between the York and James Rivers, including Jamestown Island, Yorktown Battlefield, and the Colonial Parkway, is known as the Colonial National Historical Park. The 22-mile (37-kilometer) Colonial Parkway links Jamestown, Williamsburg, and Yorktown; this scenic Parkway has several natural trail loops, with explanatory markers (a free "Historic Triangle Bike Map" is available from the State Bicycle Coordinator).

Begin this tour in Yorktown, home of the Yorktown Victory Center, a museum of the American Revolution, and Yorktown Battlefield, where the last major battle of the War for Independence was fought.

Pedal west on the Colonial Parkway to Williamsburg, where a variety of colonial homes and shops line the main thoroughfare, Duke of Gloucester Street. Sections of the restored city of Colonial Williamsburg, which recreates the vitality and historic significance of the eighteenth century town, are accessible only to bicycles and pedestrians, which makes the sightseeing even more enjoyable.

Continue west from Williamsburg to Jamestown, on the western tip of the Colonial Parkway. Jamestown was founded in 1607, and ruins of the seventeenth century town are still visible. Statues of John Smith and Pocahontas grace Jamestown Island.

Leaving Colonial National Historical Park, ride northwest on No. 5, along the James River, to Sherwood Forest; this working plantation is the former residence of two U.S. presidents (William Henry Harrison and John Tyler). Continue northwest on No. 5 to Berkeley Plantation, which is the ancestral home of President Benjamin Harrison and the birthplace of President William Henry Harrison. Then ride to Shirley Plantation (Virginia's oldest) and Edgewood Plantation; guided tours of these historic sites are available.

Continue on No. 5 to Richmond, Virginia's capital and home to several historically significant buildings, including the Capitol, Agecroft Hall, John Marshall House, St. John's Episcopal Church, Wilton House, and the Governor's Mansion (where four U.S. presidents have lived—Harrison, Jefferson, Monroe, and Tyler). The Cultural Link Trolley connects many of Richmond's landmarks. Other points of interest in this area include Monument Boulevard (with sculptures of Arthur

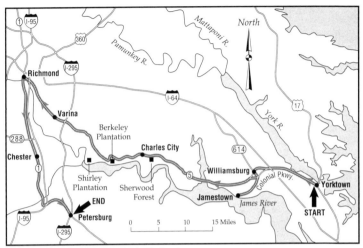

Historic Virginia—Yorktown to Petersburg

Ashe, Robert E. Lee, and Stonewall Jackson), the Valentine Museum, the Museum of Fine Arts, the Museum of the Confederacy, Richmond National Battlefield Park (site of the fight for possession of the Confederate capital), and Hollywood Cemetery (the burial place of many significant Virginians, including presidents Tyler and Monroe).

Ride south on No. 1 and No. 301 from Richmond to Chester, Colonial Heights (site of Robert E. Lee's headquarters for five months), and Petersburg. About 30,000 Confederate soldiers are buried in the Old Blandford Cemetery in Petersburg. The Siege Museum depicts the deprivations suffered by the people surrounded for months during the Civil War. Petersburg National Battlefield commemorates General Robert E. Lee's famous last stand, which led to the fall of Richmond; part of the 4-mile (7-kilometer) self-guiding Battlefield Tour Road is reserved for cyclists and hikers; walks from this tour road lead to major battle sites.

You'll cross a landscape of rolling hills as you pedal from Yorktown to Petersburg on this trip through American history.

Other Tours

• **The Blue Ridge Parkway**

The Blue Ridge Parkway is a 470-mile (784-kilometer) scenic route that connects Shenandoah National Park to the Great Smoky Mountains of North Carolina and Tennessee. You can ride a 200-mile (333-kilometer) section of this Parkway in Virginia by cycling north from Fancy Gap to Waynesboro. The curvy road makes for long, strenuous climbs and steep descents. It takes you by several scenic outlooks, Visitor Centers, campgrounds, and a lodge (Peaks of Otter Lodge). For more information, contact: Blue Ridge Parkway, National Park Service, 2551 Mountain View Road, Vinton, VA 24179; phone (703) 982-6458.

This covered bridge is found near Mount Jackson, Virginia.

• Shenandoah National Park

Shenandoah National Park has its highs and lows, taking you from mountain summits to deep valleys and chasms. The park presents opportunities for horseback riding, hiking, and mountain biking. More than 500 miles (850 kilometers) of trails (including a section of the Appalachian Trail) crisscross the park, which is home to about 40 kinds of mammals, 200 varieties of birds, and 100 species of trees. For more information (and trail maps), contact: Skyline Drive (Shenandoah National Park, National Park Service, Route 4, Box 292, Luray, VA 22835; phone (703) 999-2229.

Begin this strenuous trip by cycling north from Waynesboro on the spectacular Skyline Drive, which follows along the crest of the Blue Ridge Mountains through the park. At Big Meadows you will find a Visitor Center with displays on the history of the park. Skyland is an excellent place to begin a horseback trip. The 105-mile (175-kilometer) route ends at Front Royal, at the north end of Skyline Drive.

• The Shenandoah Valley

Parallel to much of the Blue Ridge Parkway and Skyline Drive, but nestled in a valley, is No. 11, which offers a far less challenging, but still very pretty passage from Roanoke northeast to Strasburg. This gently rolling route, with its majestic views of the Blue Ridge Mountains, passes through many interesting towns and near several tourist attractions (including Natural Bridge, Endless Caverns, and Shenandoah Caverns). I found this 159-mile (255-kilometer) route to be a very pleasant contrast to the mountainous terrain of the Blue Ridge Parkway and Shenandoah National Park.

• Virginia's Eastern Shore

Trails are available in the Chincoteague National Wildlife Refuge (where you can observe a great variety of wildlife, including the famous

Chincoteague ponies) and on Assateague Island National Seashore. For more information, contact: Refuge Manager, Chincoteague National Wildlife Refuge, P.O. Box 62, Chincoteague, VA 23336; phone 804-336-6122; Assateague Island National Seashore, National Park Service, P.O. Box 38, Chincoteague, VA 23336; phone (804) 336-6577.

• **Northern Virginia**

Here are three suggested possibilities for bike trips in Northern Virginia:

1. The 17-mile (28-kilometer) Mount Vernon Trail includes a visit to George Washington's home on the Potomac River. A pamphlet describing this route is available from: the National Park Service, George Washington Memorial Parkway, Turkey Run Park, McLean, VA 22101; phone (703) 358-3699.

2. Arlington County has miles of on- and off-road trails, detailed on a map available from the county. Contact Arlington County Trails, Arlington County Bicycle Coordinator, 2100 Clarendon Blvd., Suite 717, Arlington, VA 22201; phone (703) 358-3699.

3. The Northern Virginia Regional Park Authority maintains many miles of biking, hiking, jogging, horseback riding, and nature trails of varying lengths in the Washington and Old Dominion Railroad Regional Park. A trail guide detailing these is available by contacting Washington and Old Dominion Trail, Northern Virginia Regional Park Authority, 5400 Ox Road, Fairfax Station, VA 22039; phone (703) 352-5900.

• **New River Trail**

This 57-mile (95-kilometer) rails-to-trails route in southwestern Virginia, from Pulaski south to Galax, has 2 tunnels and 32 bridges and trestles. For more information, contact: New River Trail, Rte. 1, Box 81X, Austinville, VA 24312; phone (540) 699-6778.

Virginia Contacts

Colonial National Historical Park; phone (804) 898-3400.

Manager of Marketing Services, Colonial Williamsburg Foundation, Box C, Williamsburg, VA 23187.

Metro Richmond Convention and Visitors Bureau, 300 East Main Street, Richmond, VA 23219; phone 1-800-365-7272.

Petersburg, Virginia; phone (804) 733-2400.

State Bicycle Coordinator, Virginia Department of Transportation, 1401 East Broad Street, Richmond, VA 23219; phone (804) 786-2964.

Virginia State Chamber of Commerce, 9 S. 5th Street, Richmond, VA 23219; phone 1-800-VISIT VA.

Virginia Trails Association, 12 West Maple Street, Alexandria, VA 22310; phone (703) 548-7490.

West Virginia
• The Greenbrier River Trail
Distance: 130 miles/217 kilometers
Duration: 3–4 days
Rating: Strenuous
Type: One-way Tour
Access: White Sulphur Springs is in southeastern West Virginia, near the Virginia border. It's accessible by road and air.
Accommodations: Lodging facilities are available in White Sulphur Springs, Lewisburg, Snowshoe, and Elkins.
Route Description: Following an extinct railroad grade along the beautiful Greenbrier River, the Greenbrier River Trail (which has a generally hard-packed gravel surface) is particularly popular for hiking and mountain biking. You can bike directly on the trail (which traverses 2 tunnels and 35 bridges) or follow the back roads described here.

The Greenbrier River Trail is near White Sulphur Springs, a fashionable health resort since the late 1700s, and the starting point for this trip. Cycle west to Caldwell and Lewisburg (where some of Lewisburg's old buildings still bear scars from the Civil War's Battle of Lewisburg). Bike north to Lost World Caverns, which contain a number of rooms with stalactite, stalagmite, and flowstone formations; tours are available.

Head northeast to Frankford, and then ride on No. 219 to Renick and Spice. Cycle past Watoga State Park to Buckeye, Edray, and Slatyfork. Bike east on No. 66 to Snowshoe (a major ski area) and Cass. You might like to take a logging locomotive from Cass Scenic Railroad Park to the top of Bald Knob and stay overnight in a refurbished turn-of-the-century logger house (for more information, phone: 1-800-CALL WVA). There are also extensive trail systems for mountain biking in this area (Pocahontas County).

Cycle northeast on No. 92 from Cass to Green Bank (in Deer Creek Valley), Arbovale, and Boyer. Then bike northwest to Durbin, Cheat Bridge, and Mill Creek. Finally, cycle north on No. 219 to your destination of Elkins, on the Tygart Valley River in the Potomac Highlands. This region contains many of West Virginia's highest mountains, so you will face some tough climbs in this popular skiing and resort area.

This challenging, picturesque road tour takes you from White Sulphur Springs to Elkins, and part of this route runs parallel to the Greenbrier River Trail.

Other Tours
• The Midland Trail—Charleston to White Sulphur Springs
Ride scenic No. 60, following the Kanawha River, as you bike this pretty 105-mile (175-kilometer) route from Charleston (the state capital) to White Sulphur Springs (which is near the Greenbrier River Trail, for cyclists, and the Allegheny Trail, for hikers).

• New River Gorge National River
The New River Gorge National River winds through the Appalachian Mountains east of Beckley; this river is considered one of the best in the

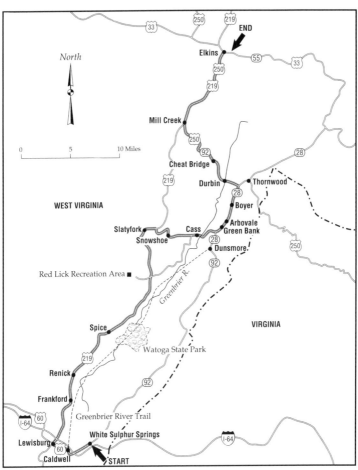

The Greenbrier River Trail

state for bass fishing and one of the most challenging for white-water rafting. This 105-mile (175-kilometer) loop tour begins in Beckley (in southwest West Virginia), a coal mining area. Ride east to Grandview State Park, where a musical drama recreates the family feud between the "Hatfields and McCoys." Pedal on No. 41 to Lawton, Layland, Landisburg, and Clifftop. Turn southeast on No. 60 to Rainette, and then ride southwest on No. 20 to Bellwood, Meadow Bridge, Sandstone Falls State Park, and Hinton (where you'll find a Visitor Center for the New River Gorge National River). Whitewater tours of the New, Gauley, and Bluestone Rivers can be arranged (for more information about the Hinton area, contact: Hinton Visitor Center, New River Gorge National River, Hinton, WV; phone 304-466-0417). Ride northwest on No. 3 from Hinton to Jumping Branch, Shady Spring, Daniels, and then back to Beckley.

129

• **Valleys of the Potomac River**

This scenic route of about 150 miles (250 kilometers) follows long pastoral valleys, surrounded by mountains, but only crosses them in the south (between Franklin and Brandywine). Begin this tour at Romney, on the south branch of the Potomac River. Ride west on No. 50 and southwest on No. 220 to Petersburg. Then take No. 28 through the Seneca Rocks National Recreation Area. Bike on No. 33 to Franklin,

The Greenbrier River Trail, in West Virginia, follows an extinct railroad grade along the beautiful Greenbrier River.

then climb through the mountains near Brandywine. Ride northeast, along the south branch of the Potomac River, to Moorefield. Cycle northeast on No. 29 to Rock Oak, and then ride north back to Romney.

• **Harpers Ferry Loop**

The town of Harpers Ferry is at the confluence of the Potomac and Shenandoah rivers, which separate West Virginia, Virginia, and Maryland. Ride north to Shepherdstown. Take No. 480 southwest to Kearneysville and No. 1 south to Summit Point. Then ride east to Rippon and north (on No. 25 and No. 27) back to Harpers Ferry, completing this 52-mile (87-kilometer) loop tour of West Virginia's eastern corner.

• **To Washington, D.C.**

In West Virginia's northeast corner, you can cross the Potomac River by way of a bike/pedestrian bridge from Harpers Ferry National Historic Park and join the C&O Canal Towpath, which will take you to Washington, D.C., (and which is described under tours of Maryland).

West Virginia Contacts

Elkins-Randolph County Chamber of Commerce, WV; phone (304) 636-2717.

Lewisburg Visitor Center, 105 Church Street, Lewisburg, WV; phone (304) 645-1000.

Pocahontas County Tourism Commission, Marlinton, WV; phone (304) 799-4636 or 1-800-336-7009.

Potomac Highlands Convention and Visitors Bureau, WV; phone 304-636-8400 or 1-800-347-1453.

State Bicycle Coordinator, West Virginia Department of Transportation, 1900 Kanawha Blvd. E., Capital Complex, Bldg. No. 5, Rm. A550, Charleston, WV 25305; phone (304) 558-3063.

West Virginia Convention and Visitors Bureau, P.O. Box 1799, Beckley, WV 25802; phone (304) 252-2244 or 1-800-VISIT WV.

Chapter 7

Western Interior States

Arizona, Colorado, Idaho, Montana, Nevada, New Mexico, Oklahoma, Texas, Utah, and Wyoming comprise a vast territory of desert, mountain and plains. Some of the most spectacular scenery and most magnificent natural wonders in the world are found here. The American West also embraces some of the most remote and wild areas left in the country.

This area encompasses dramatic extremes in weather. There are parts of Arizona, New Mexico and Texas that could be cycled year-round—but even in these states, at high altitudes and on the open plains, howling blizzards and sub-zero temperatures are a distinct possibility in winter. At the other extreme, summertime heat makes parts of the territory equally forbidding. Careful planning is important—make sure that you're picking the right time of year for your trip. Also remember that weather is unpredictable at any time of year in alpine regions. The higher the altitude, the more unpredictable. (July snowstorms in Wyoming? In the mountains, it's not unheard of.)

Arizona
• The Grand Canyon
Distance: 204 miles/340 kilometers
Duration: 3–6 days
Rating: Strenuous
Type: Loop Tour
Access: Flagstaff, south of the Grand Canyon and north of Phoenix, serves as a gateway to many of the area's scenic attractions.
Accommodations: Full services are available in Flagstaff, and a variety of accommodations are available near the area's scenic attractions.
Route Description: One of the world's most outstanding spectacles, the Grand Canyon of the Colorado River is 277 miles (462 kilometers) long and averages 10 miles (17 kilometers) in width. Opportunities abound for hiking, horseback riding, mule back trips, camping, rafting, and helicopter tours.

Ride northwest on No. 180 (Fort Valley Road) from Flagstaff into the mountainous terrain, where you will face some tough climbs. At Snow Bowl (15 miles or 25 kilometers from Flagstaff), you can take a chairlift to a magnificent view of the area. Continue riding on No. 180 to Valle. Then head north to Tusuyan, just outside the park (where you might plan your park activities).

You will enter Grand Canyon National Park near Grand Canyon Village, on the west rim (minibus service is provided). You will see such points of interest as Mohave Point, Hopi Point, Powell Memorial, Hopi House (a reproduction of a Hopi Indian dwelling), and the Visitor Center (just east of the village). As you head east, you will see the Shrine of the Ages Chapel, Yavapai Point, Tusayan Ruin and Museum (which traces the history of the Anasazi Indian culture at the canyon), Desert View, and Watchtower (with spectacular views of the canyon, river, the Painted Desert, and Kaibab National Forest).

Upon exiting the park, continue east on No. 64, crossing a section of the Navajo Reservation, to Cameron. Cycle south on No. 89, past Gray Mountain, into Wupatki National Monument, where hundreds of ruins are found; the original inhabitants of Wupatki are thought to have been ancestors of the Hopi Indians.

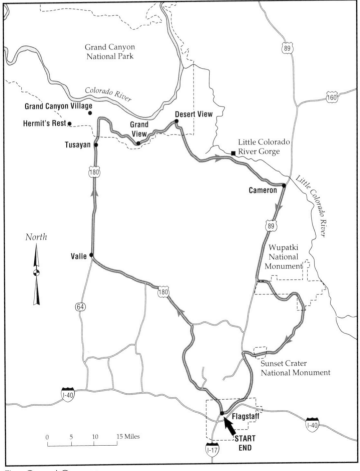

The Grand Canyon

Ride on the paved road that connects Wupatki National Monument to Sunset Crater Volcano National Monument, crossing the lava flow. A high cylinder cone dominates the area, with fields of cinders around it.

Rejoin No. 89 and ride south to Flagstaff, completing this magnificent route through what is sometimes referred to as "The Grandest Canyon of Them All," Grand Canyon National Park.

Other Tours
• Red Rock Country Loop

Arizona's Verde Valley provides the setting for this spectacular mountain-bike trip. Be prepared because you will find few conveniences

Cycling through historic downtown Bisbee, a renowned copper mining town in southern Arizona. *Photo courtesy of Arizona Department of Tourism*

on this 210-mile (350-kilometer) route. Take No. 3 southeast from Flagstaff to Mormon Lake; then descend by fire roads (dirt) to Sedona, situated amid the red-hued rocks of Oak Creek Canyon. Sedona serves as a starting point for many trips into Red Rock Country, including mountain-biking routes, hot-air balloon rides, Jeep tours, and llama treks (for more information, phone Red Rock Pathways: (520) 284-4202; and contact: Sedona Chamber of Commerce, Forest Road and U.S. 89A, P.O. Box 478, Sedona, AZ 86336; phone (602) 542-4174).

Follow the red dirt road through the Red Rock Secret Mountain Wilderness to Tuzigoot National Monument, a fascinating ruin of a pueblo, and up the long grade to Jerome, virtually a ghost town since the closing of the copper mines. Continue north on the back roads, through Prescott National Forest and Kaibab National Forest, to Williams. You will then cycle east, on a paved road, back to Flagstaff.

• Saguaro Country

If you are biking here during the summer, carry plenty of fluids. Ride southwest on No. 86 from Tucson to the exit for Tucson Mountain Park (15 miles or 25 kilometers west of Tucson). Some of the rock formations in this area are marked by pictographs. Ride through Saguaro National Monument (the Tucson Mountain section), viewing the cactus and other desert vegetation on the 6-mile (10-kilometer) Bajada Loop. Return through the park to Tucson, completing this relatively short loop tour. For more information about the area, contact: Metropolitan Tucson Convention and Visitors Bureau, 130 South Scott Street, Tucson, AZ 85701; phone (602) 624-1817.

• The Tucson Area

Tucson is rated as one of North America's top cities for cycling (according to *Bicycling Magazine*). There are more than 200 miles (333 kilometers) of bike lanes, routes, and paths for road bikes, and nearly the same amount of trail for mountain bikes. Another plus is more than 300 days of sunshine each year, the normal amount for the Tucson area.

• The Phoenix Area

There are about 400 miles (660 kilometers) of bicycle trails in the Phoenix area, including a 28-mile (47-kilometer) multi-use trail along the Arizona Canal Diversion Channel, which takes cyclists through Glendale, Phoenix and Scottsdale; tunnels go under many of the streets on this particular route, providing an uninterrupted ride.

• Cochise County

The southeastern corner of the state provides more spectacular scenery as you ride west from Bisbee (famous during the mining rush of the 1880s) to Coronado National Memorial, at the southern tip of the Huachuca Mountains. A panoramic view of the area is available from Montezuma Pass, 3 miles (5 kilometers) west of the Visitor Center (which can be reached by road and by hiking trail). For more information, contact: Coronado National Memorial, R.R. No. 2, Box 126, Hereford, AZ 85615; phone 602-366-5515.

Ride north on No. 90 to Sierra Vista, known as "The Hummingbird Capital of America." It's nestled in the slopes of the Huachuca Mountains and overlooks the San Pedro River Valley. (For more information, contact: Sierra Vista Chamber of Commerce, 77 Calle Portal, Sierra Vista, AZ 85635; phone 1-800-288-3861). Cycle northwest to Tombstone, known as "The Town Too Tough To Die," where you can visit reminders of the rough days of the mining camps, such as the O.K. Corral and Boot Hill Graveyard. Complete this 80-mile (133-kilometer) loop tour by cycling south, back to Bisbee.

- **Visit Mexico**

Just 11 miles (18 kilometers) south of Bisbee is Naco, Mexico (a small border town). You can complete a loop tour by cycling to Agua Prieta (Mexico), Douglas (Arizona), and back to Bisbee.

Arizona Contacts

Arizona Bicycling Association, P.O. Box 3132, Tempe, AZ 85280; phone (602) 990-7468.

Arizona Office of Tourism, 1100 West Washington Street, Phoenix, AZ 85007; phone (602) 542-8687.

Arizona State Parks, 800 West Washington Street, Suite 415, Phoenix, AZ 85007; phone (602) 542-4174.

The famous "Boothill Graveyard" is found at Tombstone, Arizona.

Flagstaff Visitor Center, 101 West Santa Fe Avenue, Flagstaff,
AZ 86001; phone (602) 774-9541 or 1-800-842-7293.
Greater Arizona Bicycling Association, P.O. Box 43273, Tucson,
AZ 85773; phone (602) 749-2177.
State Bicycle Coordinator, Arizona Department of Transportation,
206 South 17th Avenue, Rm. 340B, Phoenix, AZ 85007; phone
(602) 255-8010; an excellent bicycle touring map is available free.
Superintendent, Grand Canyon National Park, P.O. Box 129, Grand
Canyon, AZ 86023.

The Grand Canyon is one of the great natural spectacles of the world.

Colorado
• **Colorado's San Juan Mountains**
Distance: 247 miles/412 kilometers
Duration: 4–7 days
Rating: Strenuous
Type: Loop Tour
Access: The San Juans are in the southwest corner of Colorado, and they present a jagged, precipitous appearance. Durango serves as the gateway to this scenic area.
Accommodations: Full facilities are available in the resort area of Durango. This route is best suited to the camper, but some lodging facilities are available at Silverton, Telluride, Ouray, and Mancos.
Route Description: Each year Durango cyclists sponsor the "Bicycle Tour of the San Juans," a three-day road loop that travels through resort towns, former mining towns, ranching country, and mountainous terrain. The described route that follows allows you to take your own personal tour of the San Juans any time that is convenient.

Begin your tour in Durango, which was a mining and smelting center during the gold and silver booms. Durango now serves as the gateway to this scenic area of Colorado, and it's a great place from which to begin a back country or white-water rafting trip.

Take No. 550 (known as the San Juan Skyway), and climb through two mountain passes to Silverton. This route is very steep, and there are no guard rails along some sections, so be careful. If you prefer, a narrow-gauge train climbs to Silverton, following the course of the Animas River.

Several false-fronted buildings recall the successful era of Silverton, after its silver strike in 1871. Nearby, on No. 110, is Eureka, another reminder of the mining past (but now a ghost town).

As you leave Silverton on No. 550, you will climb through the Red Mountain Pass and then descend to the town of Ouray, the "Little Switzerland of America"; this section of the route is called "The Million Dollar Highway." You will then face two moderate climbs on your 49-mile (82-kilometer) ride from Ouray to Telluride. If you prefer off-road cycling, you can do your tour of the San Juans by biking on old mining roads from Silverton to Ouray, then to Telluride, and then back to Silverton; you will face some tough climbs on this shorter, off-road loop.

Telluride had a reputation as a rough-and-tumble town of the Old West (Butch Cassidy robbed a bank here in 1889).Today it's preserved as a National Historic Landmark and is a popular ski resort. Jeep tours are offered to the nearby mining ghost towns. Mountain bikers and hikers can take an old mining road up the canyon to Bridal Veil Falls.

After exploring the Telluride area, cycle on No. 145, through the Lizard Head Pass, to Rico. Follow the Dolores River into cattle country. Bike south on No. 145, and then ride east on No. 160, through Mesa Verde National Park, past preserved cliff dwellings and ruins; guided tours are available. Here you'll find petroglyphs made by the "Ancient Ones" (Anasazi). Continue east on No. 160, back to Durango.

This spectacular trip has taken you through several breathtaking mountain passes and into magnificent valleys as you have cycled through the San Juan National Forest area and the San Juan Mountains.

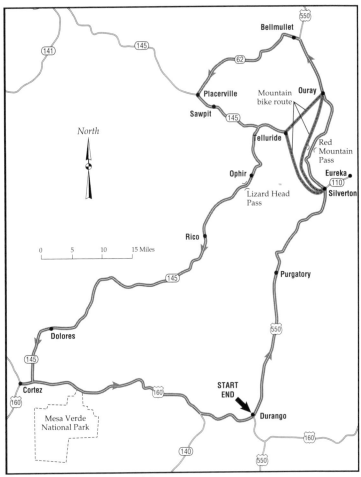

Colorado's San Juan Mountains

Other Tours
• Rocky Mountain National Park

Begin this trip in Granby, near the western entrance to Rocky Mountain National Park, and cycle on No. 34 (the Trail Ridge Road) through the park. This wildlife sanctuary is home to elk, black bear, bighorn sheep, deer, bobcat, and mountain lion. You'll find many opportunities for hiking, mountain biking, mountain climbing, and horseback riding in one of the most popular parks in America. Follow the north fork of the Colorado River as you bike past creeks and mountains, through the Milner Pass, to Trail Ridge High Point. Continue past Iceberg Lake to Hidden Valley, Aspenglen, and Estes Park (where you exit the park). Ride southeast on No. 36 to Lyons and Boulder, the destination of this 102-mile (170-kilometer) tour. For more information about the Boulder area, contact: Boulder Bicycle Program, Division of Transportation, P.O. Box 791, Boulder, CO 80306; phone (303) 441-3216.

• The Colorado Springs Loop—Gorges and Gardens

For a rather unique beauty, take this 126-mile (210-kilometer) loop tour from Colorado Springs. Cycle southwest on No. 115 to Penrose, Florence, and Canon City. West of Canon City (on No. 50) is Royal Gorge Bridge, billed as the world's highest suspension bridge. There is an aerial tram across the canyon and an incline railway to the bottom of the gorge. After exploring the gorge, return to Florence, and then take the Phantom Canyon Highway (No. 67) north; this gravel road is narrow, so take care as you cycle on this challenging route; several tunnels are cut through the red rock, and the road twists for about 35 miles (58 kilometers) through a canyon to Cripple Creek. Another very challenging ride lies ahead as you now take the Gold Camp Road over the mountainous terrain of Pikes National Forest; this route is steep and winding, and there are no protective guardrails. You will exit near Seven Falls, where water cascades down a steep canyon in seven distinct steps (illuminated at night). Returning to Colorado Springs, cycle through the spectacular scenery of the Garden of the Gods, an area of massive red sandstone formations, including Balanced Rock and Cathedral Spires. The Garden of the Gods is also a great place for horseback riding. For more information on the Colorado Springs area, contact: Colorado Springs Visitor Bureau, 104 S. Cascade No. 104, Colorado Springs, CO 80903; phone (719) 635-7506; Colorado Springs Cycling Club, P.O. Box 49602, Colorado Springs, CO 80949; phone (719) 594-6354 or 1-800-997-2453.

• Gunnison River Territory

Gunnison is in a broad, fertile valley. Ride west on No. 50, through the Curecanti National Recreation Area, to Montrose (where a 35-mile or 58-kilometer side trip offers you awe-inspiring overlooks of the Black Canyon of the Gunnison). Then ride northwest to Delta, a fruit-growing area, and site of a discovery of dinosaur bones. Take scenic No. 92 and No. 133, cycling northeast through the Gunnison National Forest and the West Elk Mountains, to Carbondale. Bike southeast on No. 82 to Basalt, Snowmass, and Aspen. A popular off-road trip takes you from Aspen to Crested Butte; you climb through the Pearl Pass. A very tough climb will take you from Aspen, through Independence Pass, and then you descend to Twin Lakes. Turn south on No. 24, cycling through Granite to Buena Vista, Nathrop, and Poncho Springs. Bike west on No. 50 back to Gunnison, completing this challenging 379-mile (632-kilometer) route. For more information on the Gunnison area, contact: Gunnison Country Chamber of Commerce, 500 E. Tomichi Avenue, P.O. Box 36, Gunnison, CO 81230; phone 1-800-274-7580.

• Summit County

Summit County has a paved bike path system of more than 50 miles (83 kilometers) that meanders between the communities of Breckenridge, Frisco, Keystone, Dillon, Silverthorne, and Copper Mountain. There's even a paved trail over the Vail Pass, into Vail. For the mountain bike enthusiast, there is also an extensive network of dirt trails winding through the Arapaho National Forest.

• The Denver Area
The city of Denver has more than 80 miles (133 kilometers) of paved bike paths. The backbone of Denver's system is the Cherry Creek Path, which takes the cyclist more than 16 miles (27 kilometers) from the junction of the South Platte River and Cherry Creek to the Cherry Creek Reservoir. The Platte River Greenway takes the cyclist from Confluence Park to the Chatfield Reservoir, covering 10 miles (17 kilometers).

• Mountain Biking on Kokopelli's Trail
The trail starts along the Colorado River just west of Grand Junction and takes the mountain biker 128 miles (213 kilometers) to Moab, Utah (described under trips in Utah).

Colorado Contacts
Bicycle Colorado, 5249 E. Eastman Avenue, Denver, CO 80222-7550; phone (303) 756-2535; FAX (303) 756-3063; ask about "Colorado Bikeways Map Series."

Bicycle Colorado hot-line; phone (970) 256-7430 or 1-800-997-BIKE; ask about "The Bike Card" and request a Bicycle Colorado packet (maps, a helpful magazine, etc.).

Bicycle Colorado Magazine, P.O. Box 698, Salida, CO 81201; phone (719) 530-0051.

Colorado Tourism Board, 1625 Broadway , Suite 1700, Denver, CO 80202; phone (303) 592-5510.

Mesa Verde-Cortez Visitor Information Bureau, Drawer, H.H., Cortez, CO 81321; phone 1-800-253-1616.

San Juan National Forest, Box 341, Federal Bldg., Durango, CO 81301; phone (303) 247-4874.

State Bicycle Program Manager, Colorado Department of Transportation, 4201 E. Arkansas, Rm. 212, Denver, CO 80222; phone (303) 757-9982; a state-wide on-highway bicycle route map is available; ask for a free copy of *Bicycle Colorado Magazine.*

Idaho
• **The Sawtooth Scenic Route**
Distance: 295 miles/492 kilometers
Duration: 5–7 days
Rating: Strenuous
Type: One-way Tour
Access: Boise is in southwestern Idaho, on the Boise River (not far from the Oregon Border). It's accessible by boat, air, and motor vehicle.
Accommodations: All types of lodging are available in Boise, Ketchum, Sun Valley, and Twin Falls. Camping is available in the Sawtooth National Recreation Area, as well as near Boise, Idaho City, Lowman, Ketchum, Bellevue, and Twin Falls.
Route Description: Boise, Idaho's capital, has a beautiful 13-mile (22-kilometer) bicycle and pedestrian path (The Boise Greenbelt) that follows the Boise River. Points of interest in Boise include the World Center for Birds of Prey, Old Idaho Penitentiary, Idaho Historical Museum, Boise City Zoo, and Idaho Botanical Garden. One day tours can be arranged for a Hell's Canyon River adventure, Payette River rafting, Snake River Birds of Prey Tour, or an Oregon Trail expedition.

You will face some tough climbs as you cycle northeast on No. 21 from Boise to Idaho City, Pioneerville, Lowman, Cape Horn, and Stanley, the entrance to the Sawtooth National Recreation Area.

Bike south on the Sawtooth Scenic Route (No. 75) to Obsidian, Yellow Belly Lake, and Pettit Lake. The Sawtooth Valley, with its spectacular views of snow-capped mountain peaks, is an excellent area for a white-water wilderness float trip or off-road biking on scenic trails that loop the sagebrush flatlands and connect old silver mines.

Complete your journey through the Sawtooth National Recreation Area by climbing to the Galena Summit and then descending into Ketchum, where Ernest Hemingway spent his last years (his grave is found in the Ketchum Cemetery). Cycle northeast to Sun Valley, which resembles an alpine village with its Swiss chalet-style architecture, quaint shops, and many art galleries. Continue northeast to Trail Creek, where you'll see a memorial to Hemingway. The Trail Creek area is another excellent opportunity for off-road biking on fire roads and single track trails; other popular pastimes here include horseback riding, hot-air ballooning, glider riding, and fly fishing.

Return through Sun Valley to Ketchum. Rejoin No. 75, cycling south to the Shoshone Ice Caves; as you might guess, the caves of ice are cold, so wear a jacket or a heavy sweater for your guided tour. Then ride south to the town of Shoshone, where several of the buildings are made from the local lava rock.

Head south on No. 93 from Shoshone to your destination, Twin Falls. In a fertile valley by the Snake River, Twin Falls is a pretty place to base yourself for exploring. Start with a raft ride down the wild Snake River. Perrine Memorial Bridge offers spectacular views of Snake River Gorge, waterfalls, and the sheer cliffs. Just a mile east of the bridge is the spot where daredevil Evel Knievel unsuccessfully tried to leap across the Snake River Canyon in 1974. Shoshone Falls, called the "Niagara of the West," is 5 miles (8 kilometers) northeast of Twin Falls; the water plunges more than 200 feet into the gorge.

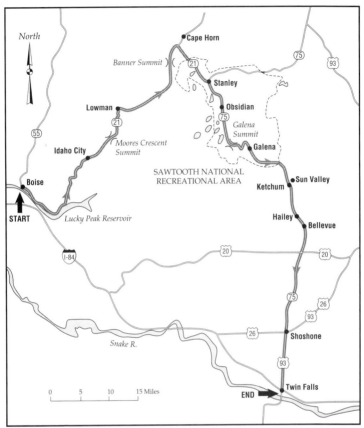

The Sawtooth Scenic Route

Other Tours

• Craters of the Moon National Monument

At the base of the Pioneer Mountains, basaltic lava sites distinguish the otherworldly landscape. A loop road and trails allow you to explore. You can view the cinder-cone chain from the summit of Inferno Cone, and a trail leads to the Devil's Orchard cinder fields. Exhibits in the Visitor Center explain the geology, plants, and history of the area. Cycle south on No. 75 from Ketchum and east on No. 20 and No. 93 to the Craters of the Moon National Monument. After exploring the area, complete your 80-mile (133-kilometer) trip by cycling east to Arco, where you can tour a nuclear reactor at the Idaho National Engineering Laboratory.

• Hells Canyon National Recreation Area

Begin this adventure in western Idaho in Cambridge. Ride northwest on No. 71 to Oxbow, Oregon, crossing the Snake River near Brownlee Dam. You will soon return to Idaho as you follow the Snake River north to Hells Canyon Dam (55 miles or 92 kilometers), where

143

you will find good opportunities for mountain biking. Several outfitters here provide float and jet boat trips on the Snake River.

• Coeur d'Alene—Sandpoint Resort Area

Two beautiful resort towns on two picturesque lakes are the focal points of this intriguing route that begins in Couer d'Alene, about 35 miles (60 kilometers) east of Spokane, Washington. The route ends in Sandpoint. Lake Couer d'Alene is 25 miles (42 kilometers) in length and averages about 2.5 miles (4 kilometers) in width. It is surrounded by forests and mountains, and is often described as one of five most beautiful lakes in the world. You will cycle northeast on No. 95 from Coeur d'Alene to Hayden, Chico, Athol, Granite, Algoma, and on to your destination of Sandpoint (47 miles or 78 kilometers). Sandpont is on the north end of Pend Oreille Lake, one of the largest freshwater lakes in the Pacific Northwest. Consider a visit to the Cedar Street Bridge Public Market (where a city bridge has been transformed into a mall).

If you wish to make this tour into a loop, you could head southwest on No. 2 to Spokane, Washington, and return to Coeur d'Alene by taking No. 90 east; if you wished to travel on quieter roads, you could take No. 200 east from Sandpoint to Clark Fork, and then cycle south through Lakeview, returning to the Couer d'Alene area by back roads.

Idaho Contacts

Boise Convention and Visitors Bureau, P.O. Box 2106, Boise, ID 83701; phone 1-800-635-5240.

Idaho Travel Council, 700 W. State Street, 2nd Floor, Boise, ID 83720; phone 1-800-635-7820.

Ketchum Chamber of Commerce, Ketchum, ID; phone 1-800-634-3347.

Sawtooth National Forest, 2647 Kimberley Road E., Twin Falls, ID 83301; phone (208) 737-3200.

State Bicycle Coordinator, Idaho Transportation Department, P.O. Box 7129, Boise, ID 83707; phone (208) 334-8484.

Sun Valley Chamber of Commerce, Sun Valley, ID; phone 1-800-634-3347.

The Cedar Bridge Mall at Sandpoint, Idaho.

Montana
• **Glacier National Park**
Distance: 115 miles/192 kilometers
Duration: 2–4 days
Rating: Strenuous
Type: One-way Tour
Access: The starting point, Kalispell, lies between two mountain ranges in the Flathead Valley. It's at the junction of No. 2 and No. 93. The destination of Browning is east of the park, at the junction of No. 2 and No. 89.
Accommodations: As a resort area, Kalispell has many lodging choices. There are several camping opportunities along this route. The destination, Browning, has limited facilities.
Route Description: Situated in northwestern Montana on the Canadian border, Glacier National Park is renowned for its spectacular mountain scenery and is home to a great variety of birds and wildlife. Going-to-the-Sun Highway, only open during the summer, takes you through the park via the Logan Pass. The park links with Waterton

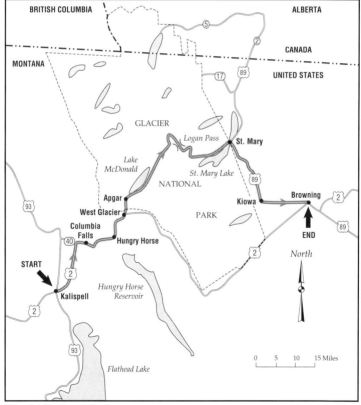

Glacier National Park

Lakes National Park in Alberta, Canada, to form the Waterton-Glacier International Peace Park, although each park is administered separately.

Begin this adventure in Kalispell. Ride northeast on No. 2 through Columbia Falls (entrance to Bad Rock Canyon) and Hungry Horse to West Glacier, the western entrance to the park. Take the challenging (and often jammed with RVs) Going-to-the-Sun Highway through Glacier National Park. You'll pedal past Avalanche Creek (site of a narrow gorge), climb Logan Pass, cross the Continental Divide, pass Going-to-the-Sun Mountain, and depart the park at St. Mary. The dangers of this road are not limited to the steep grades and heavy traffic: the mesmerizing scenery has been known to distract riders and drivers alike.

After leaving the park, continue cycling east to your destination of Browning, on the Blackfeet Indian Reservation. Browning is the headquarters of the Blackfeet Tribal Business Council and Bureau of Indian Affairs Blackfeet Agency. It's also the site of the Museum of the Plains Indians and Scriver's Museum of Montana Wildlife and Hall of Bronze.

Other Tours
• Waterton-Glacier International Peace Park
If you decide to visit the adjoining Canadian park, ride north on No. 89 after exiting Glacier National Park, and cross the Alberta border into Canada at Carway. Ride north on No. 2 to Cardston, west on No. 5, and southwest on No. 6. You will face some very challenging climbs and possibly very discouraging head winds. For more information about biking in Waterton Lakes National Park, contact: Canadian Parks Service, Western Regional Office, P.O. Box 2989, Station M, Calgary, Alberta, Canada T2p 3H8; phone 403-292-4401. Return to the States by taking No. 17 and No. 89 to Browning. I have run into a snowstorm in July in the mountainous terrain of the Waterton-Glacier region, so be prepared.

• Big Sky Country
Big Sky is a resort town near Yellowstone National Park and surrounded by the forested slopes of Gallatin National Forest. Follow the Gallatin River as you cycle south on scenic No. 191 to West Yellowstone. Enter the northwest corner of Yellowstone National Park by crossing the border into Wyoming and riding to Madison. Bike northwest along the Gibbon River to Gibbon Falls, through the Norris Geyser Basin, and on to park headquarters at Mammoth Hot Springs (site of intriguing formations created by limestone deposits). Then cross the border back into Montana, exiting the park at Gardiner, the park's northern entrance. Ride north on No. 89, stopping to view and photograph the Devil's Slide, an unusual rock formation. Continue through the Gallatin National Forest, passing through Corwin Springs and Emigrant, and arriving at your destination of Livingston, in the lush Paradise Valley. It's a 158-mile (263-kilometer) ride.

• From Parks to Peaks—Across Montana
This strenuous 495-mile (825-kilometer) tour takes you through Glacier National Park in Montana's north and through a section of Yellowstone National Park just below the south end of the state. Begin in West Glacier, at the western entrance to Glacier National Park. Take

Going-to-the-Sun Highway through the park, exiting at St. Mary. Ride southeast on No. 89 and No. 287 to Augusta. Cycle the back roads to Helena, and then take No. 287 all the way to West Yellowstone and the Wyoming border. Enter Yellowstone National Park and ride to Madison. Ride north to Mammoth Hot Springs. Cross the border back into Montana, and exit the park at Gardiner, your destination. This is a rigorous itinerary, but it takes you to two of the world's most beautiful alpine parks.

• **The Great Divide Mountain Bike Route**
  A planned mountain-bike route, from the Canadian border to the Mexican border, will parallel the Great Divide and stretch for almost 3,000 miles (5,000 kilometers). The Montana section will be somewhat parallel to the "Across Montana" route previously described, beginning near Babb and ending near West Yellowstone. The route will use dirt paths and gravel roads. For more information about this long distance off-road touring route, contact: Adventure Cycling Association (address previously given).

Montana Contacts
Adventure Cycling Association, P.O. Box 8308, Missoula, MT 59807; phone (406) 721-1776.
State Bicycle Coordinator, Montana Department of Transportation, 2701 Prospect Avenue, Helena, MT 59620; phone (406) 444-6123.
Superintendent, Glacier National Park, West Glacier, MT 59936; phone (406) 888-5441.
Travel Montana, 1424 9th Avenue, P.O. Box 20053, Helena, MT 59620; phone (406) 444-2654 or 1-800-541-1447.

Entering Yellowstone National Park from Gardiner, Montana.

Nevada

• **Lake Mead National Recreation Area**

Distance: 183 miles/305 kilometers

Duration: 3–5 days

Rating: Easy to Moderate

Type: Loop Tour

Access: The main routes to Las Vegas are No. 95, No. 93, and No. 15. McCarran International Airport is just 5 miles (8 kilometers) south of the business district. Daily train service is available through Amtrak (phone 1-800-872-7245). The main bus carriers are Greyhound (phone (702) 382-2640) and Trailways (phone (702) 385-1141). The Las Vegas Transit System provides access to most parts of the city.

Accommodations: There is no shortage of hotels in Las Vegas. Lodging is also found at Boulder City and Henderson. Camping is available in the Overton area.

Route Description: This loop tour, best avoided during the intense summer heat, takes you to the gambling resort oasis of Las Vegas, a beautiful recreation area, one of the world's largest artificial lakes in volume (Lake Mead), and one of the world's highest dams (Hoover Dam).

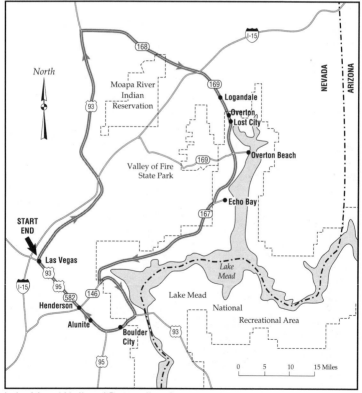

Lake Mead National Recreation Area

148

Las Vegas is a gambler's paradise, with many large resort hotels and gambling casinos on display. If you're not a gambler, Las Vegas still has much to offer, with star-studded shows and gaudy tourist attractions. Las Vegas receives only about 4 inches of rain per year, so expect lots of sunshine (an average of about 320 days per year).

Ride northeast on No. 604, past Nellis Air Force Base, north on No. 93, southeast on No. 168, crossing a section of the Moapa Indian Reservation, and then on No. 169 to Overton, just north of Lost City. Stop to visit the Lost City Museum, on a restored part of Pueblo Grande de Nevada. It displays relics and tools excavated from the Lost City pueblos. Pueblo-type houses of wattle and daub have been reconstructed on some of the original foundations.

You can explore the picturesque Valley of Fire State Park as you continue on No. 169. The red sandstone rocks can appear on fire as they reflect the sun's rays. Petroglyphs are found on some of the cliffs and rocks within the park.

Ride along the shore of Lake Mead on No. 167, passing Echo Bay as you ride to the Hoover Dam. Take a tour to learn about this engineering marvel. You can cross the canyon at the crest of the dam to see it from both sides. A boat excursion to the dam is also available from the Lake Mead Marina.

After your visit to the Hoover Dam, you face a very tough climb out of the canyon. Ride northwest on No. 93 and No. 582 back to Las Vegas to complete this loop tour.

Other Tours
• Red Rock Canyon
Cycle west from Las Vegas, via Charleston Boulevard. for 20 miles (33 kilometers) to the scenic Red Rock Canyon Loop. There is an informative Visitor Center, and you can bike the on and off-road trails through the magnificent rock formations in brilliantly colored sandstone. Bike rentals are available in Las Vegas (phone 702-596-2953).

• Mount Charleston
Escape the Las Vegas heat by cycling northwest on No. 95 and southwest on No. 157 to Mount Charleston, where summer temperatures average 30 degrees cooler than in Las Vegas. Bike on No. 158 to Lee Canyon, which is a winter ski area. Ride northeast on No. 156 and then southeast on No. 95 back to Las Vegas, completing this 102-mile (170-kilometer) loop tour.

• To Laughlin
Just 90 miles (150 kilometers) southeast of Las Vegas, in the corner of the state, is yet another gambling resort area. Reach Laughlin by cycling on No. 582 to Henderson and then on No. 95 and No. 163 to the destination.

• Nevada's Historical and Resort Areas
This 195-mile (325-kilometer) loop tour begins in Reno, another gambling oasis, and takes you through the historically significant "Old West" and to some of Nevada's finest resort areas. Ride north on No. 445 from Reno to Pyramid Lake, one of Nevada's most interesting

recreation areas. Surrounded by red and brown sandstone mountains and punctuated by rock islands, Pyramid Lake is Nevada's largest natural lake. Bike east on No. 446 to Nixon, south on No. 447 to Wadsworth, and south on No. 95 to Silver Springs. Nearby is Fort Churchill State Historic Park, an army outpost built in 1860 to protect settlers against Indian attacks; a Visitor Center now reconstructs the fort's history through interpretive exhibits. Pedal southwest on No. 50 and northwest on No. 341 to Virginia City, a gold and silver boom town in the 1870s, laden with many reminders of its history, including the Delta Saloon, the Bucket of Blood Saloon, the Ponderosa Saloon, Chollar Mine, The Way It Was Museum, and the Wild West Museum. Bike south on No. 342 through Silver City and southwest on No. 50 to Carson City, named after Kit Carson. Cycle south on No. 395 to Stewart and west on No. 50 to Glenbrook, on the shore of Lake Tahoe. Lake Tahoe is a deep, clear blue lake ringed with snow-capped mountains; about one-third of Lake Tahoe is in Nevada, with the remainder being in California. Follow the shoreline of Lake Tahoe as you cycle north on No. 28 to Incline Village, site of Ponderosa, a western theme park featuring the re-created Cartwright ranch house from the TV show *Bonanza*. Ride northeast on No. 431 and No. 395 back to Reno, completing the loop.

Nevada Contacts

Lake Mead National Recreation Area Headquarters Office,
    601 Nevada Hwy., Boulder City, NV; phone (702) 293-4041.
Las Vegas Chamber of Commerce, 2301 E. Sahara Avenue, Las Vegas,
    NV; phone (702) 457-4664.
Nevada Commission on Tourism, Capitol Complex, Carson City,
    NV 89710; phone (702) 687-4322 or 1-800-NEVADA-8.
State Bicycle Coordinator, Nevada Department of Transportation,
    1263 S. Stewart Street, Carson City, NV 89712; phone (702) 687-4997.

The Mirage Hotel in Las Vegas, Nevada.

New Mexico
• The Capital, the Enchanted Circle, and the Wild West

Distance: 143 miles/238 kilometers
Duration: 3–5 days
Rating: Strenuous
Type: One-way Tour
Access: Santa Fe is the capital of New Mexico and is in the north-central part of the state (northeast of Albuquerque). Routes No. 84, No. 285, and No. 25 meet here. There is also a municipal airport. Cimarron is northeast of Santa Fe (where No. 58 and No. 64 meet); bus service is available.
Accommodations: There are many facilities in Santa Fe, but limited facilities in Cimarron. There are several opportunities for camping along this route. You will find a hostel in Taos (by the ski area).
Route Description: From Santa Fe, around the Enchanted Circle, and on to Cimarron, you'll ride through lush forests, across mountainous terrain and painted mesas, past ancient Spanish villages and Indian pueblos, and on to the Wild West residence of several celebrated outlaws of the past.

Your tour begins in Santa Fe, where the distinctive buildings, Spanish and Indian shops, and narrow streets recall the colonial past; while here visit the Palace of the Governors, Sanctuario De Guadalupe, Cathedral of St. Francis Assisi, and the Mission of San Miguel of Santa Fe (on the Old Santa Fe Trail).

After exploring fascinating Santa Fe, which is nestled in the foothills of the Sangre de Cristo Mountains, ride north on No. 285 and No. 84 to Santa Cruz. Then go east on No. 76 to the Spanish town of Chimayo, famous for its fine weaving. At the east end of the town of Chimayo is El Sanctuario De Chimayo, an adobe chapel that still attracts many pilgrims who come for the sacred dirt within it; this earth is believed to have special healing powers, and the chapel is lined with cast-off crutches and braces.

Continue east on No. 76, known as the "High Road to Taos," past two villages famous for their crafts (Cordova, for its woodcarving; Truchas, for its weavers). You will ride through spectacular mountain scenery on this challenging, twisting route.

Take No. 518 north to Ranchos de Taos, a farming community; the local mission church is renowned for its massive buttresses. Then bike on No. 522 to Taos, home to many artists and a starting point for many river rafting trips on the nearby Rio Grande. Taos was the residence of Kit Carson, and the Kit Carson Home is open to the public; the Kit Carson Memorial State Park includes his grave.

Continue on No. 522, and you will begin cycling the Enchanted Circle, a picturesque area north of Taos that writer D. H. Lawrence once remarked was "the most beautiful" that he had ever encountered. You will face some very tough climbs and marvel at the magnificence of the mountain scenery. You'll climb the Palo Flechads Pass, ride across the Moreno Valley, and then climb the Bobcat Pass before descending into the resort town of Red River. Continue riding around New Mexico's highest mountain (Wheeler Peak) on No. 38 to Eagle Nest, on Eagle Nest Lake (renowned for its excellent trout fishing).

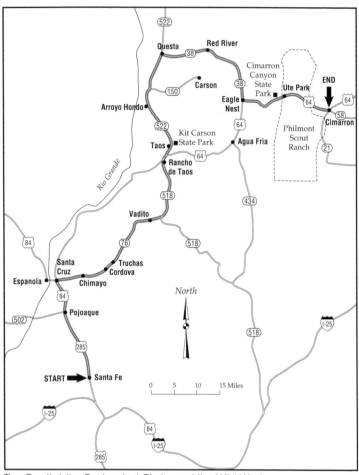

The Capital, the Enchanted Circle, and the Wild West

Having completed this section of the Enchanted Circle, bike east on No. 64, past Cimarron Canyon State Park and Ute Park, and enjoy the long descent into Cimarron, this trip's destination. From here, a 5-mile (8-kilometer) side trip will take you to the Philmont Scout Ranch, the world's largest Boy Scout Camp.

Cimarron means "wild" or "untamed," and this town seemed to live up to the name in the late 1800s when several notorious outlaws, including Billy the Kid, came to town; his bullet holes still adorn the metal ceiling in the Hotel St. James. Several range wars and gunfights occurred in the area. The *Las Vegas Gazette* contributed to Cimarron's image when it stated, in an article of the era, that "Things are quiet in Cimarron; nobody has been killed in three days."

Other Tours
• **Silver City-Gila Cliff Dwellings Loop**

The southwestern New Mexico town of Silver City prospered in the late 1860s when silver was discovered. It's also known as the boyhood home of William Bonney, who later gained notoriety as Billy the Kid. Ride east from Silver City on No. 180 and No. 152. Consider a stop at the open pit copper mine 15 miles (25 kilometers) east of Silver City to see how the mine operates before continuing your ride to Rita. Bike northeast on No. 35, through the Mimbres Valley, down Sapillo Creek, past Copperas Vista, and on to Gila Cliff Dwellings National Monument. A 1-mile (2-kilometer) loop trail leads to the dwellings, constructed in the 13th century. After examining the Gila Cliff Dwellings, complete this 110-mile (184-kilometer) loop tour by cycling south on No. 15, past the Gila Hot Springs area, over the Pinos Altos Range, and back to Silver City. You will have biked through a rather remote area , but there are several camping spots and developed recreation areas in Gila National Forest.

• **The Four Corners Monument**

The only place in the United States where four states meet is at the junction of New Mexico, Colorado, Utah, and Arizona. Complete a 73-mile (123-kilometer) loop of this monument area by cycling west on No. 64 from Shiprock (in the northwest corner of New Mexico) to Teec Nos Pos (in Arizona), northeast on No. 160 to the actual junction of the four states, on into Colorado and, finally, south on No. 666 back to Shiprock.

New Mexico Contacts
Bicycle Coordinator, New Mexico Highway and Transportation Department, Special Studies Section, P.O. Box 1149, Santa Fe, NM 87504; phone (505) 827-5248 or 1-800-827-5514.

Carson National Forest Supervisor's Office, P.O. Box 558, Taos, NM 87571; phone (505) 758-6200.

New Mexico Tourism and Travel Division, Joseph M. Montoya Bldg., Room 106, 1100 St. Francis Drive, Santa Fe, NM 87503; phone (505) 827-0291 or 1-800-545-2040.

Red River Chamber of Commerce, Box 868, Red River, NM 87558; phone (505) 754-2366 or 1-800-348-6444.

Santa Fe Visitors and Convention Bureau, Box 909, Santa Fe, NM 87504-0909; phone (505) 987-6760 or 1-800-777-CITY.

Oklahoma
• **Indian Heritage-Tulsa Loop**
Distance: 216 miles/360 kilometers
Duration: 4–5 days
Rating: Easy
Type: Loop Tour
Access: Tulsa is accessible by several major roads (including No. 44, No. 64, and No. 75), by air, and by rail.
Accommodations: Full facilities will be found in Tulsa and Muskogee. Camping is available in the Okmulgee, Tahlequah, and Salina areas.
Route Description: Some consider Tulsa, Oklahoma's second largest city, to be the "Oil Capital of the World" because there are more than 1,200 oil-associated companies in the area. But the biggest days of the boom have passed. Also known as the home of Oral Roberts, Tulsa celebrates its roots with a number of yearly events, including the Tulsa Indian Art Festival, the Tulsa Pow-Wow, and the Gilcrease Rendezvous.

Cycle south on No. 75 from Tulsa to Okmulgee (a Creek Indian word meaning "bubbling water"), the capital of the Creek Indian Nation; it's the site of Old Creek Indian Council House, containing early documents and craftwork, and the annual Creek Nation Festival.

Bike northeast on No. 62 to Muskogee, where perhaps you'll hear some proud Oklahoman singing, "I'm proud to be an Okie from Muskogee!" and Fort Gibson, where Fort Gibson Military Park includes a reconstructed fort near the site of the original, built in 1824; the Fort Gibson National Cemetery includes the grave of Sam Houston's Cherokee wife, Talihina.

As you continue riding on No. 62, you will arrive at the Cherokee Heritage Center (near Tahlequah), where you can learn a great deal about the history of the Cherokee; the center is operated by the Cherokee National Historical Society and includes a replica of a 17th century Cherokee settlement (Tsa-La-Gi), an outdoor drama ("Trail of Tears") about the forced march of Indians from Georgia and North Carolina to Oklahoma in 1838–39, and the Cherokee National Museum.

Ride into Tahlequah, the capital of the Cherokee Indian Nation, in the foothills of the Ozark Mountains. Then cycle north on scenic No. 10, following the Illinois River. Bike northwest to Leach, and then north to Kenwood and the Kenwood Indian Reservation. Ride west to Salina and on No. 20 to the Snowdale Recreation Area, Pryor, and Claremore (home of a health resort and the site of several artesian mineral wells). While in Claremore, you might like to visit the J. M. Davis Gun Museum, the Will Rogers Memorial (actor, author, vaudevillian, and rodeo performer), and the Lynn Riggs Memorial (the author who inspired the musical *Oklahoma* by writing *Green Grow the Lilacs*). Then complete this loop tour by riding southwest on No. 66 from Claremore back to Tulsa.

Other Tours
• **Kiamichi Mountains Loop**
Although Oklahoma is considered to be a prairie state, it also has mountains, and this particular loop tour of 246 miles (410 kilometers) takes you on one of the most scenic routes in Oklahoma's mountain

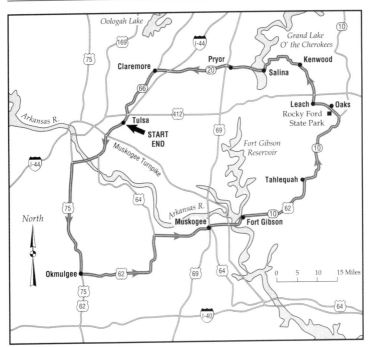

Indian Heritage-Tulsa Loop

country. The trip begins in Broken Bow. Ride north on No. 259 to Beavers Bend State Park, where you can visit the Forest Heritage Center, Broken Bow Lake, and through a deeply forested area to Big Cedar. Bike north on No. 59 to Heavener, at the base of Poteau Mountain, and Poteau , in a valley between mountains. Ride southwest on No. 271 to Wister, Talihina, Clayton Lake, and Antlers. Cycle east on No. 3, past Pine Creek State Park and North Pole, and return to Broken Bow.

This area also offers the mountain biker ample opportunities for exploring, including the scenic Winding Stair Recreation Area and the many trails and old ranch roads near Lake Wister.

• Amish Country Tour

In an area north of Texoma, near the Texas border, some communities of Amish continue their traditional lifestyle. Tour Amish Country by cycling north from Kingston to Madill (on No. 177) and Tishomingo (on No. 99), the historic capital of the Chickasaw Nation; cyclists can pitch their tents only a block off Main Street in the Tishomingo City Park. Ride north on No. 99, east on No. 7, and northeast on No. 7D to Bromide, where you will find the Amish Country Store, with its great homemade pies. Bike south on No. 48 to Wapanucka (the nearby Boggy Depot State Park contains grave markers dating back to before the Civil War), Coleman, and Durant. Then complete this 95-mile (158-kilometer) loop tour by cycling west on No. 70 back to Kingston.

155

• **Oklahoma Prairie Loop**

This tour includes three unique state parks in the midst of the Oklahoma prairie. Begin your trip at Woodward, in northwestern Oklahoma, and ride east to Boiling Springs State Park. Ride north on No. 50 to Alabaster State Park (known for its underground caves), Freedom, and Camp Houston. Bike east on No. 64 and south on No. 14 and No. 281 to Little Sahara State Park (which contains marvelous sand dunes). Complete this relatively flat, 106-mile (177-kilometer) loop tour by heading west on No. 412 back to Woodward.

• **Lake Murray Area**

Just southeast of Ardmore is Lake Murray State Park, which has a full service lodge, camping facilities, and several cabins. Pedal north on No. 77 and east on No. 53 to visit Gene Autry's original Flying A Ranch. Bike north on No. 53, through the Chickasaw National Recreation Area, to Sulphur. Ride west on No. 7 and south on No. 77 to Turner Falls Park (with its natural caves and dramatic waterfalls). Complete this loop tour by continuing south on No. 77 back to Lake Murray State Park. An easy, pleasant 25-mile (42-kilometer)s ride around Lake Murray will take you past Tucker Tower, campgrounds, and several beaches.

Oklahoma Contacts

Cherokee Heritage Center; phone (918) 456-6007.

Oklahoma Bicycle Society, 4505 N. Utah, Oklahoma City, OK 73112; phone (405) 942-4592.

Oklahoma Tourism and Recreation Department, 2401 N. Lincoln, Suite 500, Oklahoma City, OK 73105-4492; phone (405) 521-2409 (in Oklahoma) or 1-800-652-OKLA (out of state); an "Oklahoma Bicycle Route Map" is available.

State Bicycle Coordinator, Oklahoma Department of Transportation, 200 N.E. 21st Street, Oklahoma City 73105-3204; phone (405) 522-3797.

Tulsa Bicycle Club, P.O. Box 471, Tulsa, OK 74101; phone (918) 662-0905.

Tulsa Wheelmen, P.O. Box 52242, Utica Square Stn., Tulsa, OK 74152; phone (918) 584-0076.

Texas
• **Deep in the Heart of Texas Tour**
Distance: 270 miles/450 kilometers
Duration: 5–7 days
Rating: Moderate
Type: Loop Tour
Access: San Antonio is in south-central Texas. The San Antonio International Airport is served by U.S. and Mexican airlines. Greyhound Bus Line (phone [512] 226-7791) and Via Metropolitan Transit (phone [512] 227-5371) both serve the area. Rail service is also available (phone Amtrak at 1-800-872-7245).
Accommodations: Full facilities in San Antonio and many accommodations available along this route.
Route Description: This loop tour begins in the architecturally diverse and historically significant city of San Antonio. Once the capital of the Spanish province of Texas, San Antonio came under the control of Mexico after the Mexican Revolution of 1821. Mission San Antonio de Valero, the oldest of San Antonio's missions, became better known as the Alamo, a symbol of Texan liberty. When Texas declared independence from Mexico in 1836, many men died for the cause at the Battle of the Alamo (including Davy Crockett and James Bowie), and the loss inspired other Texans to fight on for independence. Other points of interest in this area include the Institute of Texan Cultures, Witte Museum, Fort Sam Houston, La Villita, Spanish Governor's Palace, San Antonio Mission National Historical Park, San Antonio Zoological Gardens and Aquarium, and San Antonio Botanical Gardens.

After exploring San Antonio, cycle northwest on No. 16 to Bandera, the "Cowboy Capital of the World." In the days of the big cattle drives, the drives often formed here and went through the Bandera Pass and along the Western Trail to Kansas and Montana. Bandera is now a dude ranch area; horseback riding and quarter-horse races are popular pastimes.

Ride north on No. 173 to Camp Verde. The cycling will be tougher as you ride through hilly terrain to Kerrville (on the Guadeloupe River). Bike northeast on No. 16 to Fredericksburg (a very pretty little German town in an area of very fertile land), and then ride east on No. 290 to Lyndon B. Johnson National Historical Park (where a bus will take you to the former president's boyhood home and to the family ranch and cemetery). Continue east to Austin, the state capita and a growing center for popular music. Ride south on No. 183 to Lockhart and west on No. 142 to San Marcos. Nearby, at San Marcos Springs, 200 million gallons of ice-cold water are produced daily. Another site in the area worth seeing is Wonder World, where you can see one of the largest caves in the United States, formed by an earthquake. Ride west on No. 12 and No. 484 to Spring Branch, and then complete this loop tour by cycling south, past Guadeloupe River State Park, back to San Antonio.

The relatively easy cycling terrain found on much of this tour will help you to enjoy this journey deep in the heart of Texas.

Other Tours
• **Big Bend National Park**
Next to the Mexican border, Big Bend National Park, named after

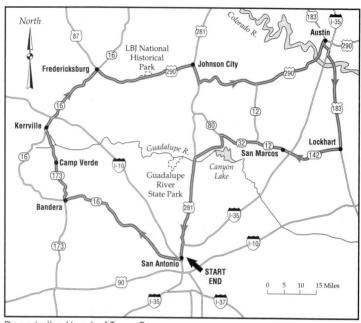

Deep in the Heart of Texas Tour

the U-shaped bend that the Rio Grande River takes there, is composed of mountain and desert. Your challenging loop tour of 190 miles (317 kilometers) begins in Alpine, in a picturesque valley, surrounded by the Texas Alps. You will cross the Glass Mountains as you cycle east on No. 90 to Marathon. Then ride south on No. 385 to park headquarters at Panther Junction (in the Chisos Mountains Basin). Many trails are available in the park for off-road biking, hiking, and horseback riding, and several of these trails will take you into desert terrain. There are also hard surfaced roads that will lead you into the major canyons. Raft trips through the park's major river canyons can also be arranged. (For more information on the park, contact: Superintendent, Big Bend National Park, TX 79834; phone (915) 477-2251). Exit the park via Study Butte. Bike west to Terlingua, once a booming mining town. Ride north on No. 118, through the Christmas Mountains, and return to Alpine.

• Gulf of Mexico Tour

Begin this 205-mile (342-kilometer) one-way tour at Port Aransas, near Corpus Christi, on the Gulf of Mexico. This quaint fishing village on Mustang Island is separated from the mainland by a causeway. Ride southwest on the island to Mustang Island State Park. At the south end of the park is the entrance to Padre National Seashore, a finger of sand that stretches almost to the Mexican border. After exploring Mustang Island, cross the causeway to Aransas Pass, and then ride northeast on No. 35 to Rockport (a picturesque resort town that attracts many artists), Aransas National Wildlife Refuge (thought to be home to more species of birds than any other of the coastal refuges), Bay City (where you can arrange a van tour of the site of the South Texas Project Nuclear Plant), and Angleton. You'll be riding on flat terrain across the coastal prairie. Ride south to Surfside, and then follow along the coast to Galveston, where you'll find miles of sandy beaches. For more information on the Galveston area, contact: Galveston Convention and Visitors Bureau, 2106 Seawall Blvd., Galveston, TX 77550; phone (409) 763-4311 or 1-800-351-4236 (in Texas) or 1-800-351-4237. Ride along the seawall to visit Galveston Island State Park.

• **East Texas Rails to Trails**
    A rugged, natural 19-mile (32-kilometer) trail for mountain bikers takes you from Tyler to Jacksonville. If you wish to make this into a loop tour, you can return by road (No. 69). For more information, write: East Texas Rails to Trails, P.O. Box 7293, Tyler, TX 75711.

Texas Contacts

Austin Cycling Association, P.O. Box 5993, Austin, TX 78763

Bandera Convention and Visitors Bureau, P.O. Box 171, Bandera, TX 78003; phone 1-800-364-3833.

Bicycle Information Committee, Texas Committee on Natural Resources, 5934 Royal Lane, Suite 223, Dallas, TX 75206.

San Antonio Convention and Visitors Bureau, 317 Alamo Plaza, San Antonio, TX 78205; phone (512) 270-8478 or 1-800-444-3372.

State Bicycle Coordinator, Texas Department of Transportation, 125 East 11th Street, Austin TX 78701-2483; phone (512) 416-2342.

Texas Trails Network, P.O. Box 2858, Grapevine, TX 76099; phone (214) 698-8733.

Tourism Division, Texas Department of Commerce, Box 12728, Austin TX 78711; phone 1-800-8888-TEX.

One of the many Texas oil wells.

Utah

• **Bryce Canyon and Zion National Parks**

Distance: 190 miles/315 kilometers

Duration: 4–6 days

Rating: Strenuous

Type: One-way Tour

Access: Hurricane is near the southwestern corner of Utah, 17 miles (29 kilometers) northeast of St. George (where air service is available). Hurricane is at the junction of No. 9 and No. 59. The destination, Escalante State Park, is northeast of Bryce Canyon National Park, just off No. 12.

Accommodations: Full facilities are found in St. George, near Hurricane. Although some lodging facilities are found along this route, it's best suited to the self-sufficient camper.

Route Description: Two of the most photographed parks in North America are visited on this exquisite bicycle trip through Bryce Canyon and Zion National Parks. The route will include some challenging climbs, but the awesome splendor of the area is more than just compensation.

Hurricane, the starting point of this trip, is named for the Hurricane Fault, a jagged escarpment that rises above the town. In a canyon near Hurricane (just north of the town) is Pah Tempe Springs, one of the world's largest springs.

Ride northeast on No. 9 to Zion National Park, where you'll pass through a spectacular gorge in an enchanting landscape of sandstone, shale, and limestone. You will pass the giant stone masses of the West Temple and The Watchman, climb the slope of Pine Creek Canyon in six switchbacks, cycle through the Zion Tunnel, and then continue to ascend, passing several scenic outlooks and opportunities for hiking (including Angels Landing Trail, Canyon Overlook Trail, and the Gateway to the Narrows Trail). The canyon narrows at the Temple of Sinawava.

Exit the park on No. 9 and ride to Mount Carmel Junction. Cycle north on No. 89 and southeast on No. 12, through Red Canyon, to Bryce Canyon National Park, which is a personal favorite. Many scenic outlooks within this park offer you an opportunity to drink in the beauty of this spellbinding canyon, with its display of colorful rocks sculpted by erosion.

Hiking and horseback riding trails within Bryce Canyon National Park allow you to descend below the rim, bringing you up close for views of the colorful and unique rock formations. Also, a 37-mile (67-kilometer) round trip by bicycle on park roads follows the high rim to several scenic vistas, including Inspiration Point, Bryce Point, Sunset Point, and Rainbow Point.

Exit this beautiful park, and continue cycling on No. 12 to Escalante, your destination. This town, on the Kaiparowits Plateau (an area of highly eroded rock formations), was named after a Spanish priest who explored sections of Utah. The nearby Escalante State Park is a showcase of petrified wood and fossilized dinosaur bones.

You will experience a variety of colors on the roads themselves and in the canyons as you ride on this visually stunning route.

Other Tours

• **Capitol Reef National Park**

If you wish to continue your trip from Escalante, ride north on No. 12 to Torrey, which *Car and Driver* magazine called "one of America's most

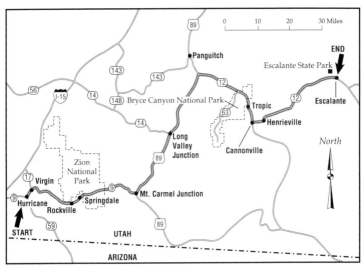

Bryce Canyon and Zion National Parks

scenic routes," and east on No. 24 to Hanksville. This challenging route will take you into Capitol Reef National Park, where there are many opportunities for mountain biking. There is also a 25-mile (42-kilometer) scenic roadway to Capitol Gorge. For more information on the park, contact: Capitol Reef National Park, Torrey, UT 84775; phone (801) 425-3791.

• The Burr Trail
Scenic No. 12 provides access (at Boulder) to the famous 66-mile (110-kilometer) off-road cycling route of the Burr Trail. It winds through the Waterpocket Fold of Capitol Reef National Park and on to Lake Powell (at Bullfrog Basin Marina).

• Natural Bridges Loop
Near Utah's southeastern corner is Natural Bridges National Monument, a scenic area 42 miles (70 kilometers) west of Blanding (on No. 95). There's a 9-mile (15-kilometer) loop road, with short hiking trails to overlooks for views of each of the three natural rock bridges. There's an informative Visitors Center, and camping is available. To complete this 150-mile (250-kilometer) loop tour, cycle southeast on No. 95 and southwest on No. 276 to Halls Crossing Marina, where a ferry will take you across Lake Powell to Bullfrog Basin Marina, and then return in a loop by cycling north on No. 276 and northeast on No. 95.

• Four Corners Monument
A loop tour of 117 miles (195 kilometers) in Utah's southeastern corner will take you to the Four Corners Monument, the only point in the United States at which four states meet. Begin at Bluff, and ride on No. 163 and No. 262 into Colorado. Cycle southwest on No. 160 to the Four Corners Monument and into New Mexico. Ride north on No. 191, returning to Bluff.

• **Coral Pink Sand Dunes State Park and Johnson Canyon**

This 50-mile (85-kilometer) scenic trip will take you from Mount Carmel Junction to Johnson Canyon, and will include a side trip into scenic Coral Pink Sand Dunes State Park.

At Mount Carmel Junction, ride southeast on No. 89, and then ride south, following the directional signs for Coral Pink Sand Dunes State Park, with its sea of coral pink sand stretching along the base of a sandstone cliff. This popular dune buggy area also offers hiking trails, Indian pictographs, and interesting cliff dwellings. (For more information, phone: 1-800-322-3770 or 1-800-874-2408).

Returning to No. 89, cycle east to Kanab and on toward Lake Powell. Take the turnoff for Johnson Canyon, your destination, and enjoy spectacular views of Lake Powell as you ride along the canyon's paved road.

• **Great Salt Lake Country**

Several cycling opportunities are available in the Salt Lake City area. A free "Salt Lake City Bikeways Map" is available from Utah's Bicycle Coordinator (address given). "The Davis County Bicycle Trail Guide" (also available from Utah's Bicycle Coordinator) outlines a roadway route from North Salt Lake Park to Clinton Park, a 34-mile (57-kilometer) route that takes you along the shore of Great Salt Lake.

• **The Moab Area**

Moab, in southeastern Utah, overlooks the Colorado River, and sits at the foot of red cliffs and the La Sal Mountains. It serves as the base for many mountain biking, hiking, Jeep, plane, rafting, and canoe trips. For more information, contact: Moab Visitor Center, 805 N. Main Street, Moab, UT 84532; phone (801) 259-8825 or 1-800-635-6622.

Although it's best to avoid the intense summer heat, this is a fantastic area for cycling (either on the roads with the wide, paved shoulders—or on the network of mountain biking trails that are also offered). Here are five specific bicycle trips that use Moab as base:

1. Arches National Park

Ride north on No. 191 to Arches National Park, a rugged area just 5 miles (9 kilometers) from Moab. You will face a very tough, twisting climb as you pedal into the park that contains the largest number of natural stone arches in the country; there are also several balancing rocks, spires, and red rock canyons. You will find several short hiking trails to scenic outlooks. As you head east in the park, you will leave the paved road to get to the viewpoint for Delicate Arch (15 miles or 25 kilometers from the park entrance. Complete this tour of about 40 miles (67 kilometers) by riding back to Moab. For more information on the park, contact: Superintendent, Arches National Park, P.O. Box 907, Moab, UT 84532; phone (801) 834-5322.

2. Castle Valley Loop Tour

Another spectacular day trip is to ride south on No. 191 to Hole in the Wall, a home excavated from sandstone. A likeness of Franklin Delano Roosevelt is carved on a rock near the home. Leave No. 191 just south of Hole in the Wall, and follow the La Sal Mountains Loop Trail to Castle Valley and to No. 128; then ride southwest on No. 128 and No. 191 and south on No. 191 back to Moab to complete this 50-mile (83-kilometer) loop tour.

Another way to complete this tour is to connect up with the network of mountain biking trails in this area. You could begin on a section of Kokopelli's Trail (one of mountain biking's best long trails), descending through forests to junipers and sagebrush. Passing the white cliffs of Polar Mesa, climb the Thompson Canyon and then descend on the Onion Creek Trail, splashing through the creek several times. After arriving at Castle Valley, climb the Sand Flats Trail and then descend to Moab through a panorama of sandstone spires and red rock canyons. Another popular mountain biking trail in the area is Slickrock Bike Trail, where the cyclist rides over smooth stones.

You have a clear option on this tour—you can ride on the designated roads or choose to follow the described mountain bike routes. You can't make a bad choice here.

3. Canyonlands National Park

Ride north on No. 191 and southwest on No. 313 to Canyonlands National Park, where you will find many opportunities for hiking and mountain biking. Ride past Upheaval Dome to Grand View Point (which offers a vista of the Colorado River, Cataract Canyon, and the Needles). You will pedal on paved roads as you pass through the area known as the Island in the Sky District. There are no services within the park, so carry lots of water and supplies with you.

4. Dead Horse State Park

Ride on No. 191 and No. 313 to Dead Horse State Park (a trip that can easily be combined with the tour to Canyonlands National Park). Dead Horse Point provides a panoramic view of the area, with its sandstone cliffs, pinnacles, and canyons (you might have seen some of this area in the film, *Thelma and Louise*). After exploring the Dead Horse State Park area, return 32 miles (54-kilometers) to Moab.

5. Mountain Biking on Kokopelli's Trail

One of mountain biking's best long trails takes you from Moab, Utah to near Grand Junction, Colorado. For more information about this mountain biking route, contact: Bureau of Land Management, 2815 H Road, Grand Junction, CO 81503; phone (303) 244-3000 or phone the Colorado Plateau Mountain Bike Trail Association at (303) 241-9561.

Utah Contacts

Bicycle Utah, P.O. Box 738, Park City, UT 84060; phone (801) 649-5806; FAX(801) 649-8805; ask for a free "Bicycle Utah Vacation Guide."

State Bicycle Coordinator, Utah Department of Transportation, 4501 South 2700 West, Salt Lake City, UT 84119-5998; phone (801) 965-3897.

Superintendent, Bryce Canyon National Park, Bryce Canyon, UT 84717; phone (801) 834-5322.

Superintendent, Zion National Park, Springdale, UT 84767; phone (801) 772-3256.

Utah Travel Council, Council Hall, Capitol Hill, Salt Lake City, UT 84114; phone (801) 538-1030.

Wyoming
• **Yellowstone and Grand Teton National Parks**
Distance: 240 miles/400 kilometers
Duration: 5–8 days
Rating: Strenuous
Type: One-way Tour
Access: Cody, the starting point, is in northwestern Wyoming, at the intersection of No. 120 and No. 20; it's also accessible by air. Jackson, the destination, is in western Wyoming (near the Idaho border), south of Grand Teton National Park.
Accommodations: Because you are cycling through two national parks, many opportunities for camping are available. Full services are found at both Cody and Jackson, and there are several motels, hotels and resorts along the way.
Route Description: One of the most spectacular and varied areas of North America is found in northwestern Wyoming, site of Yellowstone and Grand Teton National Parks. This marvelous cycling adventure will take you through both magnificent parks as you bike from Cody, near the east entrance to Yellowstone National Park, to Jackson, just south of Grand Teton National Park.

Cody was founded by Col. William 'Buffalo Bill' Cody, and points of interest here include the Buffalo Bill Historical Center and the Buffalo Bill Statue. You might enjoy attending a rodeo and studying some of the western heritage of the area before departing from Cody by riding west on No. 20. You will pass Buffalo Bill State Park, ride through the lovely Wapiti Valley (near many unusual rock formations), cross a section of the Shoshone National Forest (the nation's first national forest), and bike to Pahaska Tepee (the eastern entrance to Yellowstone National Park, the nation's first national park). According to former President Theodore Roosevelt, this route from Cody to Pahaska Tepee is "the most scenic 52 miles in America."

As you enter my favorite park, cycle through the Sylvan Pass to Fishing Bridge, where you'll find a Visitor Center that explains the biological life in the park. Ride north to Canyon. You will then cycle northeast, through a particularly scenic area, with several spectacular outlooks, including Inspiration Point, Artist's Point, and Lookout Point—a great place from which to view the magnificent Lower Falls. You will bike on relatively narrow roads as you proceed through Dunraven Pass to Tower Junction, viewing the inspiring Grand Canyon of the Yellowstone; nearby is the famous Petrified Tree and Tower Falls, another breathtaking view. Ride northwest to park headquarters at Mammoth Hot Springs.

One of the most fascinating features of Yellowstone National Park is its display of thermal basins; some bubble and spit, while others spurt scalding water high into the air. There are about 10,000 thermal features in the park, including hot springs, mud pots, and geysers. Another highlight of this park is the abundance of wildlife, including bear, elk, and buffalo; traffic often comes to a stop to photograph these magnificent animals. Of course, the spectacular scenery and varied terrain within this park also offer the cyclist special challenges because the roads tend to be narrow, winding, hilly, and busy.

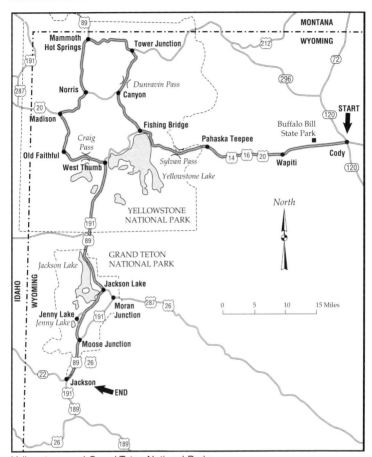

Yellowstone and Grand Teton National Parks

See more of the beauty and variety of Yellowstone National Park by riding south from Mammoth Hot Springs. You will pass Obsidian Cliff and ride through the Norris Geyser Basin to Madison. You will then bike on a relatively flat road to Gibbon Falls. Continue south to Fountain Paintpot (a large spring filled with hot clay), Upper Geyser Basin, Midway Geyser Basin, and Old Faithful, where the Visitor Center explains geyser activity and its effects. Ride past the Shoshone Geyser Basin and through the Craig Pass to West Thumb Geyser Basin and the Grant Village Visitor Center (where the fire of 1988, which destroyed a large section of the park, is detailed). You will ride past blackened trees and past patches of new growth as you ride through a section of the park that was touched by that fire. Continue south, past Shoshone Lake, Lewis Lake, and Yellowstone Lake, and exit the park.

Continue riding south (on No. 191) into Grand Teton National Park, with its magnificent mountain views. Turn southwest onto Teton Park

From the top of the ski lift, you will receive a magnificent view of the Jackson, Wyoming, area in the Grand Tetons.

Road at Jackson Lake Lodge, and bike past Signal Mountain (with its panoramic view of the area), Leigh Lake, Jenny (where nearby trails will take you to Inspiration Point and Hidden Falls), Bradley Lake, and on to park headquarters, at Moose Junction. The Chapel of the Transfiguration, at Moose Junction, has a window that frames a spectacular view of the mountains, a great photo spot. Continue south and exit the park.

In addition to the specific cycling route described here through Yellowstone and Grand Teton National Parks, both parks also provide the mountain biker with opportunities for off-road riding on many trails.

Complete your very challenging cycling adventure by descending into the beautiful resort town of Jackson, nestled in a valley, surrounded by mountains; the Snake River flows through this picturesque town. A chair-lift will take you to the summit of Snow King Mountain for a spectacular view. Opportunities abound in the Jackson area for scenic flights, float trips, mountain biking, and hiking.

Other Tours
• From Cody to Shoshoni
The ride from Cody to Shoshoni, on No. 120, is a very scenic 115 miles (192 kilometers). Near Thermopolis is Hot Springs State Park, which contains hot mineral springs and waterfalls. South of town is Wind River Canyon, a landscape of monumental rock formations.

• From Laramie to Cheyenne
The Wyoming Territory Park, in Laramie, is a re-creation of an 1890s wild west town, including a restored prison and several shops. Stagecoach, trail, and pony rides are available. (For more information on the Laramie area, phone: 1-800-445-5303). It's worth a visit before you ride east on No. 210 for 38 miles (63 kilometers), through the Medicine Bow

National Forest, past Gowdy State Park, to Cheyenne, named for the tribe of Indians that once inhabited southeastern Wyoming.When you arrive, check out the Cheyenne Frontier Days Old West Museum and the Wildlife Visitor Center.

• **Devils Tower**

Begin this tour in Sundance, at the foot of Sundance Mountain. It's believed that Harry Longabaugh assumed his nickname, "The Sundance Kid," while serving a sentence here for horse stealing. You'll be pedaling through the Bear Lodge Mountains as you take No. 14 northwest to Devils Tower Junction. Ride north on No. 24 to Devils Tower National Monument, which is known as Bear Lodge to the Lakota. Used as the spaceship's landing site in Spielberg's film, *Close Encounters of the Third Kind,* Devils Tower is a huge monolith that resembles a colossal stone tree stump; it's over 850 feet high, and the almost perpendicular sides are fluted columns; sagebrush and grass grow on the 1.5 acre top. After exploring the Devils Tower, return to Devils Tower Junction, passing a fascinating prairie dog colony. Then cycle southwest on No. 14 to Keyhole State Park (near Moorcroft) and southeast on No. 16 to Upton (which is in a section of Thunder Basin National Grassland). Complete the 109-mile (182 kilometer) loop tour by riding northeast on No. 116 back to Sundance.

Wyoming Contacts

Cody Country Chamber of Commerce, P.O. Box 2777-AAA, Cody, WY 82414; phone (307) 587-2297.

State Bicycle Coordinator, Wyoming Transportation Department, P.O. Box 1708, Cheyenne, WY 82003; phone (307) 777-4719.

Superintendent, Grand Teton National Park, P.O. Drawer 170, Moose WY 83012.

Superintendent, Yellowstone National Park, P.O. Box 168, Yellowstone National Park, WY 82190; phone (307) 344-7381.

Wyoming Division of Tourism, I-25 at College Drive, Cheyenne, WY 82002; phone (307) 777-7777 (in Wyoming) or 1-800-225-5996 (out of state).

Chapter 8

Pacific Coast States

K nown for their dense forests (including California's giant sequoias and redwoods), rugged mountains (including those of Washington's Olympic National Park, Oregon's Crater Lake National Park, and California's Yosemite National Park), and dramatic ocean shoreline, the Pacific Coast States offer the cyclist spectacular scenery and a relatively mild climate (cooler and wetter in the north). Bring your rain gear because the heaviest rainfalls in the U.S.A. occur along the coast area of Washington and Oregon.

In California, two parallel chains of Pacific Coast Ranges are divided by a particularly fertile area, where a large portion of the nation's wine grapes, fruits, nuts, and vegetables are produced. In contrast, California's desert areas are extremely hot and dry (the average summer temperature in Death Valley, for example, is more than 90 Fahrenheit (36 Celsius), and the annual rainfall averages less than 2 inches (5 centimeters).

The Pacific Coast is a very popular cycling area; you'll find a detailed Pacific Coast Tour in Chapter 11.

California
• **Yosemite National Park**
Distance: 120 miles/200 kilometers
Duration: 3–5 days
Rating: Strenuous
Type: One-way Tour
Access: Lee Vining is a small town in the Mono Basin, on Mono Lake, near the east entrance to Yosemite National Park (and not far from the Nevada border). Yosemite Village, within the park, has shuttle bus service and designated bicycle routes.
Accommodations: As a center for the Mono Lake National Scenic Area and the eastern gateway to Yosemite National Park, Lee Vining offers a variety of facilities. Camping and lodging facilities are plentiful within the park.
Route Description: If you enjoy the challenge of tough mountain climbs and the beauty of magnificent scenery, then this cycling adventure is for you. Many tourists visit the Yosemite Valley, but this ride will take you through the high mountains of the park before your descent into the much-photographed valley.

Begin this tour at Lee Vining, just east of the park. Take the Tioga Road into the park, climbing for about 12 miles (20 kilometers); enjoy a spectacular view of the valley below. As you cycle above the

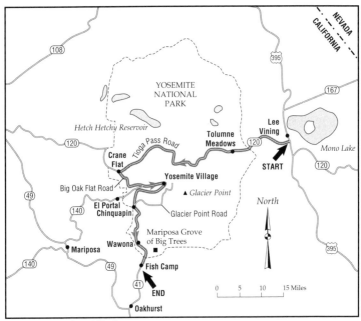

Yosemite National Park

rim of Yosemite Valley, you will find several spectacular overlooks. With more than 750 miles (1250 kilometers) of trails, the park provides many opportunities for hiking, mountain biking, and camping. Continue west through the mountainous terrain to Tuolumne Meadows, an excellent starting point for fishing, hiking, and mountain climbing trips; horseback rides or hikes will take you to such interesting area sights as Waterwheel Falls, Mount Lyell and Lyell Glacier, Lembert Dome, Muir Gorge, Soda Springs, and Glen Aulin. Descend to Tenaya Lake; then continue riding west, past Porcupine Flat, Yosemite Creek, and Tamarack Flat to the end of Tioga Pass Road. Explore the Tuolumne Grove (with its giant sequoias, including the Dead Giant) via Big Oak Flat Road (17 miles or 28 kilometers from Yosemite Valley).

Ride into Yosemite Valley, where you can marvel at the sheer immensity of the precipices on each side of the valley floor, the majesty of the granite walls, the great domes and pinnacles (including El Capitan, North Dome, Half Dome, Cathedral Spires, and Three Brothers), and the height and beauty of the many waterfalls (including Upper and Lower Yosemite Falls, Vertical Falls, Bridalveil Falls, Ribbon Falls, and Nevada Falls). Yosemite Valley is a very popular area for photography, horseback riding, hiking, cycling, and mountain climbing. Tram tours and "flightseeing" are available. Crowding is a problem in the summer months, so be sure to have campsite or other lodging reserved in advance.

Also be sure to try the beautiful bicycle route in Yosemite Valley. It takes the cyclist to Mirror Lake and past magnificent views of Lower and Upper Yosemite Falls. If you are ready for another strenuous climb, you could take the Glacier Point Road to Glacier Point (a round trip of about 60 miles or 100 kilometers). Glacier Point offers a panoramic view into the valley below.

Exit Yosemite National Park by cycling south on No. 41 to Chinquapin (where the exit to Glacier Point is found) and Wawona (where the Pioneer Yosemite History Center is). The Wawona Tunnel provides another scenic view of the valley. Continue south to Mariposa Grove (a giant sequoia grove, including a tunnel tree), where you depart the park to Fish Camp, ending this spectacular adventure through central California's Yosemite National Park.

Other Tours

• **California's Coastline**

This route is detailed (from Crescent City to Big Sur) as part of the Pacific Coast Tour, described in Chapter 11. You can continue cycling south on No. 1 and No. 101 to the outskirts of Los Angeles, where you will find a series of bicycle paths that will take you (with minor breaks) all the way from Marina del Ray to San Diego. The section from La Jolla to Oceanside is a particularly popular, scenic route, where you remain very close to magnificent beaches. A free map of area bicycle paths is available from Commuter Computer of San Diego, P.O. Box 82358, San Diego, CA 92138; phone (619) 231-BIKE.

• **Angel Island State Park**

Set in the beautiful San Francisco Bay, Angel Island is just a short ferry ride from San Francisco. The island's beaches, forested slopes, and hiking trails are a delight for the outdoor enthusiast. Bike rentals are available. For more information about the park, phone (415) 897-0715. For ferry service information, phone the Red and White Fleet (from Pier 43.5, San Francisco, CA) at (415) 546-2628.

• **Santa Cruz Loop**

Santa Cruz is a scenic coastal town on Monterey Bay (south of San Francisco). Take No. 9 up through the Santa Cruz Mountains to Boulder Creek. Turn left on No. 236 and ride through Big Basin Redwood State Park (phone (408) 335-3174 for park information). You'll pass through the tall redwoods and views of the San Lorenzo Valley. Once through the park, you'll rejoin No. 9 and bike to the Saratoga Gap. Ride north on No. 35 and then southwest on No. 84 (La Honda Road); a steep descent will bring you to No. 1, and then you will head south, back to Santa Cruz (for bike information, phone the Santa Cruz County Bike Club at (408) 423-0829). You will face some very tough climbs at the beginning of this 105-mile (175-kilometer) route, but you will have a very exhilarating descent later in the trip—and there's also a good chance you'll have the wind at your back on No. 1 (which has more traffic but good bike lanes).

• **The Los Angeles Area**

There are several bicycle trails within the city. San Vincente Boulevard, in Santa Monica, has a nice wide lane for cyclists. Bike paths are found in area parks, such as Balboa Park in the San Fernando Valley. Another bike path takes the cyclist from Temescal Canyon to Redondo Beach. For more information, contact: Caltrans District 7-Los Angeles, 120 South Spring Street, Los Angeles, CA 90012; phone (213) 897-0235.

• The Palm Springs Area

There are more than 36 miles (60 kilometers) of bicycle trails, with six mapped-out city tours; trail maps are available from Palm Springs Recreational Department, 401 South Cerritos, Palm Springs, CA; phone (619) 323-8276.

• The Sacramento Area

The American River Bicycle Trail is about 30 miles (50 kilometers) long and has access points to several parts of Sacramento. Cyclists can cross their own suspension bridge (for joggers and bicyclists) into Cal State University. For more information, contact: Sacramento Rideshare, P.O. Box 942874, MS41, Sacramento, CA 94274; phone (916) 445-POOL.

A nice loop tour is to cycle southwest on No. 160 to Walnut Grove and Isleton, cross by ferry to Rio Vista, and then return to Sacramento (on the other side of the river).

• The High Sierras

The mountainous terrain of this challenging tour takes you from Mount Shasta (in north-central California) to Tahoe City (on Lake Tahoe, next to the Nevada border). You will climb Dead Horse Summit as you bike on No. 89 from Mount Shasta to Old Station. Then ride east on No. 44 and south on No. 89, to Lassen Volcanic National Park (where the Cascades meet the Sierra Nevada). Lassen Park Road winds around Lassen Park, providing interesting views of the volcano, lava flows, hot springs, and mud pots. Cycle through the strenuous terrain of the park, and then bike east on No. 36 and southeast on No. 89 to the destination, Tahoe City.

• California's Wine Country

An easier trip in California, on relatively quiet roads that pass vineyards and meander through spectacular valleys, is this loop tour that begins in Cloverdale (in the Alexander Valley), about 88 miles (147 kilometers) north of San Francisco. You will pass many small, family-owned wineries as you ride southeast on No. 128 to Calistoga (a town known for its mineral springs and mud baths). Travel south, through the Napa Valley, past Stag's Leap and Clos du Val (wineries) to the town of Napa. Bike northwest on No. 121 to Boyes Hot Springs, Kenwood, and Santa Rosa (site of the Sonoma County Museum). Ride north on No. 101 to Healdsburgh (where several winery tours are available), and then complete this 128-miles (214-kilometer) loop tour by returning to Cloverdale. Take time to tour some of the wineries and sample some of the California wines as you ride through this rich farmland in California's Wine Country.

• Death Valley

Although a desert, Death Valley is an area of surprising beauty and varied terrain for the cyclist who wants to experience a place that's truly unique. You'll find a good paved road through the area, but the terrain is not the daunting element here; it's the weather. Do not try to do this trip during the intense summer heat, because Death Valley is one of the hottest, driest regions in the world. Begin your adventure in Mesquite Springs, at the north end of Death Valley. Bike southwest on No. 267 and No. 190, past large sand dunes, to Furnace Creek (where you will find an informative Visitor Center that's also a great place to get a cold drink of water!). Continue on No. 190 and take the scenic turnoff to Dante's View; you face a very steep climb before arriving at a panoramic view of the area; below, on the desert floor, is the Devil's Golf Course (with very rough terrain) and Badwater (which is below sea level and is the lowest point in the United States). In the distance, in stark contrast, you will see the Panamint Mountains. Return to No. 190, and ride west to Death Valley Junction, your destination on this journey through Death Valley. If you wish, you could continue riding southeast for about 100 miles (165 kilometers) to Las Vegas, Nevada.

California Contacts

California Association of Bicycle Organizations, P.O. Box 2684, Dublin, CA 94268; phone (916) 653-0036.

California Division of Tourism, 801 K Street, Suite 1600, Sacramento, CA 95814; phone (916) 862-2543 or 1-800-60 CALIF.

California Trails and Greenways Foundation, P.O. Box 183, Los Altos, CA 94023; phone 1-800-325-2843; includes a trail information library.

State Bicycle Coordinator, P.O. Box 942874, Sacramento, CA 94274; phone (916) 653-0036.

Superintendent, P.O. Box 577, Yosemite National Park, CA 95389.

The Hollywood Bowl, an outdoor amphitheater, is the site of many concerts in Los Angeles, California.

Oregon
• The Columbia River Gorge
Distance: 175 miles/290 kilometers
Duration: 3–4 days
Rating: Strenuous
Type: Loop Tour
Access: Portland is accessible by bus (Greyhound and Trailways: phone (503) 228-8571), train (Amtrak: phone (503) 241-4290), and plane (with transportation to and from the airport available by airport bus, limousine service, and the public bus system).
Accommodations: Portland has full facilities. Some lodgings are available in Hood River and Gresham. There are also several campgrounds along this route.
Route Description: This loop tour permits many scenic views in the canyon carved by the Columbia River; a detailed map of the Columbia River Gorge can be obtained from the Automobile Club of Oregon (through the American Automobile Association). The state's largest city (Portland), highest mountain (Mount Hood), and a magnificent waterway (the Columbia River) are all part of this lovely trip.

Begin in Portland, and consider visiting such points of interest as the Oregon Maritime Center and Museum, the Grotto, Portland Art Museum, Metro Washington Park Zoo, Washington Park, and Crystal Springs Rhododendron Gardens. You will find many bike paths winding through city parks; several of these even connect with the statewide network of paths.

A wide bicycle path parallels Interstate Highway 84 as you cycle on relatively flat terrain along the length of the Columbia River Gorge; many waysides, lookouts, and state parks permit leisurely sightseeing, but, be prepared for the possibility of stiff, constant winds out of the east. Ride to Troutdale, Crown Point State Park (which offers a beautiful vista of the gorge), Latourell Falls, Bridal Veil Falls, Coopey Falls, Mist Falls, Multnomah Falls (one of the highest in the country), Tooth Rock Tunnel, Bonneville (the Bonneville Dam spans the Columbia River between Oregon and Washington), Cascade Locks (where you can take a cruise through the Columbia River Gorge), and Hood River (which is in a major apple-growing area and is also considered to be one of the best areas in North America for wind surfing).

Turn south on No. 35, and ride through the orchards of the Hood Valley, past views of magnificent, snow-capped Mount Hood. Then bike northwest on No. 26, through the Barlow Pass, which was used by pioneers on the Oregon Trail, to Zigzag, Brightwood, Cherryville, Gresham, and back to Portland.

The variety of terrain found on this cycling adventure makes it a very interesting and photographic trip; you will encounter unusual rock formations, high cliffs, beautiful waterfalls, fertile orchards, and several scenic state parks.

Other Tours
• The Portland Area
Many paths wind through city parks, and many of them connect with the statewide network of paths. Rated in *Bicycling*'s "Top Ten

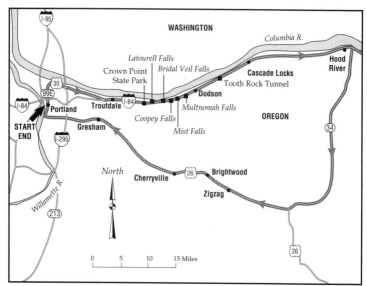

The Columbia River Gorge

Cycling Cities in North America," Portland has a number of innovative programs, including buses with front-mounted bike racks, downtown "Bike Central Stations" for bike commuters, and a "Yellow Bike Program" in which you can take a specially marked yellow bicycle to your destination within the city and leave it there for the next cyclist. Bicycles are allowed on the light-rail system, too.

• The Eugene Area
Eugene boasts more than 50 miles (84 kilometers) of bike trails, nearly 20 miles (33 kilometers) of bike routes, and 25 miles (42 kilometers) of off-street bikeways. The Willamette River splits Eugene, and there are more pedestrian and bicycle bridges across it than there are spans for motor vehicles!

• Hells Canyon National Recreation Area
This rugged route is best suited to the mountain biker because you ride on gravel logging roads for a part of this tour. Begin this adventure in Enterprise, in the northeast corner of the state. Ride on No. 82 to Imnaha, and then ride parallel to the Imnaha River on No. 3955; this route will connect with the Wallowa Mountain Loop (No. 39) and lead back to Enterprise.

• Crater Lake National Park
Crater Lake National Park is home to more than 200 species of birds and several kinds of wildflowers (Castle Crest Wildflower Trail is near the park's headquarters). The park offers more than 100 miles (165 kilometers) of maintained trails, including hiking and bicycle trails. For more information about the park, contact: Chief of Interpre-

tations, Crater Lake National Park, Box 7, Crater Lake, OR 97604; phone (503) 594-2211.

Crater Lake itself is about 6 miles (10 kilometers) long and 4.5 miles (7 kilometers) wide; it was formed by volcanic eruptions thousands of years ago; the volcanic mountain top collapsed, creating the caldera that now contains Crater Lake. Begin your loop tour at Rim Village, and circle the lake clockwise (on the 38-mile or 63-kilometer route); you will pass such points of interest as the Watchman, Hillman Peak (the highest point on the rim), Red Cone, Llao Rock (a lava flow filling an ancient explosion crater), Cleetwood Cove, Sinnott Memorial Overlook, Mount Scott, the Pinnacles (spires of cemented pumice and scoria rise above the canyon floor), and Garfield Peak before your return to Rim Village and the completion of your loop tour.

• **The Oregon Coast**
Enjoy stunning coastal panoramas, dense forested areas, fishing villages, farmland, sculpted sand dunes, and rugged promontories as you cycle along the Oregon coast (which is described as part of the Pacific Coast Tour, in chapter No. 11).

Oregon Contacts

Bicycle Program Manager, Oregon Department of Transportation, Transportation Bldg., Room 210, Salem, OR 97310; phone (503) 986-3555; FAX (503) 986-3896.

Oregon Tourism Commission, 775 Summer Street, N.E., Salem, OR 97310; phone 1-800-547-7842.

Portland Oregon Visitors Association, 26 S.W. Salmon, Portland, OR 97204; phone (503) 222-2223.

Southern Oregon Cycling Association, P.O. Box 903, Ashland, OR 97520; phone (503) 488-BIKE.

Washington
• **Puget Sound and the San Juan Islands**
Distance: 260 miles/444 kilometers
Duration: 6–9 days
Rating: Moderate
Type: One-way Tour
Access: "The Emerald City" of Seattle sits on a narrow piece of land between Puget Sound and Lake Washington. The jagged Olympic Mountains are to the west of the city, and the volcanic peaks of the Cascade Range are visible to the east. The major roads are Interstate Highways 5 and 90. Seattle is also accessible by boat (Washington State Ferries: phone (206) 464-6400 or 1-800-542-7050), plane (Seattle-Tacoma International Airport), and train (Amtrak: phone 1-800-872-7245).
Accommodations: Many facilities are available on this route.
Route Description: Puget Sound is south of the Strait of Juan de Fuca and goes nearly two-thirds of the way down the state. Its many sheltered harbors protect fishing fleets, pleasure craft, and ports of call. Several beautiful islands can be visited in Puget Sound. Before you travel, check with the Puget Sound Vessel Traffic Service, which provides twenty-four hour traffic and weather information—and don't forget your rain gear (this coastal area receives a lot).

Begin in Seattle, one of the best cities for cycling, with many paths. Ride north on No. 99 and No. 525 to Mukilteo (about 25 miles or 42 kilometers), and then take the ferry to Whidbey Island, the largest island in Puget Sound, and one of the most scenic (for more information, phone Whidbey Island at (206) 675-3535).

The moderate terrain on this island makes it a very pleasant cycling experience; you will ride on a wide paved shoulder as you pass bays and coves, fragrant fir trees and saltwater beaches, and enjoy both scenic shoreline vistas and the grandeur of the distant Olympic Mountains. Ride north on No. 525 to Langley (a charming cliff-top village), Mutiny Bay, South Whidbey State Park, and Coupeville, one of the oldest towns in the state and the location of several antique stores and art galleries. Ride north on No. 20 to Oak Harbor (the largest town on the island), Ebey's Landing National Historical Reserve (protecting a variety of historic and natural sites), and Deception Pass State Park (which contains more than 25 miles or 40 kilometers of hiking trails).

Several miles of saltwater shoreline are found along the cliff-lined channel that separates Whidbey Island and Fidalgo Island. The Deception Pass Bridge offers a panoramic view of the area. Ride to Anacortes, at the tip of Fidalgo Island, where ferry service is available to a number of the San Juan Islands.

Enjoy the natural beauty of this area as you visit some of the 172 islands (for a copy of the ferry schedule, phone (206) 464-6400 or 1-800-84-FERRY). I would especially recommend visiting San Juan Island, Orca Island, and Lopez Island. Watch for whales as you journey from island to island; you might also see salmon, seals, dolphins, bald eagles, great horned owls, and tufted puffins.

On San Juan Island, the westernmost of the major islands, you will ride on quiet roads that wind through rolling farmland and along high

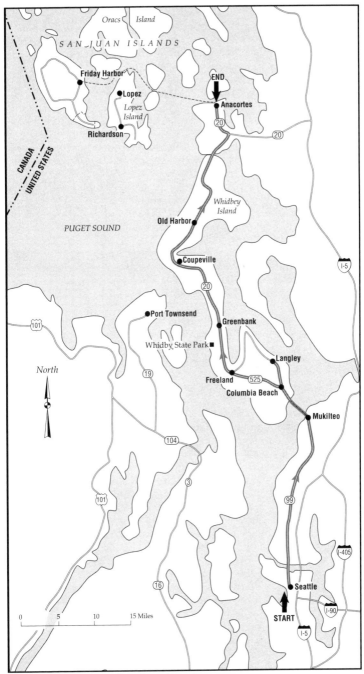

Puget Sound and the San Juan Islands

cliffs. Visit Friday Harbor (its bustling port), Lime Kiln State Park (a good place from which to view pods of whales), and Roche Harbor.

On Orca Island, visit Moran State Park, and climb the very steep hill to the top of Mount Constitution; from this vantage point, you will have a panoramic view of many of the islands. In season, you'll find bushes laden with ripe blackberries along the roads as you pass through stands of Douglas fir and white oak.

Lopez Island is particularly popular with cyclists because of its relatively flat terrain. You can enjoy a magnificent view from MacKaye Harbor.

After visiting several of the beautiful San Juan Islands in Puget Sound, return to Anacortes, your destination. Anacortes is connected to the mainland by bridge and by ferry service.

Other Tours
• The Seattle Area

Seattle is a great city for cycling. Many bicycle paths run through the city, along the waterfront, and connect with city parks. The showpiece trail is the 20-mile (33-kilometer) Burke-Gilman Trail. A 150-mile (250-kilometer) trail, re-creating the Olympia to Bellingham train route, is in the planning stages. For more information, phone (206) 522-BIKE.

• Explore Canada's Gulf Islands

You can take a ferry from Anacortes to Sidney, on Vancouver Island, in British Columbia, Canada. You could then continue your island exploration by cycling some of Canada's Gulf Islands, one of the West Coast's most spectacular cycling areas; many of these islands are linked by ferry, including Saltspring, Saturna, Pender, and Galiano. This cycling adventure is detailed in my book, *Cycling Canada*.

• Washington's Pacific Coast

This intriguing route is detailed in Chapter 11, as part of the Pacific Coast Tour.

• Mount St. Helens National Volcanic Monument

This 54-mile (90-kilometer) one-way route takes you from Morton (northeast of Portland) into Mount St. Helens National Volcanic Monument. Ride east on No. 12 to Randle and southeast on No. 26 and No. 99 to your destination.

There is a network of hiking trails around the volcano and the route for a rigorous trek to the summit of Mount St. Helens. For more information, contact: Mount St. Helens National Volcanic Monument Headquarters, 42218 N.E. Yale Bridge Road, Amboy, WA 98601; phone (206) 247-5473). The Windy Ridge Viewpoint is a great spot from which to see Mount St. Helens Crater and Spirit Lake. Aerial sightseeing tours are available from Morton.

• Mount Rainier National Park

Both the Mount St. Helens National Volcanic Monument tour (described above) and the Mount Rainier National Park tour begin from the same base (Morton), where "flightseeing" trips to the areas can be arranged. Ride northwest on No. 12 and No. 123 from Morton, and enter Mount Rainier National Park. This park has more than 140 miles (233 kilometers) of roads and more than 300 miles (500 kilometers) of trails open to the public. For more information, contact: Superintendent, Mount Rainier National Park, Tahoma Woods-Star Route, Ashford, WA 98304; phone (206) 569-2211.

Bike on the Stevens Canyon Road (with its great views of Mount Rainier and the Tatoosh Range) to Paradise (really!), where you'll find an inn and a Visitor Center. Then take the Nisqually-Paradise Road as you go west, passing a trail to Narada Falls and Comet Falls, Christine Falls, a museum at Longmire, and the Kautz Mudflow area. Exit the park, and ride west on No. 706 to Elbe and south on No. 7 back to Morton, completing this 118-mile (197-kilometer) loop tour.

• **North Cascades National Park**
You will face some tough climbs on this challenging, one-way, 90-mile (150-kilometer) tour that takes you through mountainous terrain. You'll be going from Marblemount, at the park's western entrance, to Winthrop. The park is in north-central Washington, and its many trails provide opportunities for hiking and mountain biking. Deer, black bear, grizzly bear, wolverine, mountain goat, and cougar are among the wildlife found in this park. For more information, contact: Superintendent, North Cascades National Park, 2105 Highway 20, Sedro Woolley, WA 98284; phone (206) 856-5700.

Ride northeast on No. 20 through the park, passing Newhalem, Gorge Dam, Diablo, Diablo Dam, Ross Dam, and Ross Lake, across which is Canada. As you leave North Cascades National Park, you will cycle on the North Cascades Scenic Highway, through the Okanagan National Forest, to Rainy Pass and Washington Pass. Washington Pass Scenic Overlook offers a short loop trail to a spectacular viewing point. Complete the trip by riding southeast to the destination, Winthrop (parts of which are restored to 1890s-era architecture: false-fronted buildings, old-fashioned street lights, and wooden sidewalks).

Washington Contacts
Bicycle Program Manager, Design Office, Department of
    Transportation, P.O. Box 47329, Olympia, WA 98504; phone
    (206) 705-7258.
Seattle Engineering Department, Bicycle Program, Transportation
    Services Division, Municipal Bldg., 7th Floor, 600 Fourth Avenue,
    Seattle, WA 98104; phone (206) 684-7570.
Seattle-King County Convention and Visitors Bureau, 520 Pike Street,
    No. 1300 Seattle, WA 98101; phone (206) 461-5840.
Washington State Council, Hostelling International, American Youth
    Hostels, 419 Queen Anne Avenue North No. 102, Seattle, WA
    98109; phone (206) 281-7306.
Washington State Department of Trade and Economic Development,
    Tourism Division, P.O. Box 42500, Olympia, WA 98504; phone
    (206) 586-2102.

Chapter 9

Alaska

Alaska is more than twice the size of Texas, and its coastline is longer than that of the continental United States. A vast, unspoilt landscape of mountains, glaciers, and tundra, Alaska offers a special wilderness adventure for the more daring cyclist. Here you'll find two spectacular cycling tours detailed, along with optional activities in each area and other suggested routes.

The cyclist will find paved bicycle paths and roads for much of the prescribed routes—and will find surprisingly mild summer temperatures. Pack your rain gear. The southern coast gets a lot of precipitation. Also, be prepared. You will cycle through some remote and isolated areas.

• 1. Anchorage-Prince William Sound

Distance: 348 miles/580 kilometers
Duration: 6–10 days
Rating: Strenuous
Type: Loop Tour
Access: Anchorage, Alaska's largest city, is accessible by bus, boat, rail, and air. The protective mountains and the proximity of the ocean combine to give Anchorage a surprisingly mild climate for this far north.
Accommodations: Full services are available in Anchorage, which is home to almost half the population of the state. However, services are very limited along this route, so the trip is best suited to the self-sufficient camper.
Route Description: Anchorage, Alaska's largest city and the starting point for this tour, has about 180 miles (300 kilometers) of bicycle trails. It's also the site of the Alaska Zoo, Alaska Aviation Heritage Museum, Heritage Library and Museum, and the Anchorage Museum of History and Art. Many exciting adventure tours begin here, including helicopter tours, white-water rafting trips, float trips, hot-air balloon rides, and dogsled tours.

Ride northeast to Eagle River (on bicycle trails) and Palmer, through a wilderness where it's not unusual to see bald eagles, bear, and moose. Follow the Matanuska River eastward to the massive Matanuska Glacier, and continue east to Eureka and Glenallen. The Glenn Highway (No. 1) can have quite a bit of traffic, and there is often no paved shoulder as you ride on this hilly, challenging route. Bike south on the Richardson Highway (No. 4) to Copper Center, past Mount Wrangell (Alaska's largest active volcano) and Worthington Glacier, over the Thompson Pass (a tough climb!), past Bridal Veil Falls and Horsetail

Falls, and on to the scenic coastal town of Valdez. Head winds can be a problem as you ride south, so be prepared for some tough pedaling.

Valdez is the southern terminus for the Alaska Pipeline and is Alaska's northernmost ice-free port. This coastal town is ringed by picturesque, snow-capped mountains, and it's known as the "Switzerland of Alaska."

Take the unforgettable ferry ride from Valdez, across Prince William Sound, to the Kenai Peninsula (near Kenai Fjords National Park, which encompasses a coastal mountain range that includes Harding Icefield, one of the largest icefields in the United States). While on this magnificent ferry ride, watch for seals, porpoises, sea otter, and killer whales; you will also view the Columbia Glacier's turquoise icefalls.

You will arrive at Whittier, on the Kenai Peninsula, where you will board the Alaska Railroad for a scenic journey to Portage. Then complete this wilderness loop tour by cycling north back to Anchorage. Traffic can be quite heavy on the Seward Highway, and the road is twisty, but you will have a wide paved shoulder as you ride to your destination.

Since this adventure tour takes you through bear country, take appropriate precautions with food and garbage. The awesome scenery that you witness on this wilderness tour (by bicycle, boat, and train) makes it a memorable experience.

Optional Activities

Pan for gold or take a helicopter tour, white-water rafting trip, hot-air balloon ride, dogsled tour, or float trip in the area.

Cruise the Inside Passage and visit Juneau, Alaska's capital city.

Explore Kenai Fjords National Park, Kodiak Island, and Homer: Take a ferry from Valdez to Seward Then you will enjoy views of the glacier-carved Kenai Fjords as you travel by ferry past a section of Kenai Fjords National Park to Kodiak Island. Known as the home of the Kodiak (or Alaskan brown) bear, Kodiak Island is also a habitat for bald eagles, porpoises, sea otters, sea lions, and whales. Take yet another ferry to Homer, a picturesque coastal community. After exploring the beauty of this area, a private shuttle service will take you to Anchorage.

• 2. Denali National Park and Preserve
Distance: 147 miles/245 kilometers
Duration: 3–5 days
Rating: Strenuous
Type: One-way Tour
Access: Fairbanks, near the geographical center of Alaska, is accessible by motor vehicle, plane, and rail. Several tour operators offer sightseeing trips in the area.
Accommodations: As one of the larger cities in Alaska, Fairbanks offers full services. They are limited along the route, however, so it's best suited to the self-sufficient camper. Several campgrounds are found within Denali National Park and Preserve.
Route Description: Fairbanks, the northern terminus of the Alaska railroad, is the starting point for this spectacular adventure tour. Fairbanks' location allows the local semipro baseball team (the "Goldpanners") to play its annual Solstice Game at midnight (on the weekend nearest June 21) without extra lighting. Fairbanks is also the location of

one of the northernmost golf courses in the world. Annual events here include the Festival of Native Arts, Golden Days, the North American Dog Sled Championships, and the World Eskimo Indian Olympics.

Cycle south on the George Parks Highway (No. 3) to Nenana, Anderson, Clear Site, and Healy. Enter the eastern boundary of Denali National Park and Preserve via the Denali Park Road, and cycle on a paved road for 15 miles (25 kilometers) to Savage River. You can continue on this road for another 75 miles (125 kilometers) to the semi-abandoned mining town of Kantishna; however, this section of the road is unpaved, twisting, and narrow, and it could prove to be quite a problem to a road cyclist after a rain.

During the summer, sled-dog demonstrations are conducted daily in Denali National Park and Preserve. More than 150 species of birds and 35 species of mammals are found here (including wolf, grizzly bear, moose, caribou, and Dall sheep).

Excellent views of Denali, or Mount McKinley, are possible along the park road, weather permitting. Known to the early Athabascan Indians as "Denali," "the high one," the mountain actually has two peaks: South Peak (the true summit) and North Peak. Much of this mountain is covered by ice and snow all year. You will also observe several other mountains and glaciers on your journey (including Muldrow, the largest northward-flowing glacier in Alaska). The many hours of daylight during this summer tour will give you extra time to marvel at the incredible scenery.

Optional Activities

Travel by rail to Anchorage (via Denali National Park and Preserve), take a "flightseeing" tour of the park, or enjoy a tundra wildlife tour within the park.

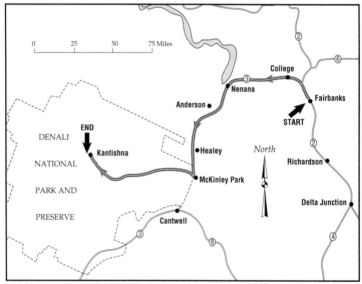

Denali National Park and Preserve

Take a riverboat ride or a canoe trip on the Chena or Tanana Rivers.

Visit the University of Alaska, Chena Hot Springs, or see abandoned gold dredges along the roads to Chatanika and Ester.

Other Tours
• The Denali Highway

For adventurous cyclists who want to get away from the many summer tour buses in Alaska, try riding the Denali Highway, a 133-mile (222-kilometer) dirt road. (Note: The first 21 miles or 35 kilometers are paved). This route takes you through very remote country as you ride from Paxson to Cantwell, mostly biking above the tree line. Services are very limited, so you must be self-sufficient. You will pass a few lodges and campgrounds, and you can also camp on the public land beside the road; remember that this is bear country—be careful with your food! It's best to avoid doing this trip alone. Several companies offer organized cycling tours; for example, Adventure Cycling (phone (406) 721-1776) offers a 14-day, 450-mile (750-kilometer) camping trip from Anchorage that includes the Denali Highway and ends at Denali National Park and Preserve.

The mileposts on the Denali Highway begin at 0 in Paxson. Some of the highlights on your journey will include the Maclaren Summit at mile 36; the Valdez Creek Mine at mile 83 (thought to be the world's largest gold mine); the Watershed Divide at mile 95.6 (it's the dividing line for water running to the Cook Inlet or the Bering Sea); an exquisite view of Denali at mile 130. Several mountain bike trails and many blueberries will also be found along this wilderness route.

A view from the ferry, near Haines, Alaska

• **The Pacific Coast**
    This long tour, down the coast, all the way to California, is detailed in Chapter 11.

• **Anchorage-Fairbanks-Glenallen Triangle**
    This very challenging 900-mile (1,500-kilometer) trip will take you from Anchorage (via No. 3), north to Denali National Park and Preserve, and on to Fairbanks. Ride south on No. 2 and No. 4 to Gulkana Junction, and then bike southwest on the Glenn Highway (No. 1) back to Anchorage. This route offers spectacular scenery, and you will often find yourself on paved roads with a wide shoulder. Be forewarned, however, that winds can pose serious pedaling problems, particularly in the area of Isabell Pass on the section from Delta Junction to Paxson.

• **The Klondike Highway**
    Since the winds here are often from the south, it's best to ride this challenging 667-mile, (1110-kilometer) one-way route from Skagway to Dawson City. You will face very tough climbs as you cycle through the White Pass and the Chilkoot Pass on your route to Whitehorse, in Canada's Yukon Territory. Bike northwest on the Klondike Highway (No. 2) to your destination. The last section of this trip (between Whitehorse and Dawson City) will often find you riding without a good paved shoulder, but the traffic should be relatively light. Some areas offer few facilities, so this tour is most suitable for the self-sufficient camper.

• **Skagway-Whitehorse-Haines Triangle**
    With a little help from the Alaska Marine Highway, you will complete a challenging, spectacular 558-mile (930-kilometer) loop tour that begins and ends in Skagway. You will face very tough climbs as you cycle through the White Pass and the Chilkoot Pass to Whitehorse, in Canada's Yukon Territory. Ride west on the Alaska Highway (No. 1) to Haines Junction, and then bike southeast on the Haines Highway, through the Chilkat Pass, another tough climb, to Haines, a beautiful coastal town, with a tranquil, picturesque harbor and a background of snow-capped mountain peaks. Complete this magnificent loop tour by taking the ferry back to Skagway.

Alaska Contacts

Alaska Division of Tourism, P.O. Box 110801, Juneau, AK 99811; phone (907) 465-2010.
Alaska State Park Information, P.O. Box 107001, Anchorage, AK 95510-7001.
Denali National Park, P.O. Box 9, Denali Park, AK 99755; phone (907) 683-2294.
Juneau Freewheelers Bicycle Club, P.O. Box 34475, Juneau, AK 99803.
Kenai Fjords National Park, P.O. Box 1727, Seward, AK 99664; phone (907) 224-3175.
Log Cabin Visitor Center, 4th Avenue and F Street, Anchorage, AK; phone (907) 274-3531.
State Bicycle Coordinator, 3132 Channel Dr., Juneau, AK 99801-7898.

Chapter 10

Hawaii

The state of Hawaii is, generally, an alluring place of warmth and beauty. It's about 2,400 miles (4,000) kilometers southwest of the continental United States and consists of eight major volcanic islands and about 120 smaller ones; the islands are the summits of a great volcanic mountain range that stretches across the floor of the Pacific Ocean.

Hawaii is world famous for its tropical beauty and pleasant climate. Except in the mountains, the semitropical climate of Hawaii allows little seasonal variation in temperatures. For example, the average maximum and minimum temperatures in Honolulu can vary only a few degrees from January to July. This makes the state of Hawaii a pleasant, year-round cycling destination.

Three cycling tours (on three separate islands within the state) are detailed here, along with optional activities to do on each trip, including suggestions for other bicycle tours.

• 1. Around Hawaii
Distance: 235 miles/392 kilometers
Duration: 5–8 days
Rating: Moderate to Strenuous
Type: Loop Tour
Access: Transportation from one island to another is by air. Aloha Airlines (phone (808) 836-1111) and Hawaiian Airlines (phone (808) 537-5100) offer safe, fast, and extensive service.
Accommodations: Lodging facilities are available at Kailua-Kona, Hilo, and Waimea. Camping is available at Hookena, Kalopa State Recreation Area, and in Hawaii Volcanoes National Park.
Route Description: Hawaii is the largest of the chain of islands that make up the State of Hawaii; it's the easternmost island (and the southernmost point in the United States. To avoid confusing the island of Hawaii with the state, this island is often referred to as "The Big Island" or "The Orchid Island." Begin your trip at the resort area of Kailua-Kona, on the west coast; it's the center of the island's coffee industry and is also the host of the "World Triathlon Championship" each autumn.

Cycle south, past the Kona Coffee Mill and the Captain Cook Memorial, to Pu'uhonua o Honaunau National Historical Park (tikis mark this ancient place of sanctuary). Continue riding along the coast (on No. 11); the narrow road will take you past beaches, sugar-cane fields, coconut trees, and macadamia orchards. Ride around the southern tip of the island to Naalehu. Head northeast to Whittington Beach

Park and Punaluu Black Sand Beach Park, through a desert landscape of scrub brush and ferns. You will face a long, steep climb before reaching Hawaii Volcanoes National Park.

Bike to the rim of the Kilauea Crater, one of the world's most active volcanoes. Crater Rim Road encircles Kilauea Caldera, passing lava flows, rain forests, and craters. The Kilauea Iki Crater is a pond of molten lava, and the Thurston Lava Tube is part of a prehistoric tunnel of cooled lava. This loop road will take you to the Kilauea Visitor Center, Volcano Art Center, Jaggar Museum, Vuvekahuna Bluff (site of the Hawaiian Volcano Observatory), and the Kilauea Overlook. West of Kilauea is Mauna Loa, the world's largest volcano; a very demanding hiking trail leads to the summit, passing barren lava fields.

After exploring Hawaii Volcanoes National Park, ride northwest on No. 11 (Volcano Road) to Keaau and then north to Hilo, the island's capital city. While in the Hilo area, you might like to see such points of interest as Liliuokalani Gardens Park, Rainbow Falls (where a rainbow

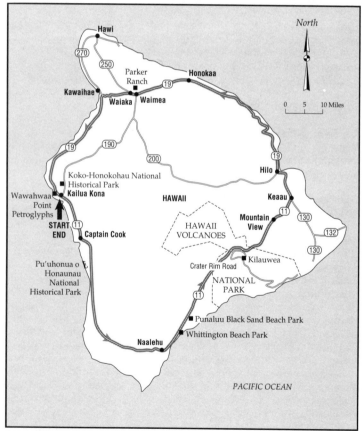

Around Hawaii

often appears in the falls' mist), Akaka Falls State Park (with two high waterfalls), Kaumana Caves (lava tubes), Boiling Pots, Nani Mau Gardens, Hawaii Tropical Botanical Gardens, and the Mauna Loa Macadamia Nut Plant.

Ride northwest, along the coast, where you will cross some one-lane bridges and pass lava rock beaches and several rugged hills. The scenery will change dramatically when you leave the coast and go west on No. 19 from Honokaa to Parker Ranch, oddly enough the largest privately owned cattle ranch in the country. Now you find yourself riding in vast, rolling ranch country.

Continue west on No. 19 to the coast. Bike southwest alongside the ocean, passing beautiful bays and inlets as you ride on the Queen Kaahumanu Highway to Wawahiwaa Point (where there are petroglyphs) and Kaloko Honokohau National Historic Park. You will then complete your loop tour by cycling south, back to Kailua-Kona.

This trip has it all: rolling highlands, mountains, lush forests, fields of orchids, cascading waterfalls, fiery volcanoes, white sand beaches, dense jungle trails, fields of lava, and groves of sugarcane.

Optional Activities

Take a dinner cruise aboard a Royal Polynesian canoe at Kailua-Kona.

Consider a hike to the summit of Mauna Loa, the world's largest volcano.

Arrange a helicopter tour of Hawaii Volcanoes National Park.

• **Cycle to Hawi**

At Walaka (on No. 19), cycle north through the Kohala Mountains to Hawi, the northernmost community on the island. Then follow the coast (on No. 270), cycling through the Pololu Valley, with its spectacular gorges and views of mountain summits. Ride south to Kawaihae, and then rejoin your previous route (on No. 19).

• **2. Southern Oahu**

Distance: 65 miles/108 kilometers
Duration: 2-3 days
Rating: Moderate/Strenuous
Type: Loop Tour
Access: The islands are connected by air. Both Aloha Airlines (phone (808) 836-1111) and Hawaiian Airlines (phone (808) 537-5100) offer flights.
Accommodations: Full facilities are available in Honolulu. Camping is available in Waimanalo Bay State Recreation Area.
Route Description: The best-known and most heavily populated of Hawaii's islands is Oahu, where you will find Honolulu, Waikiki Beach, Diamond Head, and Pearl Harbor. Oahu means "gathering place," and this island attracts the largest gathering of tourists.

This tour begins in Oahu's largest city, Honolulu. Visit such points of interest as Bishop Museum, Chinatown, Honolulu Academy of Arts, Iolani Palace State Monument, King Kamehameha's Statue, National Memorial Cemetery of the Pacific, Royal Mausoleum State Monument, State Capitol, U.S. Army Museum of Hawaii, Kawaiahao Church (Honolulu's oldest), Dole Cannery Square (where tours of the pineapple cannery are available),

Foster Botanic Garden, Paradise Park, Ala Moana Park, Kapiolani Park, Kewalo Basin, Diamond Head State Monument (a famous landmark that is actually an extinct volcanic crater), and Waikiki Beach.

After exploring the state's capital city, cycle east on No. 92 and on Kalakalia Avenue, along the coast, passing Diamond Head State Monument. Ride northeast on No. 72 to Koko Head Regional Park (a popular spot for scuba diving, swimming, and snorkeling, and site of Koko Crater, Koko Crater Botanical Garden, and Halona Blowhole). Cycle around Makapuu Point (a popular hang-gliding area) to Sea Life Park (with shows and lectures featuring sea lions, turtles, seals, and penguins), Waimanalo (a challenging area for surfing), and Olamana. Then bike west on No. 61 to Pali Tunnels and Pali Lookout. This is a very challenging section of the route because of the possibility of strong head winds and the certainty of mountainous terrain. You will climb through a gap to a panoramic view of the valley and coast. Continue to the National Memorial Cemetery of the Pacific, which offers an excellent view of the city of Honolulu. The graves of service personnel are arranged in concentric circles on the floor of the crater of an extinct volcano.

The Pali Highway will become Bishop Street as you ride toward Honolulu Harbor. Bike northwest on No. 92 and No. 99 to Pearl Harbor, where you can visit Submarine Memorial Park and the *Arizona* Memorial Visitor Center. Offshore is the U.S.S. *Arizona* Memorial, which is dedicated to all the service personnel who were killed during the attack on Pearl Harbor on Dec. 7, 1941; most are still entombed in the sunken ship.

After your visit to Pearl Harbor, return to Honolulu. This loop tour of southern Oahu has taken you to many of the state's most popular attractions.

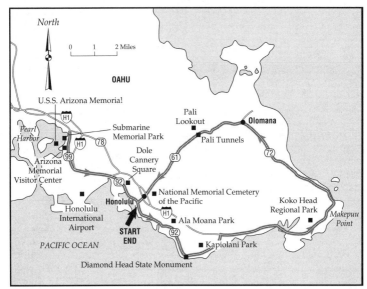

Southern Oahu

Along the way you've probably noticed that surfing is a very popular activity; however, strong currents and turbulent water can make surfing very dangerous, so be cautious. Many of the beaches post signs describing surfing conditions; when conditions are dangerous, a red flag is displayed on the beach.

Optional Activities

The ocean offers almost endless possibilities.

Enjoy snorkeling, swimming, surfing, sailing, or scuba diving.

Take a boat tour of Pearl Harbor and (or a guided tour of the island).

Go deep-sea fishing for marlin or tuna.

If you get sea sick, go hang gliding at Makapuu Point or take a horseback ride in the Koko Crater.

• Cycle Northern Oahu

Instead of riding southwest on the Pali Highway (No. 61), continue northeast (on No. 83) along the eastern coast. Sacred Falls State Park, near Hauula, offers a grueling 2-mile (3-kilometer) hiking trail up a rocky mountain ravine. Further north, Laie is the site of the Mormon Temple, the Hawaii campus of Brigham Young University, and the Polynesian Cultural Center, where the heritage of the South Seas is preserved and shared. After cycling around the northern tip of the island, you will arrive at Waimea Falls Park, where kahiko hula shows, cliff-diving demonstrations, and guided tours are available. Continue riding southwest to Haleiwa, a popular resort area, and a good place from which to charter a boat for deep-sea fishing. Ride southeast on No. 99 to Wahaiwa, inland on the Leilehua Plain, and a shopping center for

Honolulu, Hawaii, is a very popular tourist area.

surrounding villages). Then complete this extended loop tour by returning to Honolulu.

• 3. Northern Maui
Distance: 45 miles/75 kilometers
Duration: 1-2 days
Rating: Moderate
Type: One-way Tour
Access: Aloha Airlines (phone (808) 836-1111) and Hawaiian Airlines (phone (808) 537-5100) both provide flights from island to island.
Accommodations: Lodgings are available at Kahana Beach, Kaanapali Beach, Lahaina, and Kahului.
Route Description: A short flight will take you from Honolulu, on Oahu, or from Kailua-Kona, on Hawaii, to Kapalua, on Maui. Kapalua, near the northwest tip of the island, is considered to have one of the safest beaches on Maui for swimming, diving, and surfing.

Arguably the most picturesque of the Hawaiian Islands, Maui is often referred to as "The Valley Isle," and the island has several beautiful

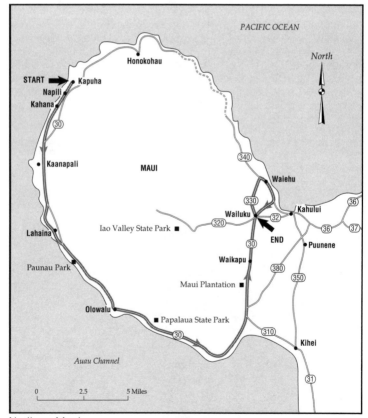

Northern Maui

resorts. Maui also has a strong agricultural base, which includes the raising of cattle and thoroughbred horses and such crops as sugarcane, pineapple, russet potatoes, and Maui onions.

As you cycle south from Kapalua to Napili Bay, Kahana, Kaanapali, and Lahaina, you can notice humpback whales frolicking off the coast. At Lahaina, you can visit the Lahaina Art Gallery, Lahaina Jodo Mission, Carthaginian II Floating Museum, Wo Hing Temple and Museum, Hale Paaho (originally used as a jail for drunken sailors), and Banyon Tree (which marks the center of town and is the largest on the islands).

Continue southeast on No. 30 from Lahaina to Paunau Park, Olowalu, Papalaua State Park, and Papawai Point. Then bike north on the Hondapilani Highway (No. 30) to the Maui Plantation (where samples of the Hawaiian Islands major crops are grown), Waikapu, and Wailuku (site of the Maui Historical Society Museum, with missionary-era furnishings and Hawaiian artifacts).

Ride west on the winding road from Wailuku to Iao Valley and Iao Valley State Park, riding through a densely forested area. This valley is known for unusual rock formations; some people say one looks like the profile of former President John F. Kennedy. Another is Iao Needle, which juts more than 1200 feet above the floor of Iao Valley.

Return to Wailuku, and then bike north on No. 330 to Waiehu. Cycle south, following the shoreline, to Kahului, this tour's destination, and site of another airport. Kahului offers helicopter tours of Maui's mountains, valleys, waterfalls, and secluded coves; you can even get a video of your actual flight. The spectacular scenery of northern Maui makes this tour on Hawaii's second largest island very memorable.

Optional Activities
• Enjoy an airplane tour of Maui's remote beauty, a deep-sea fishing charter from Lahaina, a whale-watching expedition, or go surfing at Kapalua or at Kanaha Beach Park.

• **Cycle to Surf**
Instead of cycling north on No. 30 to Kahului, continue southeast on No. 31 (the Pilani Highway) to Kihei, and then take the Kihei Road, along the coast, where you will pass several excellent surfing areas. Return on No. 31 from Wailea to Kihei, and then complete your route by biking to Kahului.

• **Explore Haleakala National Park**
Cycle from Kahului (on No. 37) to Pukalani. Then bike southeast on No. 377 and No. 378 into the park. Haleakala is an enormous dormant volcano. The Kalahaku Overlook, 2 miles (4 kilometers) below the Visitor Center, offers panoramic views of the crater's cinder cones. Several interesting hiking trails are available in Haleakala National Park; they range from 14-mile day hikes that include steep climbs to easy strolls to scenic waterfalls.

• **Cycle to Hana**
This 95-mile (158-kilometer) return trip takes you along the coast (on No. 32, No. 36, and No. 360) from Kahului to Hana and back. The

entire road is paved, but be prepared for narrow, twisty, hilly sections as you follow the rugged coastline. You will pass tiny fishing villages, ravines, bamboo forests, scenic gorges, and majestic waterfalls. The Wailua Valley Lookout, 34 miles (56 kilometers) east of Kahului, offers a panoramic view of the valley of banana groves far below.

County of Hawaii, Department of Parks and Recreation, 25 Aupuni Street, Hilo, HI 96720; phone (808) 961-8311.

Division of State Parks, Department of Land and Natural Resources, 1151 Punchbowl Street, Honolulu, HI 96813; phone (808) 548-0300.

Hawaii Bicycling League, P.O. Box 4403, Honolulu, HI 96812; phone (808) 735-5756.

Hawaii Visitors Bureau, 2270 Kalakaua Avenue, Suite 700, Honolulu, HI 96815; phone (808) 923-1811; for a surf report, phone (808) 836-1952.

Maui Visitors Bureau, 250 Alamaha Street, Kahului, Maui, HI 96732; phone (808) 871-8691.

State Bicycle Coordinator, Hawaii Department of Transportation, 869 Punchbowl Street, Honolulu, HI 96813.

Superintendent, Hawaii Volcanoes National Park, P.O. Box 52, Hawaii Volcanoes National Park, HI 96718; phone (808) 967-7311.

Chapter 11

Long Tours of the U.S.A.

Y ou will find a list in the Appendix of several commercial bicycle tour operators who offer organized tours in the U.S.A., but four specific contacts will be given here.

"The Pacific-Atlantic Cycling Tour" (PAC) does a rapid 140-mile (230-kilometer) per day journey across America each summer. Lon Haldeman began this tour in 1985 because he liked rapid transcontinentals and reasoned that "one thing all cyclists should do before they die is cross America in three weeks or less to appreciate what it is to ride." The tour varies each year (one year going from Huntington Beach, California, to Tybee Island, Georgia, and another year beginning in Seattle, Washington, and ending in Williamsburg, Virginia). For more information, contact: PAC Tour, P.O. Box 303, Sharon, WI 53585.

"Pedal for Power," another organized tour group, became John Terosian's method for raising money for cycling education and safety and, at the same time, a way to dip his bicycle wheels in a couple of oceans each year. This ride for charity takes cyclists from Maine to Florida each autumn. For more information, contact: Pedal for Power, 190 West Ostend Street, No. 120, Baltimore, MD 21230-3731; phone 1-800-288-BIKE.

Another charity fund-raising tour across the United States is "The Southern Cross Bicycle Classic" (which, in 1996 went from Anaheim, California, to Orlando, Florida—from Disneyland to Disney World); in fact, Tim Kneeland and Associates organize several group cycling fundraisers of various distances each year. For more information, contact: Tim Kneeland and Associates, Inc., 200 Lake Washington Blvd., Suite 101, Seattle, WA 98122-6540; phone (206) 322-4102 or 1-800-433-0528; FAX (206) 322-4509.

Adventure Cycling offers a 93-day, trans-America, self-supported camping tour and several other organized group tours. Maps can be purchased for several specific bicycling routes, including the "TransAmerica Bicycle Route," "California to Florida Bicycle Route," and the "Great Parks Grand Tour." For more information, contact: Adventure Cycling Association, P.O. Box 8308, Missoula, Montana 59807; phone 1-800-721-8719; FAX 1-800-721-8719.

This book will also provide you with specific routes for longer tours, which can be enjoyed by the individual cyclist or a group. Four specific long tours will be detailed in this chapter: "The Pacific Coast Tour—Alaska to California," "Coast-to-Coast Route—Washington to Maine," "The Atlantic Coast Tour—Maine to Florida," and "My Route from Canada to South Carolina."

• 1. The Pacific Coast Tour—Alaska to California

This magnificent "trip of a lifetime" adventure takes you from Anchorage, Alaska, to Big Sur, California. The route is very challenging but has spectacular scenery. Be prepared for rain and fog as you cycle along the coast; however, winds will be more favorable by cycling south into California.

Anchorage to Vancouver

Distance: 2,173 miles/3,622 kilometers (shorter option: 1,715 miles/2,858 kilometers)

Your adventure begins in Anchorage, Alaska's largest city, where you will find about 180 miles (300 kilometers) of bicycle trails. Bike northeast to Eagle River (on bicycle trails) and Palmer, through a wilderness that can offer you sightings of bald eagles, bear, and moose. Take the Glenn Highway (No. 1) east, following the Matanuska River, and ride through the Tahneta Pass and on to Glenallen. The summer traffic can be quite heavy, and much of this section does not have a wide paved shoulder, so be cautious.

Continue riding on No. 1 to Tok, and then bike southeast on No. 2 (the Alaska Highway) into Canada's Yukon Territory, where the Alaska Highway becomes No. 1. Ride on No. 1 to Whitehorse, founded during the Gold Rush, and almost to Watson Lake, site of a famous collection of town signs. Turn south on No. 37 (Stewart Cassiar Highway), continuing to ride through relatively isolated wilderness in Canada's north, as you cycle through northern British Columbia. Join the Yellowhead Highway (No. 16) and ride east to Prince George. Then ride south on No. 97 to Cache Creek and south on No. 1 (the Trans-Canada Highway) to Hope. Bike west on No. 7 to Vancouver.

Option: A certainly less taxing route for the cyclist is to use the Alaska Marine Highway for part of this section. Cycle to Whitehorse, as above, but then ride southwest on No. 2, through the Chilkoot Pass and the White Pass, to Skagway, Alaska. Skagway is the northern terminus of the Alaska Marine Highway, and you can take a ferry and cruise the Inside Passage down the Alaskan coast. You can even stop at Juneau, Alaska's capital, or at such picturesque towns as Sitka, Petersburg, Wrangell, and Ketchikan. Disembark at Prince Rupert (in northern British Columbia, Canada) and then cycle east on No. 16 to Prince George. Complete this section of the trip by riding south on No. 97 and No. 1 to Hope and then east on No. 7 to Vancouver (as described above). This option saves you about 460 miles (765 kilometers) of cycling.

Vancouver to Astoria

Distance: 270 miles/450 kilometers

Take a ferry from Tsawwassen (south of Vancouver) to Swartz Bay, on Vancouver Island. If you wish, you can explore several of the Gulf Islands (detailed in my book, *Cycling Canada*) or several of the San Juan Islands, described in this book under the tours of the State of Washington, before continuing this specific route.

Cycle from Swartz Bay to Victoria, and then take a ferry back into the United States, arriving at Port Angeles, Washington. Port Angeles provides access into Olympia National Park. Take No. 101 from

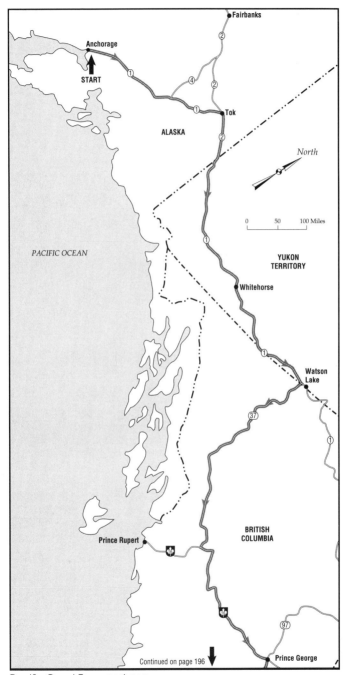

Pacific Coast Tour, part one

Continued on page 196

Continued from page 195

Pacific Coast Tour, part two

Port Angeles, around a section of Olympia National Park, and then ride south, along the coast, passing scenic vistas and sandy beaches. You will ride through the twin cities of Hoquiam and Aberdeen (which share the well protected Grays Harbor), Raymond, Chinook (where Lewis and Clark camped on their famous transcontinental journey) and Fort Columbia State Park (a military post during the Spanish-American War) before you cross the Columbia River into Astoria, Oregon.

Astoria to Crescent City
Distance: 370 miles/617 kilometers

Astoria is the northernmost Oregon city on scenic No. 101. You will enjoy stunning coastal panoramas, dense forested areas, sculpted sand dunes, rugged promontories, and tranquil fishing villages as you cycle south along the coastline. Along the way you'll see Tillamook, Lincoln City (with 7.5 miles/12 kilometers of public beach), Newport (at the entrance to Yaquina Bay), Waldport, Florence, the Oregon Dunes National Recreation Area (an extensive area of high sand dunes), North Bend (on a peninsula jutting into Coos Bay), Bandon (where the Oldtown Harbor District houses art galleries and craft shops), Port Orford, Gold Beach, and Brookings, known as "The Banana Belt of Oregon" because of its mild temperatures.

An optional route at Tillamook is to continue along the coast, to explore three area capes, by taking Three Cape Road to Cape Meares, Cape Lookout, and Cape Kiwanda State Park (and then rejoin No. 101).

Your trip through Oregon will include riding through two tunnels. Flashing signs, activated by the cyclist before entering, warn motorists that a bicycle is in the tunnel. But these tunnels are still hazardous. Before entering, turn on your bicycle light, remove your sunglasses, wait for a lull in the traffic, and then ride through as quickly as possible.

After cycling along the Oregon coastline, you will cross the border and continue into California.

Crescent City to Big Sur
Distance: 530 miles/883 kilometers

Ride south on No. 101 through Redwood National Park, where more than 100 miles (170 kilometers) of trails provide access to magnificent redwood groves. You can take the Klamath Beach Road exit to Coastal Drive, 8 miles (13 kilometers) of spectacular coastal scenery, with vistas of rock promontories, sea-lion colonies, whales, seabirds, and redwood forests.

You will exit Redwood National Park near Orick and continue south to Arcata, Eureka (on Humboldt Bay), Ferndale, Scotia (site of the world's largest sawmill), Humboldt Redwood State Park, the "Avenue of Giants" (redwoods), Garberville, and Leggett. Here you will take the coastal route (No. 1), climbing to the top of the Leggett Pass before descending along the coastal bluffs to Fort Bragg and Mendocino. Traffic on No. 1 is usually light, but there are several steep sections and lonely stretches of road etched into the cliffs.

Continue south through Little River and Gualala to the deep coastal gulches in Salt Point State Park. At Point Reyes National Seashore, 70 species of mammals and 300 species of birds inhabit a wilderness of beaches, bays, dunes, and forests.

Ride over Mount Tamalpais and the Marin Headlands to the skyline of San Francisco. Follow the bike route signs as you cross the Golden Gate Bridge and cycle along San Francisco's waterfront. While in this fascinating city, you can choose to see such points of interest as Golden Gate Park, Lincoln Park, Presidio, Fisherman's Wharf, Japan Center, Chinatown, Telegraph Hill, Lombard Street (thought to be "the crookedest street in the world"), and Alcatraz Island.

The Oceanfront Promenade Bike Path parallels Park Road, and you will eventually find a broad bicycle lane when you get to No. 35. Ride south to Daly City, rejoin No. 1, and follow the coastline to Santa Cruz (with its beach boardwalk, popular surfing waters, and Natural Bridge State Park). Cycle around Monterey Bay to Watsonville and Monterey (primarily on bike paths). Monterey was made famous by writer John Steinbeck (*Cannery Row*); it was once considered to be the "Sardine Capital of the World."

Bicycle paths follow some of the most picturesque shoreline, including Pacific Grove and the exquisite Seventeen Mile Drive to Carmel (passing windswept cypress trees and such points of interest as Seal Rock, Cypress Point, Lone Cypress, and the renowned Pebble Beach Golf Course). The picturesque village of Carmel is home to many artists, and local shops and galleries display their works.

As you bike from Carmel to your destination of Big Sur, you will pass Point Lobos State Reserve (which contains groves of the nearly extinct Monterey Cypress and is a sanctuary for seals and sea otters). This section of No. 1 is often winding and narrow, with steeply rolling terrain.

Writer Robert Louis Stevenson said that the coastline between Monterey and Big Sur was "the greatest meeting of land and water in the world;" it therefore provides a suitable climax to this journey along the Pacific coast.

• 2. Coast to Coast Route—Washington to Maine

To truly "cycle the U.S.A.," you should ride across this vast land from coast to coast. Winds will be more favorable if you ride from west to east—from the Pacific Ocean to the Atlantic Ocean. There are, of course, several possible cycling routes that will take you from ocean to ocean, but one of the best takes you across the northern states, biking from Anacortes, Washington, to Acadia National Park, in Maine.

Anacortes to Crookston
Distance: 1,560 miles/2,600 kilometers

This transcontinental journey begins at Anacortes, on Washington's west coast. You can dip your wheels in the Pacific Ocean before heading east on No. 20 and cycling through magnificent North Cascades National Park, home to black bear, grizzly bear, deer, wolverine, mountain goat, and cougar. You will find many trails for hiking and mountain biking. You will face some very tough climbs as you continue east on scenic No. 20, across the state, through the mountainous terrain. At Newport, you will begin riding on No. 2, across Idaho (to Sandpoint and Bonners Ferry) and into Montana, where you will take the spectacular Going-to-the-Sun Highway through the incredible grandeur of Glacier National Park (detailed in this book in tours of Montana). Take No. 89 southeast, return

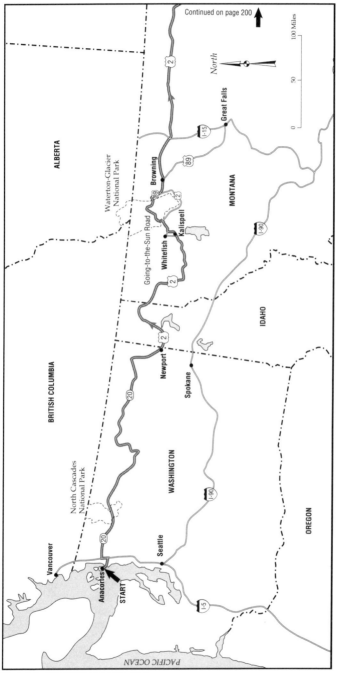

Continued on page 200

Coast to Coast Tour, map one

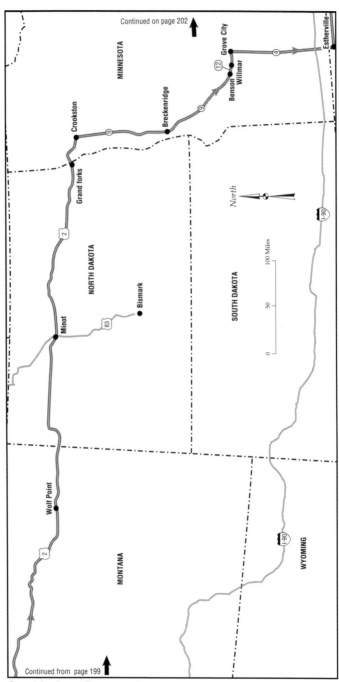

Coast to Coast Tour, map two

National Geopgraphic once stated that Lake Couer d'Alene, Idaho, was "one of the five most beautiful lakes in the world."

to No. 2, and continue on it as you cycle east across Montana, North Dakota, and on to Crookston, Minnesota.

Crookston to Greenville
Distance: 1,356 miles/2,260 kilometers

Ride south on No. 9 to Benson, and then ride southeast on No. 12 to Grove City. You'll be riding on relatively quiet roads in Minnesota, through many small towns, so careful planning will be necessary if you are not camping. Take No. 4 south through the remainder of the state and into Iowa (to Estherville). Ride No. 9 east and No. 69 south to Des Moines. Then cycle southeast on No. 163 to Oskaloosa and east on No. 92 to Muscatine (on the bank of the Mississippi River). Cross into Illinois (to Illinois City). Once again, you'll be on relatively quiet rural roads, visiting many small communities, as you bike south on No. 9 to Joy and east on No. 17 to Kanakee. Continue on No. 17 and then on No. 114 to the state border. Ride east on No. 10 to Warsaw, Indiana, then take No. 30 to Columbia City. Head northeast on No. 205 to Auburn. Take No. 8 to the state border and No. 18 to Brunersburg, Ohio. Cycle southeast on No. 15 to Defiance and east on No. 281 to Bradner. Bike No. 6 east to Fremont and No. 20 east to Monroeville. Take No. 18 east to Akron and No. 59 northeast to Ravenna. Near Ravenna, you will cycle on No. 88 northeast to the state border, and you will then take No. 358 east to Greenville, Pennsylvania.

Greenville to Alburg
Distance: 612 miles/1020 kilometers

Ride north on No. 18 to Albion and east on No. 6N to Edinboro. Ride east on No. 6 to Corry and on No. 957 to Russell. Then bike north on No. 62 and cross into the state of New York. The terrain will be very

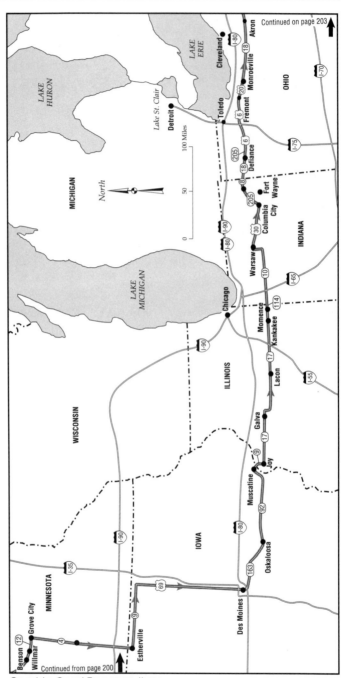

Continued on page 203

Continued from page 200

Coast to Coast Tour, map three

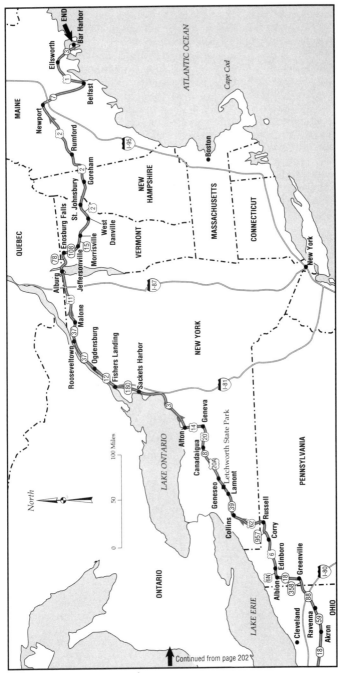

Coast to Coast Tour, map four

hilly as you ride northeast on No. 62 to Collins, and then ride east on No. 39 to Lamont. Take a slight detour to Portageville, where you will enter Letchworth State Park, an oasis of scenic roads and bicycle trails. The towering walls of the Genesee River Gorge offer wonderful views of the area, including three waterfalls. After exploring the park, continue north to Geneseo. Take No. 20A and No. 5 northeast to Canandaigua and No. 20 east to Geneva. Cycle north on No. 14 to Alton. Then bike on No. 104, No. 104A, No. 104B, and No. 3, along the shore of Lake Ontario, to Sackets Harbor. Ride northeast on No. 180 almost to the Canadian border. Cycle northeast on No. 12 and No. 37 (following along the St. Lawrence River) to Rooseveltown. Continue east on No. 37, No. 122, and No. 11 across northern New York state, through the foothills of the Adirondacks; this route provides a wide paved shoulder as you cycle to the Vermont border.

A side trip worth considering in this area is to go south on No. 30, east on No. 3, northeast on No. 86 and No. 9N, and north on No. 9. This detour allows you to drink in the beauty of the Adirondacks, including the towering Whiteface Mountain and the resort towns of Saranac Lake and Lake Placid.

At Rouses Point, cross by bridge over Lake Champlain (the largest body of fresh water east of the Great Lakes). You are now entering the state of Vermont. Ride southeast to Alburg on No. 2.

Alburg to Acadia National Park
Distance: 440 miles/740 kilometers
Take No. 78 east to Swanton and Enosburg Falls. Then go south on No. 108 to Jeffersonville and southeast on No. 15 to Morrisville. You are now in a very popular Vermont skiing area that includes Smugglers Notch and Stowe (Mount Mansfield); many trails in this area are shared by skiers, hikers, equestrians, and mountain bikers. You will face some tough climbs as you cycle through Vermont's Green Mountains, with the toughest ones being on No. 15 between Hardwick and Walden.

Continue southeast on No. 15 until you meet No. 2, and then ride east on No. 2 to St. Johnsbury, where you will experience the ecstasy of a long descent into the town. Take No. 2 to the state border and into New Hampshire. You will bike through a particularly picturesque area, viewing the Presidential Range in the White Mountains as you ride to Randolph and descend into the Mount Washington Valley at Gorham, in the heart of the White Mountains National Forest and close to the Appalachian Trail and the Great Gulf Wilderness Area.

From Gorham, New Hampshire, you will continue east on No. 2, crossing into the state of Maine, and ride to Newport. The terrain will remain hilly as you bike south on No. 7 to Belfast and east on No. 1 to Ellsworth. Finally, cycle south on No. 3 to Bar Harbor, where you will find the entrance to Acadia National Park,(your destination. You can again dip your tires in the ocean, this time the Atlantic.

Acadia National Park is a natural destination for cyclists, offering paved seashore roads and a network of gravel carriage paths that meander through lush forests, around mountains and lakes, and along the Atlantic Ocean's shoreline.

Cycling is a popular activity on the paved paths and the sandy beaches of Hilton Head Island, South Carolina.

• 3. The Atlantic Coast Tour—Maine to Florida

This cycling adventure, along the coastline of the Atlantic Ocean, will take you from the northeast corner of the U.S.A., at Bar Harbor, Maine to the most southerly state, Florida, and to your specific destination of St. Augustine. You may face some bothersome head winds at times, but this route will take you through the hillier, cooler, wetter north country first as you ride toward the flatter, warmer, drier south. Don't forget your rain gear on this coastal tour.

Bar Harbor to Hartford
Distance: 450 miles/750 kilometers

Your coastal journey begins in Bar Harbor, Maine, next to Acadia National Park. Activities in the park include whale-watching, sunbathing, sailing aboard a windjammer, partaking in a lobster clambake, and exploring the rugged coastline and lobster ports.

Ride north on No. 3 and southwest on No. 1 as you bike through the state of Maine. You can face heavy summer traffic, sometimes without a paved shoulder, so be careful. Cross the state border into New Hampshire, and ride on No. 1A, along the coast, past several state parks. Bike southwest on No. 111 to North Hampton, Exeter, Kingston, and Nashua. Continue south on No. 111 into Massachusetts (to Ayer), and then take No. 110 southwest to Worcester and No. 12 south to Oxford. Head south on No. 12 into Connecticut (at Putnam). Go southwest on No. 44 to Hartford, Connecticut's state capital, which was once the home of such literary figures as Harriet Beecher Stowe (*Uncle Tom's Cabin*) and Mark Twain (*The Adventures of Tom Sawyer*).

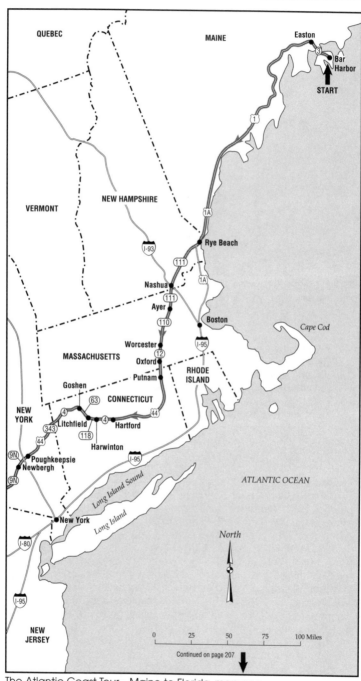

The Atlantic Coast Tour—Maine to Florida, map one

Continued on page 207

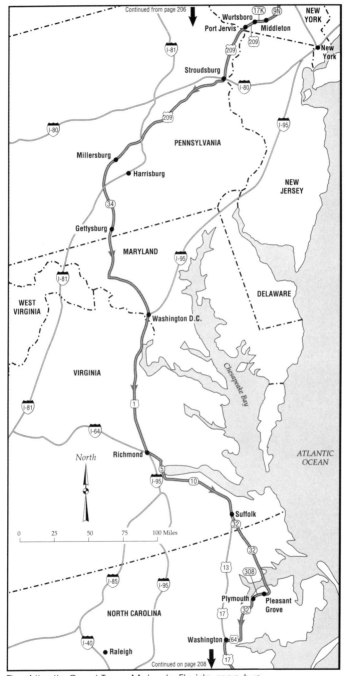

The Atlantic Coast Tour—Maine to Florida, map two

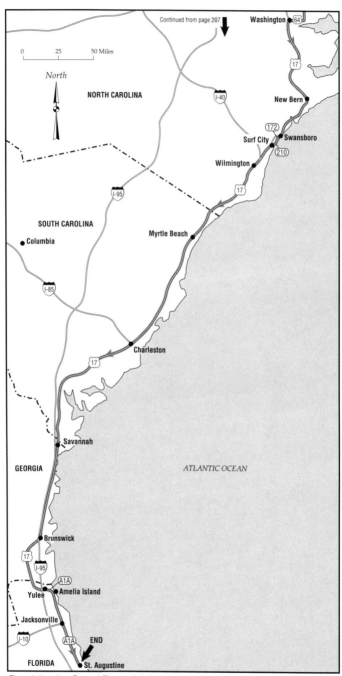

The Atlantic Coast Tour—Maine to Florida, map three

Hartford to Richmond
Distance: 690 miles/1150 kilometers

Leaving Hartford, take No. 4 and No. 118 northwest to Litchfield, (the birthplace of author Harriet Beecher Stowe and No. 63 north to Goshen. You will face some tough climbs as you continue west on No. 4 to the New York state border, where you ride west on No. 343 and No. 44 to Poughkeepsie. Cross the Hudson River here, and then cycle south on No. 9W to Newburgh. Ride west on No. 17K and southwest on No. 211 to Middletown. Bike south to No. 6, and then ride west on No. 6 to Port Jervis. Continue southwest on No. 6 to Milford, Pennsylvania. Ride southwest on No. 209, along the Delaware Water Gap National Recreation Area, to Stroudsburg, where you can visit the Quiet Valley Living Historical Farm, a Pennsylvania German farm that dates from 1765. Bike south to Scioto, and then ride southwest on No. 209 to Millersburg, on the Susquehanna River. Take the ferry across the river to Liverpool, and then ride, through the hilly terrain, south on No. 34 to Gettysburg, the site of Gettysburg National Military Park, where one of the most important and hotly contested battles of the Civil War took place. Ride south on No. 97, through Maryland, to Washington, D.C., where you will follow urban bike paths through the city and along the Potomac River to Mount Vernon, Virginia. (Washington's attractions have been discussed in the tours of the District of Columbia, found in Chapter 6). Join up with No. 1 and follow it south to Fredericksburg, site of the Fredericksburg National Military Park, and Richmond, the state capital. The traffic will be heavy in this area, and the terrain is hilly, so be careful. Richmond is the site of several interesting attractions, including the Museum of the Confederacy, Virginia Aviation Museum, the Poe Museum, and Richmond National Battlefield Park, which preserves the struggle for possession of the Confederate capital during the Civil War.

Richmond to Wilmington
Distance: 360 miles/600 kilometers

Bike southeast on No. 5 and No. 10 to Suffolk. Ride south on No. 13 and No. 32 to the North Carolina border. Continue riding south on No. 32 to Sunbury, Edenton, and across Albermarle Sound to Pleasant Grove. Take No. 308 west to Plymouth and No. 32 and No. 264 southwest to Washington. Cycle south on No. 17 to New Bern and Maysville. Bike southeast to Swansboro, and then take No. 172 and No. 210 out onto the peninsula. Ride southwest to Surf City, and then ride north to rejoin No. 17, which takes you (southwest) to Wilmington. Located on the Cape Fear River, Wilmington is the location of the U.S.S. *North Carolina* Battleship Memorial and the Wilmington Railroad Museum. You might enjoy cycling the 5-mile (8-kilometers) route around Greenfield Lake, where the gardens are particularly beautiful from February to April (azaleas; camellias; roses; cypress trees).

Wilmington to St. Augustine
Distance: 636 miles/1060 kilometers

The traffic can be heavy as you continue southwest on No. 17 into South Carolina, where you will ride to North Myrtle Beach, Myrtle Beach (a very popular resort area), Myrtle Beach State Park, Murrells

Inlet, Huntington Beach State Park, Georgetown, Charleston, and Gardens Corner. Bike south on No. 21 to Beaufort and southwest on No. 170, rejoining No. 17 near the Georgia state border.

An interesting side trip in this area is to cycle southeast on No. 278 out onto Hilton Head Island, a resort area where you will find many miles of flat, paved bicycle paths for your enjoyment.

Follow No. 17, which keeps you close to the coastline, as you cycle south through Georgia. Then cross the Florida state border and ride on No. 17 to Yulee. Bike east on No. A1A to Amelia Island. Continue to follow No. A1A as you now cycle southeast, along the coast, through Jacksonville, and on to your destination of St. Augustine, where you will find magnificent beaches for your rest and recuperation.

From north to south, you've covered a wide range of terrain—from the challenging hills of Maine, Massachusetts, and Virginia to the grueling mountainous terrain of Connecticut and Pennsylvania and, finally, to the flatter landscape of South Carolina, Georgia, and Florida.

• 4. My Route from Canada to South Carolina

My latest long tour in the U.S.A. actually began at my home, in southern Ontario, Canada, not far from New York state, and ended in South Carolina. Maintaining the same pace, I would have been to Florida in another four days. I covered about 1,000 miles (1,650 kilometers) in 12 days, averaging just more than 80 miles (130 kilometers) per day. This is perhaps a little too quick a pace for enjoying all the sights along the way, but of course you can set your own pace.

One of the purposes for my particular trip was, of course, to test a specific route for other cyclists—and to be able to share that tour with you. Another motive was the sheer pleasure I derive from my cycling expeditions!

This particular route could certainly begin with a tour of more of Canada, but I will just briefly mention two convenient ways to get from southern Ontario to New York (via the Watertown area); one route is to cycle on No. 2 to Gananoque, where you will find a wonderful paved bike path (the Thousand Islands Bikeway) that will take you right to the Ivy Lea Bridge (which takes you to New York state); the other interesting route is to ride on No. 2 to Kingston, take the ferry to Wolfe Island, cycle across the island, and take the ferry into New York state (at Cape Vincent). The route to South Carolina will begin from the Canadian border.

The Canadian Border to Williamsport
Distance: 185 miles/309 kilometers

If you begin at the Ivy Lea Bridge, take No. 180 southwest to Limerick (just northwest of Watertown). If you begin at Cape Vincent, cycle southeast on No. 12 E to Limerick. Bike south to No. 3, and then bike southwest on No. 3 to Mexico, Fulton, Hannibal and Walton, riding near the southern shore of Lake Ontario; the terrain is hilly, and most of this route has a wide paved shoulder. Bike south on No. 14 to Geneva and Watkins Glen; this is a pleasant cycling area, and you will pass many vineyards and small wineries in the resort-rich Finger Lakes Region. Continue south on No. 14, crossing into Pennsylvania, and cycling to

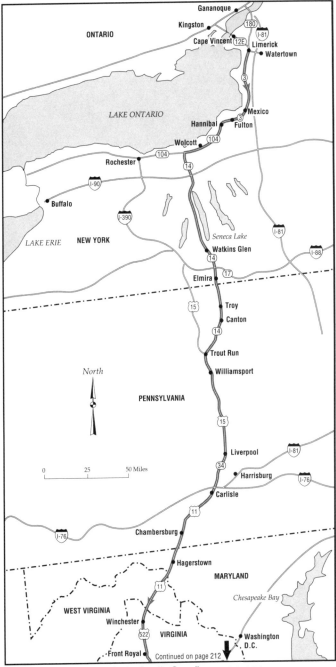

My Route from Canada to South Carolina, map one

Continued on page 212

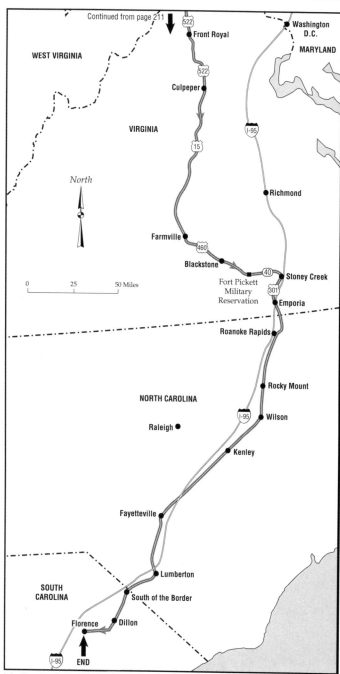

My Route from Canada to South Carolina, map two

Trout Run. There is about a 25-mile (42-kilometer) stretch here (from Canton to Trout Run) that is basically all downhill (if cycling south). At Trout Run, take No. 15 south to Williamsport, site of the annual Little League World Series.

I am going to digress a little here to give an example of the wonderful people that you can meet while touring. When I reached Trout Run by 2 p.m., I knew that my planned stop in Williamsport (about 15 miles or 25 kilometers further) would soon be realized. A severe storm suddenly erupted, however, while I was having a drink. Two older gentlemen with an enclosed truck offered me a lift. As a cyclist, I would normally say no, but because I was so close to my destination and because of the severity of the storm (complete with flash flooding and hail!), I accepted. These guys turned out to be genuinely friendly and very kind; they even recommended a motel and a restaurant and drove me right to this destination. In my haste to get my bicycle out of the truck, I forgot my helmet. Fortunately, the men found the helmet and returned it. Of course, they wouldn't even accept any gas money for their trouble. All I can do is share this anecdote and express my thanks to them again.

Williamsport to Emporia
Distance: 478 miles/797 kilometers

You will face a very tough 3-mile (5-kilometer) climb out of Williamsport (to a beautiful scenic outlook), and you will face several more climbs as you cycle through the mountainous terrain of Pennsylvania to Carlisle. Ride south on No. 15 to just below Liverpool; then leave this rather busy road for the quieter (but still very hilly!) No. 34, and ride southwest to Carlisle. The terrain will be gentler as you cycle southwest on No. 11 through the remainder of the state. Continue on No. 11 as you bike through a section of Maryland, West Virginia, and on into Virginia.

One of the many wine distilleries to be found in New York's Finger Lakes Region (this one is the Fox Run Vineyards).

Leave No. 11 at Winchester, and cycle south on No. 522 to Front Royal and Culpepper. You will face some very tough climbs between Front Royal and Culpepper (including a climb of almost 6 miles or 10 kilometers out of Front Royal), as you are biking very close to Virginia's Skyline Drive, which takes you through mountainous terrain to Shenandoah National Park and the Blue Ridge Parkway. The cycling will become less strenuous as you ride southwest on No. 15 from Culpepper to Farmville. Then you will ride on relatively flat terrain southeast on No. 460 to Blackstone and on No. 40 across the Fort Picket Military Reservation, where signs warn "Tank Crossing," to Stony Creek. Ride south on No. 301 to Emporia, as you ride parallel to No. 95 (the freeway).

Emporia to Florence
Distance: 256 miles/427 kilometers
You will ride south on No. 301 for the remainder of this trip. The paved shoulder disappears at times, but it's there most of the way. Be cautious, as the shoulder is sometimes littered with pieces of rubber tire, screws, nails, glass, and other debris.

Cross the border into North Carolina, and ride southwest on No. 301 to Rocky Mount, Wilson, Kenly, Selma, Smithfield, Benson, Dunn, Fayetteville, Lumberton, and Rowland. Continue south on No. 301 into South Carolina, and cycle to Florence, the destination.

I chose part of this particular route to avoid the coast because there was a hurricane problem at the time of this trip and that proved a prudent move, indeed. This route also avoided the heavy traffic that is often found in the Fredericksburg-Richmond-Petersburg area of Virginia and in the Wilmington area of North Carolina. In Florence, I caught a lift back to Canada.

Continue to Florida?

If you were to take the route just described, you could easily continue the trip on into Florida. Here are two suggested routes to Florida:

1. Continue south on No. 301 and No. 15 from Florence to Walterboro. Bike southeast on No. 303 to Green Pond. Cycle southwest on No. 17 to Gardens Corner. Continue on the same route to Florida that has been detailed in "The Atlantic Coast Tour."

2. Exit the No. 301 before Florence, at Lumberton, North Carolina. Then cycle southwest on No. 41 to Lake View, South Carolina. Head southeast on No. 9 to North Myrtle Beach, and then join up with the same route to Florida that was detailed in "The Atlantic Coast Tour."

Cycle North?

If you were to cycle from the southern states to Canada on this specific route, you would probably find favorable winds as you ride north. You would have the flatter terrain at the beginning of your journey and face the mountains later on; one of the toughest uphill sections would be a 25-mile (42-kilometer) stretch from Trout Run to Canton, Pennsylvania.

Appendix

1. Addresses

American Hiking Society, P.O. Box 20160, Washington, D.C.
20041-2160; phone (301) 565-6704; FAX (301) 565-6714.

American Trails, P.O. Box 200787, Denver, CO 80220; phone
(303) 321-6601; FAX (303) 321-6864; dedicated to lobbying for the
common interest of all trail users.

Bicycle Institute of America, 1506 21st Street, N.W., Suite 200,
Washington, D.C. 20036; phone 202-463-6622; promotes bicycling
in the United States.

Canadian Cycling Association, 1600 Naismith Drive, Gloucester, Ont.
K1B 5N4; phone (613) 748-5629.

Concerned Off-Road Bicycle Association (CORBA), 15236 Victory
Blvd., Box 149, Van Nuys, CA 91411; phone (818) 991-6626.

Hosteling International, 733 15th Street Northwest, Suite 840,
Washington, DC 20005; phone (202) 783-6161

International Mountain Bicycling Association (IMBA), P.O. Box 7578,
Boulder, CO 80306; phone (303) 545-9011; FAX (303) 545-9026.

League of American Bicyclists (L.A.B.), 190 West Ostend Street, Suite
120, Baltimore, MD 21203; phone (301) 539-3399 or 1-800-288-BIKE;
FAX (410) 539-3496.

National Bicycle Tour Directors Association (NBTDA), c/o Jim Jeske,
4737 Sunnyview Cresc., St. Louis, MO 63128; provides information
about week-long tours available in the United States.

National Off-Road Bicycling Association (NORBA), 1750 E. Boulder
Street, Colorado Springs, CO 80909; phone (719) 578-4717.

Rails-To-Trails Conservancy, 1400 16th Street, N.W., Washington,
D.C. 20036.

Touring Cyclists' Hospitality Directory, L.A.B., 190 West Ostend Street,
Suite 120, Baltimore, MD 21203; phone (301) 539-3399; a reciprocal
network of people offering touring cyclists a place to stay.

Touring Exchange, P.O. Box 265, Port Townsend, WA 98368; phone
(206) 385-0667; collects cyclists' tour maps from around the world
and lists resources for cyclists.

Women on Wheels, 3624 North Greenview, Chicago, IL 60613.

2. Bicycle Touring Companies

This list is not complete, but here are several bicycle tour operators who offer organized tours in the United States:

Adventure Bicycle Tours Ltd., 4931 Michele Lane, Sacramento, CA 95822; phone (916) 456-3493.

Adventure Cycling Association, P.O. Box 8308, Missoula, MT 59807; phone (406) 721-1776; FAX (721) 8754; e-mail: acabike@aol.com.

Adventures and Delights, 414 K Street, Anchorage, AK 99501; phone (907) 276-8282 or 1-800-288-3134.

American Wilderness Experience, P.O. Box 1486, Boulder, CO 80306; phone 1-800-444-0099; FAX (303) 444-3999.

Appalachian Valley Bike Touring, 31 East Fort Avenue, Baltimore, MD 21230; phone (410) 837-8068.

Back Country, P.O. Box 4029-Y, Bozeman, MT 59772; phone (406) 586-3556; FAX (406) 586-4288.

Back Roads, 1516 5th Street, Berkeley, CA 94710-1740; phone 1-800-462-2848.

Baybrook Bicycle Tours, 243 Captain Thomas Blvd., West Haven, CT 06516; phone (203) 933-4576.

Bicycle Adventure Club, 3904 Groton Street, San Diego, CA 92110-5635; phone (619) 226-2175; phone 1-800-775-2453.

Bicycle Adventures, P.O. Box 7875, Olympia, WA 98507; phone 1-800-443-6060.

Bike Arizona, 14019 N. Coral Gables Drive, Phoenix, AZ 85023; phone (602) 942-8860.

Bike Riders, Inc., P.O. Box 254, Boston, MA 02113; phone (617) 723-2354 or 1-800-473-7040; FAX (617) 723-2355.

Bike The Whites, Box 189, Tamworth, NH 03886; phone 1-800-448-3534.

Bike Vermont, Inc., P.O. Box 207 K, Woodstock, VT 05091; phone 1-800-257-2226.

Bike Virginia, P.O. Box 203, Williamsburg, VA 23187.

Blazing Pedals, P.O. Box 5929, Snowmass Village, CO 81615; phone (303) 923-4544.

California Coastal Rides, 5224 Prosperity Lane, San Diego, CA 92115; phone (619) 583-3261.

CBT Bicycle Tours, 415 W. Fullerton Pkwy., No. 1003, Chicago, IL 60614; phone 1-800-736-BIKE.

Christian Adventures, A-4380 46th Street, Holland, MI 49423; phone (616) 751-5990.

Colorado Heartcycle Association, Inc., P.O. Box 100743, Denver, CO 80210; phone (303) 267-1112.

Country Inns Along the Trail, R.R.No. 3, Box 3115-CYP, Brandon, VT 05733; phone (802) 247-3300.

Country Roads, Rt. 2, Box 186B, Fayetteville, TX 78940; phone 1-800-366-6681.

Cycle America, P.O. Box 485, Cannon Falls, MN 55009; phone 1-800-245-3263.

Cyclevents, P.O. Box 7491-TE, Jackson, WY 83001; phone (307) 733-9615.

Cycle-Inn-Vermont, P.O. Box 243-BC, Ludlow, VT 05149-0243; phone (802) 228-8799.

Cycle Kentucky Bicycle Tours, 3520 Maple Road, Louisville, KY 40206; phone 1-800-286-9107.

Elk River Touring Center, Highway 219, Slatyfork, WV 26291; phone (304) 572-3771.

Finger Lakes Cycling Adventures, P.O. Box 457, Fairport, NY 14450; phone (716) 377-9817.

French Louisiana Bike Tours, 601 Pinhook Road East, Lafayette, LA 70501; phone 1-800-458-4560.

Hawaii Bicycle Tours, c/o Doug Hansen, P.O. Box 4994, Kanehoe, HI 96744; phone (808) 739-2453.

Hells Canyon Bicycle Tours, 102 W. McCully, P.O. Box 483, Joseph, OR 97846; phone (503) 432-2453.

High Peaks Mountain Adventure Center, 331 Main Street, Lake Placid, NY 12946; phone (518) 523-3764.

Imagine Tours, 917 3rd Street, Davis, CA 95616-4202; phone (916) 758-8782 or 1-800-228-7041.

Lakeshore Bicycle Touring, R.R.No. 3, West Lake Road, Oswego, NY13126; phone (315) 343-0687.

Lancaster Bicycle Touring, 3 Colt Ridge Lane, Strasburg, PA 17579; phone (717) 396-0456.

Mammoth Adventure Connection, P.O. Box 353, Mammoth Lakes, CA 93546; phone (619) 934-0606 or 1-800-228-4947.

Michigan Bicycling Touring, 3512 Red School Road, Kingsley, MI 49649; phone (616) 263-5885.

Mississippi River Bicycle Tours, R.R.No. 2 Box 298, Greenville, IL 62246; phone (618) 664-1776.

Monadnock Bicycle Touring, Box 19 Keene Road, Harrisville, NH 03450; phone (603) 827-3925.

Nomad Expeditions, P.O. Box 773993. Steamboat Springs, CO 80477.

Off The Beaten Track, 1008 Justin Street, Pearce, AZ 85625-9712; phone (520) 826-3466; FAX (520) 826-3703.

Old Dominion Bicycle Tours, 3620 Huguenot Trail, Powhatan, VA 23139; phone (804) 598-7815.

Outdoor Adventure, 6110-7 Powers Avenue, Jacksonville, FL 32217; phone (904) 739-1960.

Out-Spokin' Adventures, 409 N. Court Street, Sparta, WI 54656; phone (608) 269-6087.

PAC (Pacific-Atlantic Cycling) Tour, P.O. Box 303, Sharon, WI 53585.

Pedal For Power, 190 West Ostend Street, No. 120, Baltimore, MD 21230-3731; phone 1-800-288-BIKE.

Progressive Travel, Inc., 224 W. Galer Street, No. C, Seattle, WA 98119-3332; phone 1-800-245-2229.

Student Hostelling Program (for Teens), Ashfield Road, Conway, MA 01341; phone (413) 369-4275 or 1-800-343-6132.

Suwanee Bicycle Tours, P.O. Drawer 247, White Springs, FL 32096; phone (904) 397-2347; FAX (904) 878-2041.

Teton Mountain Bike Tours, P.O. Box 7027, Jackson, WY 83001; phone (307) 733-0712; FAX (307) 733-3588.

Tim Kneeland and Associates, Inc., 200 Lake Washington Blvd., Suite 101, Seattle, WA 98122-6540; phone 1-800-433-0528.

Trailside Lodge Bicycle Tours, HCR 65, Coffee House Road,
    Killington, VT 05751; phone (802) 422-3532 or 1-800-447-2209.
Trails Unlimited, Inc., 299 N. Hover Road, Nashville, IN 47488; phone
    (812) 988-6232.
True Wheel Tours, P.O. Box 366, Long Lake, NY 12847-0366; phone
    (518) 624-2056.
Two For The Road Tandem Touring, Rt. 3, Box 552, Greenville,
    NC 27858; phone (919) 756-4885 or 1-800-2-BIKE-42.
Ultimate Bike Tours, 1123 Los Palos Dr., Suite 1, Salinas, CA 93901;
    phone 1-800-337-TOUR.
Vermont Bicycle Touring, Box 711, Bristol, VT 05443; phone
    (802) 453-4811.
Vermont Cycling Vacations, Villages at Killington, Killington,
    VT 05751; phone 1-800-343-0762.
Wayfarers, P.O. Box 211, Fair Lawn, NJ 07410; phone (201) 796-9344.
Wheel Power Christian Cyclists (Cross Country Tour), P.O. Box 4791,
    Lynchburg, VA 24502; phone (804) 385-7213; FAX (804) 385-7214.
WomanTours, P.O. Box 142, Driggs, ID 83422; phone (208) 354-8804.
WoodsWomen, 25 W. Diamond Lake Road, Minneapolis, MN 55419;
    phone (612) 822-3809 or 1-800-279-0555; FAX (612) 822-3814.
Worldventures, 25 E. 40th Street, Suite 7B, Indianapolis, IN 46205;
    phone 1-800-447-2866.

Bibliography

American Automobile Association. Maps and booklets.

Barnett, Gene. "Hostel Hopping the Pacific Northwest," internet (e-mail: ebarnett@hostel.com).

"Best Rides from Readers," *Bicycling,* Feb. 1995.

Bicycle Colorado Magazine, Grand Junction, CO: Jappe & Associates, Inc.

"Bicycle Utah Vacation Guide," P.O. Box 738, Park City, UT 84060.

"Bicycling in Maryland Reference Guide," Maryland State Highway Administration.

"Bike Arkansas," Arkansas Highway and Transportation Department

Bike Midwest Magazine, Columbus, OH, 1995.

"Biking Utah's Color Country," P.O. Box 1550, St. George, UT 84771.

"Blue Ridge Parkway," Virginia and North Carolina National Park Service.

Broughton, Bob. "British Columbia/Alaska Cycle Touring Frequently Asked Questions," internet (his e-mail address is roberb7@iceonline.com).

"Buckeye State Bikeways," 2nd ed. Ohio Department of Transportation, 1995.

Coello, Dennis. "Kentucky and Tennessee," *Bicycle Guide*, Oct. 1993.

Collier's Encyclopedia. Vol. 22. Toronto: P.F. Collier and Son Ltd., 1990.

Cooke, Alistair. *Alistair Cooke's America*. New York: Alfred A. Knopf, 1973.

Countries of the World and Their Leaders Yearbook. Vol. 2. U.S.A.: Gale Research Inc., 1996.

Cundall, Alan W. and Lystrup, Herbert T. *Yellowstone National Park*. Hamilton Stores Inc., P.O. Box 250, West Yellowstone, MT 59758.

"Cycling Tennessee's Highways," Tennessee Department of Transportation.

"Delaware Maps for Bicycle Users," Delaware Department of Transportation.

Drive North America. Published by the C.A.A. in conjunction with the Reader's Digest Association (Canada) Ltd., 1983.

Ellis, William S. *The Majestic Rocky Mountains*. U.S.A.: National Geographic Society, 1976.

Faubert, Jean-Pierre, "45 Days Of Solitude," *Canadian Cyclist*, Fall, 1991.

Fisher, Ronald M. *The Appalachian Trail*. U.S.A.: The National Geographic Society, 1972.

Fodor's Arizona. U.S.A.: Fodor's Travel Publications, Inc., 1986.

Fodor's California. U.S.A.: Fodor's Travel Publications, Inc., 1990.

Fodor's Cape Cod. U.S.A.: Fodor's Travel Publications, Inc. 1992.

Fodor's New England. U.S.A.: Fodor's Travel Publication's, Inc., 1993.

Fodor's Pacific North Coast U.S.A.: Fodor's Travel Publications, Inc., 1993.

Fodor's The Carolinas. U.S.A.: Fodor's Travel Publications, Inc., 1991.

Fodor's Vacations in New York State. U.S.A.: Fodor's Travel Publications, Inc., 1991.

Fodor's Washington. D.C. U.S.A.: Fodor's Travel Publications, Inc., 1993.

Fodor's Williamsburg. U.S.A.: Fodor's Travel publications, Inc., 1989.

Frech, Lisa Jo. "Upper Peninsula Dreaming," *Adventure Cyclist*, Sept./Oct. 1994.

Georgia Statewide Bicycle and Pedestrian Plan. Georgia Department of Transportation, 1995.

Goddard, Mary M. "Cruiser Bob and the Big Volcano," *Adventure Cyclist*, Aug. 1994.

Goodwyn, Lawrence. *The South Central States*. New York: Time-Life Books, 1967.

Graves, William. *Hawaii*. U.S.A.: National Geographic Society, 1970.

Hildebrand, William. *North America: Introducing the Continent*. 2nd ed. Toronto: Holt, Rinehart and Winston of Canada, Limited, 1982.

Hiller, Herb. "Traveling Easy," *National Geographic Traveler*, Nov./Dec. 1995.

Hochstein, Peter. "BAM: Ride Along on Bicycle Across Massachusetts," *Bike Report*, Aug. 1993.

Ikenberry-Aitkenhead, Donna. *Bicycling the Atlantic Coast*. Seattle, Washington: The Mountaineers, 1993.

Information Please Almanac. 48th ed. New York: Houghton Mifflin Company, 1995.

Jones, Evan. *The Plain States*. New York: Time-Life Books, 1968.

"Kansas Bicycle Guide," Kansas Department of Transportation.

Keating, Bern. *The Mighty Mississippi*. U.S.A.: National Geographic Society, 1971.

"Kentucky Bicycle Tours," Kentucky Travel.

Kirkendall, Tom and Spring, Vicky. *Bicycling the Pacific Coast* 2nd ed. Seattle, Washington: The Mountaineers, 1990.

Koch, Christopher, "Cross-Country Rides," *Bicycle Guide*, June 1991.

Landers, Rich. "The Ride of Your Life," *Adventure Cyclist*, Can, 1994.

Lands and Peoples. Vol. 5. U.S.A.: Grolier Incorporated, 1991.

Leonard, Jonathan Norton. *Atlantic Beaches*. New York: Time-Life Books, 1972.

Long-Distance Cycling. Editors of *Bicycling* magazine, Emmaus, Pennsylvania: Rodale Press, 1993.

Lynch, Jason M. "Mass Appeal: The Best of the Biggest Organized Rides in North America," *Bicycle Guide*, Apr. 1993.

Martin, Scott. "The Other Alaska," *Bicycling*, Feb. 1995.

Massachusetts Getaway Guide. Massachusetts Office of Travel and Tourism, 1996.

Matheny, Fred. "Masters of the Desert," *Bicycling*, Feb. 1996.

McCoy, Michael. "Powderhounds Across America," *Adventure Cyclist*, July 1996.

Mednick, Marc. "Philadelphia to Valley Forge Park," internet (his e-mail address is marc@panix.com).

Montgomery, Johnnye. "Taking the Long Road Home," *Adventure Cyclist*, Aug. 1955.

Motorist's Guide to Everglades National Park. The Everglades Natural History Association, Inc., 1980.

Nelson, Wade H. "Touring Northern New Mexico—Cycling Heaven!" internet (his e-mail address is wadenelson@frontier.net).

New England in Color. Don Mills, Ontario: Saunders of Toronto, Ltd., 1969.

"North Carolina Bicycling Highways," North Carolina Department of Transportation.

Oppenheimer, Evelyn. *Texas in Color*. New York: Hastings House, 1971.

Paterson, J. H. *North America*. New York: Oxford University Press, 1979.

Perrin, Noel. *Vermont In All Weathers*. New York: The Viking Press, 1973.

Roberts, Bruce and Nancy. *The Faces of South Carolina*. New York: Doubleday and Company, Inc., 1976.

Robertson, D'Avenue "The TransAmerica Trail," *Adventure Cyclist*, Nov./Dec. 1995.

Ross, Gail. "Kokopelli's Trail," *Bicycle Guide*, Nov./Dec. 1992.

Rouse, Park. Jr. *Tidewater Virginia in Color*. New York: Hastings House, 1968.

Schoenholz, Dan. "Riding With the System: Hut to Hut in the San Juan Mountains," *Bike Report*, Feb./March 1993.

Sexton, Tom and Larison, Julie. *Pennsylvania's Great Rail-Trails*, published by the Rails-to-Trails Conservancy, 1400 16th Street, NW, Suite 300, Washington, D.C. 20036, 1994.

Smith, John M. *Cycling Canada*. San Francisco, CA: Bicycle Books, 1995.

Sprague, Marshall. *The Mountain States*. New York: Time-Life Books, 1967.

Stripling, Sherry. "Cycling Through Washington," *The Edmonton Journal*, June 15, 1991.

"Ten One Day and Weekend Bicycle Tours in West Virginia," West Virginia Division of Tourism.

"The Best Cities For Cycling," *Bicycling*, Nov./Dec. 1995.

The Cyclists' Yellow Pages, Adventure Cycling Association.

The Encyclopedia Americana. International Edition. Vol. 27. U.S.A.: Grolier Incorporated, 1991.

The Marshall Cavendish New Illustrated Encyclopedia of the World and Its People. Vol. 17. New York: Marshall Cavendish Corporation, 1988.

The World Book Encyclopedia. Toronto: World Book, Inc., 1994.

The World Book Encyclopedia of People and Places. Chicago: World Book, Inc., 1992.

Thomas, Fred, "Cowboy Trail is Foreseen as Spur to Area Economies," *Omaha World-Herald*, Jan. 20,1994.

Thrasher, Barbara P. *Alaska and The Yukon*. London, England: Bison

Books, Ltd., 1985.

"Virginia—A Great Place To Bike," Virginia Department of Transportation.

Watkins, T. H. *Mark Twain's Mississippi*. Palo Alto, California: American West Publishing Company, 1974.

"Wisconsin Bicycle Maps," Wisconsin Department of Transportation.

Wohliabe, Raymond A. *High Desert and Canyon Country*. New York: The World Publishing Company, 1969.

Woodward, Bob. "Kokopelli the Prankster," *Adventure Cyclist*, June 1995.

About the Author

John M. Smith is a graduate of Wilfrid Laurier University, Waterloo, Ontario, Canada. He lives in Prince Edward County and teaches English and geography in Belleville, Ontario. An avid cyclist and traveler, he has journeyed throughout the United States and Canada, one time crossing the continent on two wheels. He has also done extensive touring in Mexico, Europe, Asia, New Zealand, and Australia. He has given many slide shows about his traveling experiences, has written extensively for magazines, and is the author of *Cycling Canada*. If interested in having a slide show and book talk presentation in your area, contact the author at: R.R. No. 1 Carrying Place, Ontario, Canada K0K 1L0.

John M. Smith

Index